T0339742

Measuring and Communicating Security's Value

Measuring and Communicating Security's Value

A Compendium of Metrics for Enterprise Protection

George Campbell

ELSEVIER

AMSTERDAM • BOSTON • HEIDELBERG • LONDON
NEW YORK • OXFORD • PARIS • SAN DIEGO
SAN FRANCISCO • SINGAPORE • SYDNEY • TOKYO

Security
Executive Council

Elsevier
Radarweg 29, PO Box 211, 1000 AE Amsterdam, Netherlands
The Boulevard, Langford Lane, Kidlington, Oxford OX5 1GB, UK
225 Wyman Street, Waltham, MA 02451, USA

Notices
Knowledge and best practice in this field are constantly changing. As new research and experience broaden our understanding, changes in research methods, professional practices, or medical treatment may become necessary.

Practitioners and researchers must always rely on their own experience and knowledge in evaluating and using any information, methods, compounds, or experiments described herein. In using such information or methods they should be mindful of their own safety and the safety of others, including parties for whom they have a professional responsibility.

To the fullest extent of the law, neither the Publisher nor the authors, contributors, or editors, assume any liability for any injury and/or damage to persons or property as a matter of products liability, negligence or otherwise, or from any use or operation of any methods, products, instructions, or ideas contained in the material herein.

ISBN: 978-0-12-802841-4

British Library Cataloguing in Publication Data
A catalogue record for this book is available from the British Library

Library of Congress Cataloging-in-Publication Data
A catalog record for this book is available from the Library of Congress

For Information on all Elsevier publications visit our website
at http://store.elsevier.com/SecurityExecutiveCouncil

For Lolly

The impact and appeal of information, quantitative or not, flows naturally from the significance and relevance of the message it contains. As a communicator, it is up to you to give a clear voice to that information and its message using language that is easily understood by your audience.

Stephen Few, Show Me the Numbers: Designing Tables and Graphs to Enlighten, Analytics Press, Oakland, CA, 2004.

Contents

About the Author..xiii
Foreword xv
Special Thanks xvii
A Short Story to Set the Stage xix
Some Notes to the Reader on Using This Book....................................xxiii

CHAPTER 1   Metrics Management—It is Not About the Numbers 1
Introduction... 1
Metrics Program Assessment.. 2
    Using This Assessment.. 6
Building Your Program 7
    Step 1: Identify the Business Drivers and Objectives for the
    Security Metrics Program.. 8
    Step 2: Determine Who Your Metrics Are Intended to Inform
    and Influence 9
    Step 3: Identify the Types and Locations of Data Essential
    for *Actionable* Security Metrics 9
    Step 4: Establish Relevant Risk-Related Metrics.................... 11
    Step 5: Focus Your Metrics on Demonstrating Security's
    Multiple Benefits to the Business.. 12
    Step 6: Establish Internal Controls to Ensure Integrity of
    All Data, Data Assessments, and Protection of
    Confidentiality 13
    A Few Closing Thoughts.. 15
Great Data, Great Opportunity but *Bad* Presentation!................ 16
What is the State of the Art in Corporate Security Metrics? 18
    Is This the State of Our Art?... 19
Benchmarking Your Metrics with Peers 27
Finding Value in Security Benchmarking..................................... 28
    Introduction 28
    The Challenge.. 29
    Established Models of Benchmarking Comparison 30
    Current State of Security Benchmarking............................... 30
    Qualitative or Quantitative?... 32
    Key Performance Indicators 32
    Key Risk Indicators 33
    Best Practices 34

Managing the Limitations of Benchmarks and
Benchmarking.. 34
Getting the Most Out of Valuable Responses......................... 36
Conclusion... 36
Benchmarking Security Metrics Programs.................................... 36
Who Is Driving the Need from above?.................................. 37
What Business Drivers Are Pushing the Need for Improved
Metrics from within the Security Organization?..................... 37
What Have Been the Roadblocks to Metrics
Development?.. 37
Observation 38
What Security Programs Are the Focus of Your Metrics?....... 38
What Best Describes the Current Status of Your Security
Metrics Program? 39
Single versus Multisector Benchmarking.............................. 42
Summary... 43

CHAPTER 2 Quantifying & Communicating on Enterprise Risk 45
Introduction... 45
Managing Enterprise-Wide Board Risk...................................... 46
A Conceptual Risk Picture 46
Enterprise Risk Council 47
Security's Role in Risk Management..................................... 48
Next Steps... 48
Operating the Radar and the Relevance of "What If".................. 50
Leading Indicators... 50
Addressing the Obvious 51
Managing Competency... 51
Protecting the Supply Chain... 51
Managing "What If?" 52
Managing Accountability 52
Managing System Reliability 52
Summary 52
Identifying Exploitable Security Defects in
Business Processes.. 52
Risk Management Strategy 53
Where Are the Data? 54
A Caution on Likelihood.. 54
Focus Your Metrics on Avoidable Risk...................................... 54
Measuring the Impact of Background Investigations 55

Tracking Preventable Risk 56
    Risk Management Strategy 57
    Cost Assignment to Preventable Security Incidents 58
Identify and Advertise the Causes of Loss....................................59
    Risk Management Strategy 60
    Measuring the Elements of Effective Access
    Management 60
    Strategy..62
Measuring Security Awareness...65
    Surveys Deliver the Data..66
    Testing Delivers the Data 67
    Risk Awareness Assures Preparedness 67
Workplace Violence 69
Advertising the Failure to Act..71
    Leveraging the Learning..72
Measuring Compliance Risk...73
    Risk Management Strategy 73
When Does an *Avoidable* Risk Become *Inevitable?*....................75
    The Idea..75
    The Business Risk Profile 76
    The Risk Management Strategy 76
Tracking Nuisance and False Alarms 77
    Reducing Nuisance Alarms 79
    Summarizing Avoidable Risk 80
Meters and Dials—Tracking and Monitoring Key
Risk Indicators 80
    Key Risk Indicators at the Enterprise Level 80
    Summary 81
    Key Risk Indicators at the CSO Level.....................................82
    Take a Deeper Dive on Multiyear Trends to
    Highlight Risk 85
    Build a Risk Indicator Dashboard 86
    Risk Management Strategy 86
    Measuring Risk Assessment Program Effectiveness...............87
    Identifying the Threshold of "Acceptable" Risk 88
Creating a Business Unit Scorecard 90
    Objective..90
    Risk Management Strategy 90
    Where Are the Data? 92

Tracking Risk in Outsourcing 92
    Information Technology Contractor Risk 92
    Where Are the Data? 93
    Tracking Key Risk Indicators in Business Continuity 94
Business Integrity and Reputational Risk 95
    Broken Windows in the Boardroom 96
Risk Personified—The Knowledgeable Insider 98
    Incident Analysis Identifies Evolving Insider Threats 101
    What Is the Cost of a Bad Employee? 103
    Use Your Metrics to Influence Policy 104
    Measuring Impact of Security Incidents on Business
    Productivity 106
    Tracking Internal Investigations 108
    Tracking Disciplinary Action 110
    Insider Risk in Outsourced Business Process 110
    Tracking Losses from Fraud, Waste and Abuse 111
    Confidential Hotline Reporting 112
    A Simple Dashboard on Reputational Risk 113
    Unintended Consequences—Another View of
    Incident Impact on Productivity 114
    Summarizing Insider Risk Measurement 115
Transitions—Moving the Lens from Risk to Performance
Indicators 115

CHAPTER 3 Measuring Security Program Performance 117
Introduction 117
Key Performance Indicators 118
    KPI Objectives 119
    Strategy 119
Communicating Program Performance with Dashboards 120
    Summary 124
Physical Security Is Measurable 124
Alerting Management to High Probability Risk 126
    Risk Management Strategy 127
Measuring and Managing Your Regional Security Team 128
    Challenges 129
Measuring and Managing Your Guard Force Performance
and Cost 130
Measuring Vendor-Based Alarm Response 133
Tracking Protective Services Key Performance Indicators 134
    Risk Management Strategy 135
    Summary 135

Security Operations Control Center Metrics 136
    Operational Criticality 136
    Performance Measurement 137
Secure Area Reliability 138
The Critical Measure of Time to Respond................................ 138
    Risk Management Strategy 139
    Summary 141
Measuring for Operational Excellence in Security Services 141
Measure Risk Exposure with Security Inspections 143
    Risk Management Strategy 143
    Where are the Data? 144
    What Do You Want to Achieve with This Information? 145
Measuring and Managing Cost.................................... 145
    Show Me the Money: Task and Time Analysis 147
    Expense Management: The Inevitable KPI........................ 148
    Slash and Burn 148
    Showing the ROI of Contract Security Forces 151
Cycle Time: An Expected Measure of Performance.................. 153
Information Security 155
Metrics are Bidirectional: Failure as a Performance
Indicator 155
Measuring Progress of Annual Plans and Objectives 156
    Summary 158
Is Compliance a Key Risk Indicator or a Key Performance
Indicator? 158
    Objective 159
    Risk Management Strategy 159
Security Contract Compliance Auditing............................. 161
    Background 161
    Risk Management Strategy 162
    Questions... 163
Measuring for Integrity: Background Investigations................. 163
    Risk Management Strategy 163
    Summary 165
Measuring Executive Protection Programs............................ 165
Business Unit Criticality, Resilience, and Continuity
Planning 166
    Summary 168
Measuring Security Awareness Programs................................ 169
    Risk Management Strategy 169
The Absence of Awareness Is a Key Contributor to Risk 171

Ability to Influence the Business Is a Key Performance
Indicator 173
  Warning Signs of Security's Decreasing Influence 174
  Measure Influence by Tracking Acceptance of
  Recommendations 177
  Risk Management Strategy 178
Security's Value Proposition: Value Is a Key Performance
Indicator 179
  Finding a Corporate Security Value Proposition 179
  Measuring Security's Value 181
  Do Business Units Value Security Recommendations? 184
Use Metrics to Demonstrate Security's Alignment with
Business Objectives 186
  Risk Management Strategy 186
  A Simple Analysis Yields Valuable Results 187
  Security's Balanced Scorecard 188
  Benchmarking Security Operations 189
  Security Expense versus Cost of Loss 191
A Few Metrics You Should Really Consider 193
  Key Risk Indicators 194
  Influence Indicators 194
  Key Performance Indicators 195
  Value Indicators and Financial Perspective 195
  Value Indicators: Customer Perspective and Business
  Process Enablement 195
Some Closing Thoughts 196

Index 197

About the Author

George Campbell has served as a member of the Emeritus Faculty of the Security Executive Council (SEC) from day 1. In addition to consulting activities with the SEC, he has focused his research and development on corporate security performance measures and metrics. He retired in 2002 as Chief Security Officer at Fidelity Investments, the world's largest privately owned financial services firm. Under George's leadership, the global corporate security organization delivered the full range of proprietary security risk management services. He previously owned his own security consulting firm and was the Group Vice President at a system engineering firm supporting high security US Government security programs from 1978 to 1989. His criminal justice career from 1965 to 1978 was spent in various line and senior management assignments within federal, state, and local government agencies.

He is a member of ASIS International since 1978 and a frequent speaker and contributor to professional security journals and seminars. He is the coauthor of the *ASIS International Chief Security Officer Standard for Organizations*, author of *Measures and Metrics in Corporate Security* published in 2005, and contributing editor of *Adding Business Value by Managing Security Risks* published in 2009 by the SEC. He was the 2006 CSO Magazine Compass Award winner and selected as Security Magazine's 25 Most Influential People in Security in 2009. George is a graduate of American University; a life member, former president, and Board member of the International Security Management Association; and an alumnus of the US Department of State, Overseas Security Advisory Council.

Foreword

For many years, one of the biggest challenges facing a chief security officer (CSO) was "having a regular seat at the table." Sure, when a crisis event occurred, they would always get their 15 minutes of fame, but once the incident or issue was under control, they would generally be forgotten until the next major event.

While the statement above is meant to be somewhat tongue-in-cheek, the reality is that a lack of visibility for CSOs within their company was not uncommon. The questions to be answered are, "why are they regularly excluded from the table?" and "what has changed for them in today's business environment?"

For many years, the security function and their CSOs were viewed within a corporation as a "business necessity." What was interesting was that in many instances, they were not held to the same performance standards as their peer leaders who worked within the profit and loss side of the business, or even led similar functions.

Business leaders within a corporation's manufacturing, engineering, or information technology groups have always been measured by corporate leadership on the value that they create within the corporate infrastructure. As such, leaders within these areas learned the necessary business acumen a long time ago that would allow them to effectively measure and communicate the value and effectiveness of their individual organization.

These leaders routinely produced metrics that "told their stories" in regard to profitability, productivity, quality, cycle time, unit cost, etc. It was an expectation that a leader in one of these areas would be able to artfully articulate all aspects of their business using metrics and be able to hold their own in any financial discussion regarding their business. Why were CSOs not held to the same expectation and what has changed?

CSOs and the business of security remained a mystery for many companies. Due to a general lack of understanding with the CEO about what a CSO should do and how security should be run, CSOs got a pass for many years. They were never expected to run security "like a business." In many ways the adage "no news is good news" was all a CEO needed to believe that their CSO and security program was doing a good job.

After 9/11, and the ensuing economic challenges over the past 10 years, the CSO position has been thrust into the limelight. Initially, company leadership needed to know that their corporation was protected from terror threats. This gave additional visibility to the security function. As time passed and the economy periodically faltered, the cost associated with the security function began to be scrutinized by company leadership with the same vigor as that of other operations within their company. No longer could the CSO, the security function, and the costs associated with that function be ignored. The expectation that CSOs run their security functions "like a business" became the norm.

CSOs who anticipated the directional change began reaching out to their peers within their own companies or professional security organizations to begin learning the necessary business skills and tools to effectively tell their story.

The seat at the table was open and leadership's expectation was that their CSO would be able to effectively communicate the value of the security function, the results it was achieving, and the return on investment it was creating for the corporation.

Many CSOs (myself included) felt the urgency to develop a suite of metrics, which was essentially a set of two-minute "elevator speeches" that could be used to quickly and concisely communicate the value of the security investment.

The initial journey of discovery was not easy. We first had to educate the middle management of our organization on the value of creating metrics. George Campbell, the author of this book, was our guide in this journey. I'll never forget George's initial assessment of our security and fire protection organization. "You have great people, a ton of data and world class services," he stated. "But, you don't do anything of value with the data. Your security and fire leaders don't understand how to create metrics and you aren't telling your story effectively at all." It was a sobering moment.

So began our metrics journey in late 2010. Fast forwarding to today, we have developed an impressive suite of metrics that capture nearly every service offering within our security and fire protection organization. These metrics allow me to quickly and effectively communicate the value, quality, cycle time, and cost avoidance created by the investment made by the company to protect our people, property, information and providing business resiliency.

The security and fire leaders in the middle who initially resisted the idea have all seen the value of being able to "tell their individual organizational story." Many have used the metric creation journey as an opportunity for employee involvement and engagement within their teams. By doing so, every member of our security organization has increased their level of business knowledge. Each of my security and fire leaders are now able to tell "the bigger story" via our metric package with our internal business partners. Leaders can now easily brief the effectiveness of security and fire protection, even if they don't manage them, because we have spent the time learning about each other's functions and how we collectively bring value to our company.

Three years ago, I had my first opportunity to walk through sections of my metric suite with our CEO and other senior leaders within our corporation. The briefing created an invaluable dialogue for our organization. It was clear that our value story resonated with our CEO and his leadership team. I truly believe the perception and expectations of our security and fire protection organization changed that day in a very positive way.

George's work within the field of security metrics is unparalleled. As you walk through his stories and examples, you will discover that each are based on years of practical learning and experience as a CSO. The knowledge you will gain will undoubtedly help you "tell your story" in the most effective way possible!

Dave Komendat, Chief Security Officer
The Boeing Company

Special Thanks

If the contents of this little book have any value, it is because of a few good people who helped make it happen. First, my thanks to Bob Hayes, the Managing Director of the Security Executive Council (SEC) who has provided the creative and supportive platform for me to practice my craft. He is a visionary with a level of energy and reservoir of ideas that dwarfs the strategic petroleum reserve. My thanks also to Kathleen Kotwica, knowledge master-in-residence who pushes the envelope on ideas, and Liz Lancaster from the SEC's excellence department, who serves as my probation officer and just make things happen.

I have had two wonderful editors throughout my writing efforts, Elaine Cummings at CSO magazine and now with Bain Consulting, and Marleah Blades from the SEC. Elaine suffered with determination through the early years of my creative efforts, fed the fire, and is both a great friend and an incredibly gifted teacher. Marleah has her competent hand on most of what you will read here and continues to make better what I am trying to convey. Both have bled gallons of editorial blood on my account and if what I have to say in these columns makes sense, it is their counsel that has skillfully clarified and improved my work. Both must have been third grade teachers in former lives.

And to the wonderful security professionals from whom I have learned and with whom I have had the privilege to follow and lead, thank you.

George Campbell
2014

A Short Story To Set The Stage

This short story originally appeared in CSO Magazine in November, 2004 under the "anonymous" authorship. While fictitious, it does fairly represent my own experience in being pushed (not dragged…) into the hunt for meaningful metrics in my diverse security programs. What is not in here is the extent to which I drove my team crazy with probing the data that were squeezed and poured forth from every data repository I could find.

We have a chief financial officer (CFO) who's always been a nut on quantitative measures. But he's recently decided to make a metrics march on all his direct reports and that includes me. So every department in the company has engaged in a great exercise identifying the metrics appropriate to their business processes. And since all the service functions (including corporate security) report to him, I determined that compliance is the better part of valor.

I first found this metrics mania somewhat vexing. Historically speaking, I am the kind of person who has proudly sported that bumper sticker proclaiming "what do you mean I'm overdrawn, I've still got checks left!"

So, I decided early on to go to the source, the CFO and chief metrics officer himself. What might he be looking for in this program? I was aware that there was a risk involved here; I didn't want to look like I was carrying a dunce cap through the door. But caution has never been my strong suit so I got right to the point in our regular one on one in his office.

FATEFUL MEETING

Me: "I know you have an endgame in mind with your measures request from your Services Group. In corporate security, we generate volumes of data on a daily basis. It would be helpful if we could kick some ideas around on how to meet your goal."

CFO (smiling): "Sure. The heart of it is that if a business process cannot be measured in one way or another, we likely ought to cast it off as wasted effort. As a business, we live or die every day on a host of measures, all of which indicate our health to shareholders, the capital markets and any manager worth his or her paycheck. I know you are thinking about replacing our global access control system. It's a significant investment. You know I need to see the return on it. What's the benefit? When is the payback? What is it going to give us that the one we've got doesn't? This is simple stuff. Digging into the essence of what we get for our global spending on security programs is far more difficult."

Me: "You've highlighted the fact that we've always been seen as a cost center. But how do you see security as being a fundamental part of our financial success?"

CFO (excited, stands up): "That's absolutely the right question! But think about it for a moment. You are in the best position to answer it. And, you need to know that I don't see security as a cost center. You are a performance center. Your department's operations are critically focused on helping our company succeed in an increasingly risky world. Every business process involves a variety of steps, actions, or transactions that can be measured. In my office, we track dozens of financial performance metrics that provide the grist for boardroom debate and business strategy. A few years ago I might have wondered aloud about the value of a comprehensive security program in a global business, but no more. The risks are all over the map, but I leave it to you to develop the metrics you believe tell the story. Come back with a focused approach and we'll go from there."

I leave the CFO's office thinking, I couldn't have asked for a more supportive charter than that, could I?

METRICS COVER MORE THAN IT SYSTEMS

The quest for the right metrics has been illuminating for a couple of reasons.

First, I knew we generated a variety of volume-related statistics, for our internal performance assessments and to support our insurance and risk management requirements. But I have to admit that we hadn't considered a more proactive use of this or other data—until it was made clear that performance metrics were going to be a much bigger deal.

Second, after some serious Web surfing and literature review, it became clear that the bibliography for "security metrics" was limited, to say the least. Limited to information security, that is.

For example, The Robert Frances Group states that "...collecting and reporting security metrics is an integral part of an enterprise security strategy. IT executives should examine their metrics collection practices to ensure that the metrics collected are useful and understandable, and cover all necessary security aspects." I thought "enterprise security strategy" covered the whole corporation? Why talk only about "IT executives"? A security metrics consortium was founded by a group of leading CSOs and CISOs and announced that "was established to define such real world metrics, giving CISOs and CSOs the ammunition to adequately protect digital assets of their organizations." Digital assets? Do you mind if I protect people, assets, and maybe reputation before all the zeros and ones? It's a damn shame that professionals with their heads screwed on straight failed to include the whole landscape of security metrics in their leadership model from the get go.

Our research on the Web confirmed that the IT security consultants and centers of technical expertise were the prime movers in security metrics. This highlights what I can only conclude is a general absence of interdisciplinary debate, benchmarking, project coordination, and collaboration among security professionals.

The dominance of the digerati is disappointing, but I have to applaud the fact that a core element of our security profession sees the wisdom of building a security metrics database. The digital side clearly has the machines to log and track metrics like intrusion attempts, virus incursions, access attempts, blocked internet sites, and sophisticated monitoring and scanning tools to check on IT health on a nanosecond schedule. But I learned early that an enterprise security metrics and measurements program has to be significantly broader and deeper than this.

DATA ON HAND, AWAITING ANALYSIS

My group wasn't totally in the dark on metrics tracking. We have always watched trends on losses, exposures, shrinkage, recovery, safety, caseloads, incidents, various measures to prioritize investigations, response times, false alarms, outages, and so on. We have a global incident reporting system that probably houses terabytes of data. We just hadn't considered how this information could be organized to make the business safer, more efficient, less costly, better managed, and more accountable. When I look at that statement, it makes me shudder at what we/I didn't know because we were just making lists and counting things.

We were sitting on reams of historical data that failed to provide real, actionable information. We fed the databases hourly without fail. My investigative team conducts hundreds of cases annually, has solid recoveries, makes successful referrals for prosecution, and documents our findings with solid conclusions. But when we reviewed several of these, it was amazing what information we had failed to pass on to business units on internal control deficiencies, managerial failures, and, most critically, actionable recommendations on vulnerability fixes. We had been missing the gold in the work—the lessons learned, the take aways, the kind of information that can lead to real, incremental improvement in protection.

Thinking more strategically about our metrics initiative also meant considering the multiple constituencies who would receive our reports and feedback. There are several stakeholders in this game. I know I could work with the CFO, but to influence the business as a whole we had to identify others who would benefit from the knowledge we could package and deliver.

HR and legal counsel were early partners and the general auditor followed. Collaborative discussions centered on our metrics both revealed new knowledge of emerging risk and also synched with their own findings and concerns. Sharing this information enabled us to *connect the dots*. The result: $1+1=3$. This simple set of discussions has invigorated an internal governance dynamic that put our security programs far more meaningfully into the enterprise risk management agenda.

LESSONS LEARNED

Some of my lessons learned as a result of this charter from the CFO:
* Engage your internal business unit clients in identifying metrics vital to their success. Consider cycle times for your processes that impact them (like background investigations), loss reduction (be specific), use of technology versus use of manpower, proactive identification of vulnerabilities that could impact uptime reliability, and increased efficiency/reduced business impact from essential security processes.

- Risk analysis is a must. If you aren't thoroughly engaged in the proactive identification of risk, I assume you have an updated resumé. These activities are the essence of security management and provide incredible opportunities for metrics to influence the quality of enterprise protection.
- Identify incident trends important to key senior managers. If you are connecting qualitatively with your leadership, you will have to know what is keeping them awake at night in your space and theirs. Your metrics are the license to influence policy, behavior, and support for security programs.
- As you consider the metrics you will build into your core presentation, make certain you are reporting on verifiable conclusions that result from analysis—not guesswork or symptoms.
- Develop a few value indicators that you can track and report on with a high degree of reliability. How is value defined for security in your company? Is that assessment accurate and complete? How is value defined for some of your service provider peers in the company? What about metrics around cost avoided, recovery above a threshold, avoidance of sanctions, reduction of risk to employees, improved cycle times, and the like are attractive to your constituents.
- Formalize the relationship with your key governance partners. Meet regularly to compare notes on emerging risks, develop shared metrics presentations, enable ongoing incident postmortem learning.
- Develop a couple of confidence indicators. There are people in your company that really know how customer satisfaction can and should be measured. Engage them and measure your team's results with your customers. Measure your success in influencing business process improvements from your risk assessments and investigative postmortems.
- Have every security manager responsible for reporting on two to three key measures of program success. Incorporate the metrics into your overall storyboard.
- Build a couple of "stretch objectives" into your annual business plan. Go for a measurable reduction in a concerning risk trend, incremental improvement in a key cycle time, reduced cost of protection.
- Lastly, keep it simple and, above all, check your numbers.

Oh, by the way, it went really well with the CFO. I've even learned to balance my checkbook.

Some Notes to the Reader on Using This Book

If there is one thematic target that should guide the metrics hunt, it is that of value—how should it be defined, measured, and presented in a portfolio of security metrics?[1] It is likely doubtful that security's value has a uniform definition for every company that has an established security department. However, it may be said that an ability to effectively communicate and advertise how enterprise protection solutions contribute value to the business is related to an ability to inform and tell stories around solid, well-crafted security metrics.

The following stories have been organized to build on a principal theme of having metrics that demonstrate the security department's value to the corporation. Many of the examples contain a variety of metric outputs related to the script or headline that serves the purpose of the chart. The objective with these examples is simply to plant seeds and prompt ideas. If there were an ideal scenario for this work, it would be around the discovery of how to put that data of yours to work in ways you have not yet tried and with positive results you had not envisioned or thought possible.

Here are brief summaries on the half dozen buckets that follow. I hope they contain a few gems that will work in your security organization.

Beginnings—The initial collection focuses on the why, what, and how of a security metrics program. Since so much of what is being learned about this subject on my own and from reviewing scores of others' programs has illustrated the lack of attention to the basics, I thought these few pages would help the reader get grounded on some key concepts I think are essential measures of a metrics program.

Risk—I am also strongly biased toward focusing our measures and metrics on risk; after all, *it is why we have a job*. We add value where we enable the business to avoid risk and an element of that enablement is actionable information and a centerpiece should be our metrics reporting. Thus, a brief cross-section of examples to consider and hopefully prompt ideas for your own risk reporting. I also link this perspective on risk to a section on our ability to influence corporate policy and behavior.

Insider Risk—This is what should keep every CEO awake at night and we have a unique perch from which to view risk exposure and influence accountability—or at least eliminate plausible denial. Depending on the reader's security program involvement, understanding our opportunities to provide a lens on reputational risk and corporate integrity is a valuable metrics product offering.

Influence—I see our ability to influence as a key performance indicator. Our metrics are the products of our marketing and communications strategy. When they

---

[1] Return-on-investment (RoI) certainly belongs in this bucket but I am biased toward a broader view; one that enables the business to see security's value as a full partner in business strategy and enterprise risk management. Compared to our business peers, we have done a lousy job in selling our value proposition to those who should know it by heart.

are accurate, timely, informative, and actionable, they can tell a story that no other member of the enterprise risk management and corporate governance team can bring to the table. I believe every security manager should consider having a few key influence indicators focused on the actionable needs of their primary customers.

How well connected are we to the business? How should we measure our partnership with core business strategy and process? If you can see how our ability to influence through metrics could serve a customer in avoiding a risk, what other information could provide a valued perspective to a business decision-maker? A faster, more secure supply chain? Improved cycle times for hiring and access? A safer workplace or elimination of hazards that cause critical process interruption? Good opportunities for metrics are here as well.

How well are security's varied programs performing and why does it make a difference? Key performance measures are an integral element of business management. Every security program has embedded objectives that define the desired results require measurement—and measurements deliver metrics. Additionally, cycle time, customer satisfaction, SLAs, regulatory compliance, benchmarking, and other means of performance provide qualitative reporting opportunities for security management.

Building your metrics for impact and results—Do not waste time building a metric unless you have a clear idea about what result you want it to achieve. The articles in this book all contain a snapshot of one or more results that should be the intent or anticipated result of the metric(s) discussed. I would hope this will prompt your consideration of a potential benefit to your program.

Searching for ideas? The table of contents is reasonably suggestive of potential points of interest but I have also provided a list of charts and a high level topical index to compliment the reader's use of this reference.

Building the knowledge base is a shared exercise—In addition to my own experience and probing, much of what you will find in here is the result of a lot of discussions and idea sharing with a lot of really smart colleagues from across global security organizations. As you consider and hopefully apply some of the concepts contained in this book, I hope you will share that experience and your applications with me. What worked and what did not and why? What is missing here that you hoped you would find? You can reach me at contact@secleader.com.

Metrics Management—It is Not About the Numbers

INTRODUCTION

During the past several years, the more I've worked with some really good security organizations to assess and develop their metrics programs, the more I'm convinced that metrics isn't about the numbers, it's about measuring performance of people, process, and performance. Don't get me wrong: We need to build and maintain lists of numbers, but this is just the beginning of the work. Like a smart colleague of mine says, "It's just counting nails." What do these numbers mean? What story do they tell, what action is required—and by whom?

This first section is focused on metrics program management in three parts. It begins with a metrics program assessment that can affirm a mature program or direct remedial action on perceived shortcomings gleaned from an honest self-evaluation. I recommend this process to the reader regardless of your level of accomplishment in our craft.

> Measuring your various programs is not something extra to do. It is a key element of management and an expectation of your position.

The next section sets forth a six-step process for putting to work what you have gleaned from this self-assessment and using the data you have waiting to be mined. Building a security metrics program keyed to the unique needs of your company is not about incident reports and spreadsheets full of activity and event data. These are just the fuel that powers the analysis and judgment that yield your metrics. You have the data. You have the ability to tell powerful stories that can influence business strategy, corporate policy, and have a measurable impact on risk. But those stories and that ability to communicate with impact are the products of a well-established connection to the business and a disciplined process of data and information management. The steps briefly outlined in this chapter are both proven and just plain common sense.

The third and final section in this management review is a discussion of my sense of the state of the art regarding *corporate* security metrics. Note the emphasis. There are some outstanding books on *information security* metrics but very few on the portfolio of work confronting the corporate Chief Security Officer (CSO). I lean on some benchmarking results along with an assembly of excuses I've heard over many years—they are excuses I've said myself and then had the audacity to complain about when I heard them from others who continue to labor at this business of corporate security.

Chapters 2 and 3 will delve into various examples of security programs and their measures and metrics.

METRICS PROGRAM ASSESSMENT

Much of what follows in this book is focused on examples of security management challenges and opportunities, and the role and contribution I see for measurements and metrics. But I think it is important to level-set where you stand in terms of your program's status, whether you are reading this as a security executive with a solid metrics program, one desiring to reinvent or build a body of security metrics, or perhaps as a student of the discipline. In working with scores of corporate security organizations over the past decade, I've found that there are about a dozen questions about the organizations' metrics programs that effectively serve to focus the manager on developmental priorities. I included this material in the second edition of my first book on measures and metrics, but repeating it here is a logical beginning to my new work, and helps us consider the potential value of the examples that are discussed throughout.

The following metrics self-assessment tool walks security managers through a number of questions about how they would rank their program's maturity. Take an honest look at each of the descriptions and see how you would assess your current security metrics program. If you think carefully about the questions and your assessment compared to the alternatives, I think you will find a roadmap for targeted improvements.

> What is the business case for your security organization and how do you want it measured? What are the quantifiable measurements that ought to apply to management's assessment of value? How would you grade your measurements and metrics?

You can work this assessment on your own if you are a sole practitioner. But if you have a team of managers leading various programs and functions, it would be advisable to develop this as a team exercise. It will get everyone (hopefully) on the same page, and will help to chart your program's strengths, weaknesses, opportunities and threats (SWOT). This self-assessment is a precursor to the metrics construction process that takes the reader through six steps in building a program. Use it to leverage your strengths and opportunities and note where each of the steps offers an approach to mitigating your weaknesses and threats.

Metrics Self-assessment Tool
Review and fill in the attached self-assessment questionnaire. Select the one statement in each section that best suits your metrics program, and designate the current level of accomplishment for your selection. For example, if you selected *1.2 Management is beginning to seek performance measures and metrics from security*, a Level 1 would indicate you are at the earliest stage of response to this need. If none fit the bill, insert your own selection as noted.

Key Metrics Program Indicators	Maturity Level		
1. Organizational Context	Level 1	Level 2	Level 3
1.1. Metrics are an accepted element within selected business operations but have not been requested from security.			
1.2. Management is beginning to seek performance measures and metrics from security.			
1.3. Performance measures and metrics are a required element of program management.			
(Insert your own performance indicator if not listed or adaptable above).			
2. Current Status of Metrics Within the Security Department	Level 1	Level 2	Level 3
2.1. Recognized need and trying to understand best first steps.			
2.2. Established objective but just in very early stages of development.			
2.3. We have a variety of data and now are moving to identify best approach for desired results.			
2.4. We have several focused metrics outputs for targeted constituents, but now want to elevate the content and management (or board) targeting.			
2.5. We have a well-established program with quality reporting, and now desire to develop a more directed and influential set of measures and metrics.			
(Insert your own performance indicator if not listed or adaptable above).			
3. Data Availability	Level 1	Level 2	Level 3
3.1. We do not currently have a centralized incident reporting system.			
3.2. We have a limited incident reporting database that is distributed among multiple security-related functions.			
3.3. We have an enterprise-wide incident reporting and case management system that enables reporting of desired metrics.			
(Insert your own performance indicator if not listed or adaptable above).			

4. Data Reliability	Level 1	Level 2	Level 3
4.1. Our incident and performance-related data do not currently have consistent standards of review and reliability.			
4.2. Although our incident and performance-related data are distributed among multiple organizational units, there are consistent standards of review and reliability for reporting up.			
4.3. We have an enterprise-wide incident and performance-related data repository with consistent standards of review and reliability.			
(Insert your own performance indicator if not listed or adaptable above).			
5. Analytical Scope and Discipline	**Level 1**	**Level 2**	**Level 3**
5.1. Current processing of incident and performance data is primarily limited to maintaining counts of various data elements for trend analysis and reporting.			
5.2. A limited number of security programs are thoroughly analyzed for qualitative and quantitative findings and targeted reporting.			
5.3. Selected security programs have established performance measurement criteria and are consistently tracked and subjected to in-depth analysis.			
5.4. All security programs are subjected to ongoing qualitative and quantitative measurement with metrics outputs available for management reporting.			
(Insert your own performance indicator if not listed or adaptable above).			
6. Analytical Benefits	**Level 1**	**Level 2**	**Level 3**
6.1. While it is an objective, we do not currently provide a measurable level of analysis to our incident and program performance data.			
6.2. We see measurable results when we provide analyses of business unit risk exposure and security advice to business units.			
6.3. Our analyses provide evidence of compliance with applicable regulations.			
6.4. Our analyses provide evidence of business unit compliance with policies related to internal controls and security.			
6.5. Our analyses of security program performance has enabled demonstrably improved management understanding of the value of security investments.			
6.6. Our ongoing analyses of risk assessment and security program performance data is a required deliverable to senior management (and the board).			
(Insert your own performance indicator if not listed or adaptable above).			

7. Reporting	Level 1	Level 2	Level 3
7.1. Reporting is primarily for internal security department program performance tracking.			
7.2. There are multiple security functions with no consolidated metrics reporting.			
7.3. Formal reporting of program performance data is limited to a select few key indicators required by management.			
7.4. We provide a variety of standardized and tailored metrics reports to management on an established schedule.			
(Insert your own performance indicator if not listed or adaptable above).			
8. Directional Performance Standards and Guidelines	**Level 1**	**Level 2**	**Level 3**
8.1. We have not found a set of security-related standards or guidelines that may be useful as measurement benchmarks.			
8.2. We currently do not use an established body of industry or locally developed performance standards or guidelines that may be used as benchmark targets for metrics.			
8.3. We have adopted a selected set of measurable performance standards or guidelines developed by others that are tracked and reported to management.			
8.4. We have both adopted externally produced performance standards and developed others appropriate to our unique business management requirements.			
(Insert your own performance indicator if not listed or adaptable above).			
9. Actionability	**Level 1**	**Level 2**	**Level 3**
9.1. Our metrics are limited to occasional reports that are primarily designed to inform on status of selected trends over time.			
9.2. We are in the process of developing a body of metrics that may be used to measure the value and effectiveness of security programs.			
9.3. Our metrics are primarily analyzed and delivered to affirm positive business unit action or advise and direct corrective actions.			
(Insert your own performance indicator if not listed or adaptable above).			
10. Resources and Tools	**Level 1**	**Level 2**	**Level 3**
10.1. Resource constraints currently limit our ability to maintain an effective security metrics program.			
10.2. Each security manager is required to maintain basic performance metrics for each of their assigned programs.			

	Level 1	Level 2	Level 3
10.3. We devote adequate staff time and employ a robust set of applications to maintain and deliver a variety of metrics reports to management.			
10.4. Our company has developed dashboard models that we are adapting to suit our security metrics reporting requirements.			
(Insert your own performance indicator if not listed or adaptable above).			
11. Data Sensitivity and Protection	**Level 1**	**Level 2**	**Level 3**
11.1. There are safeguards to protect the confidentiality of metrics data that could reveal potentially risky information to unauthorized individuals.			
(Insert your own performance indicator if not listed or adaptable above).			
12. Summary Assessment: Measuring Security's Value to the Enterprise	**Level 1**	**Level 2**	**Level 3**
12.1.We are actively seeking a body of metrics capable of demonstrating measurable value to the enterprise.			
12.2. We have a body of metrics accepted by management as demonstrating measurable value to the enterprise.			
(Insert your own performance indicator if not listed or adaptable above).			
Organization: Evaluator: Date:			

USING THIS ASSESSMENT

If you are just beginning the hunt for your few meaningful metrics, you need to carefully consider the implications of your choices. For example, consider your selection of these options:

3.1. We do not currently have a centralized incident reporting system;
4.1. Our incident and performance-related data do not currently have consistent standards of review and reliability; and
5.1. Current processing of incident and performance data is primarily limited to maintaining counts of various data elements for trend analysis and reporting.

Reliability is the heart of a metrics program, so that is your first priority in the building process.

The absence of a centralized reporting system is not a show-stopper, but lack of an effective incident reporting system is. In the former, you have the data distributed among various entities, but it will be more difficult to bring these data into a form that enables solid analysis. In the latter, you probably cannot rely on the data that are going to be difficult to even gather; thus, selection of 4.1 is likely. When you have the data and you are confident of their accuracy, remember that after you put it in a form that essentially enables counting, this is only the beginning. Counts are acceptable for trending but they fail to provide direction for alternative action; they merely serve up the fuel for your analysis and decisions. Every one of these assessment items has its own implications for your next steps. If you are alone in interpreting your results or the team needs some thoughtful advice, think about the short story above and find a mentor who can help you sort the options and be a supporter in the construction process. If you are in great shape, check out the examples, among which you may find a number of ideas for adding and improving your security metrics portfolio.

BUILDING YOUR PROGRAM

If you have come away from the assessment with a conclusion that you have a mature, well-functioning metrics program that is delivering measurable results to you as a manager and to your customers, I suggest you use the table of contents to cherry-pick topics that I hope will deliver an actionable idea or two. If the assessment helped you focus on some gaps or shortcomings, or if you are engaged in a bottom-up reinvention, perhaps a review of the following will offer an approach to set your program in the right direction.

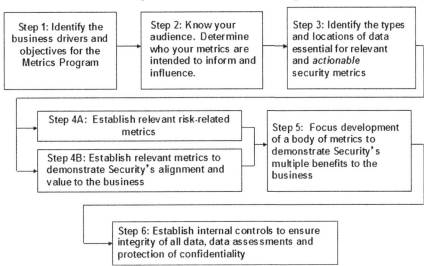

Construction Process for Implementing a
Security Measures & Metrics Program

Step 1: Identify the business drivers and objectives for the Metrics Program

Step 2: Know your audience. Determine who your metrics are intended to inform and influence.

Step 3: Identify the types and locations of data essential for relevant and *actionable* security metrics

Step 4A: Establish relevant risk-related metrics

Step 4B: Establish relevant metrics to demonstrate Security's alignment and value to the business

Step 5: Focus development of a body of metrics to demonstrate Security's multiple benefits to the business

Step 6: Establish internal controls to ensure integrity of all data, data assessments and protection of confidentiality

STEP 1: IDENTIFY THE BUSINESS DRIVERS AND OBJECTIVES FOR THE SECURITY METRICS PROGRAM

How can metrics deliver the greatest benefits for your company and its security mission?

- To make a positive impact on company policy and culture?
- Or should it be to measurably impact risk exposure?
- How about to demonstrate security's alignment with business goals and deliver value to the bottom line?
- How about all of these and more?

Look at the key words in this figure: risk, measure, value, policy, influence, impact, change, compliance, alignment, strategy. These are the high-profile targets of your metrics.

Step 1: Identify the business drivers and objectives for the Metrics Program

Business Drivers for the Metrics Program	Objectives of the Metrics Program
Measure conformance with corporate values and policy	Positively influence action, attitude and policy
Measure change from a desirable to undesirable state of risk or *vice versa*	Impact exposure to specific Risks
Measure compliance with legislative and regulatory requirements	Demonstrate Security's value through clear alignment with business strategy and objectives
Measure successes and failures of past and current security program investments	Provide assurance of cost effectiveness and benefits of security programs

Be clear on your priorities and objectives as you begin to develop your program. Talk to your boss to determine what management would value and how they would use actionable metrics from your organization. Determine who among your colleagues is measuring and reporting with quality and relevance. I'll give you a tip: Your information security partner has volumes of established metrics you can use as a model.

Don't take this step lightly. Create a formal process for identifying what management wants and needs. Think about the knowledge resident in your programs that offer quality guidance to business strategy and an improved state of risk management. There is a clear correlation between how well you identify these needs and how successful your program will be.

STEP 2: DETERMINE WHO YOUR METRICS ARE INTENDED TO INFORM AND INFLUENCE

You are well aware of what will happen if your company fails to connect with the needs of its customers. I cannot overemphasize the importance of understanding the diversity of perceptions about risk and how each of your constituents views your role in its management. Metrics are central to our ability to influence and engage our customers in their role in corporate security and brand protection. They enable a coherent set of messages focused on a targeted audience.

Each of these audiences has a unique agenda and set of needs, a "hot button," if you will. Some need to see the broader view with a clear assessment of alternatives. Others require the 10 minute laser approach to the problem and best solution. You must know your customer and what motivates them to action. Your message has to be tailored to influence, to enable them to see why your message deserves their acceptance and buy-in.

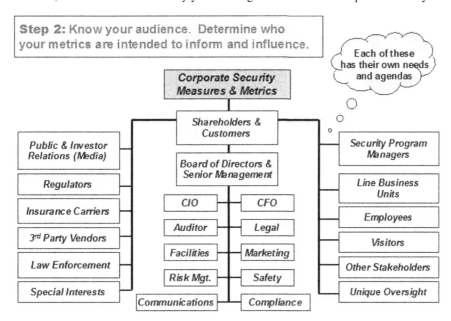

Metrics should be presented as enabling tools rather than criticisms whenever possible. Positive action is more likely if the audience feels it is being given an opportunity rather than a sharp stick in the eye. You want partnership in results more than a notch on the gun.

STEP 3: IDENTIFY THE TYPES AND LOCATIONS OF DATA ESSENTIAL FOR *ACTIONABLE* SECURITY METRICS

I have no time for the security manager who tells me there are no data to support a metrics program! Now, I'll take that back if you don't log calls, take reports on incidents, and are not accountable for reporting on how you have spent your budget—in which case the remainder of this presentation has no connection to your security program. You have a staggering amount of data in the files associated with your service portfolio. You have invested financial, personnel, and technology resources into understanding, preventing, and responding to the risks on your watch and the services you provide to your customers.

Take a look at the business drivers and objectives you outlined in step 1, and then consider the types of data you might need to create meaningful metrics that help meet those objectives. Think about the needs and hot buttons of your many constituents seen in step 2.

- How have your programs resulted in an improved state of risk management?
- What learnings can be used to modify business process and thereby eliminate future risk?
- How can your unique knowledge and perspective more directly enable alignment of security programs to the business strategy and needs of your internal customers?

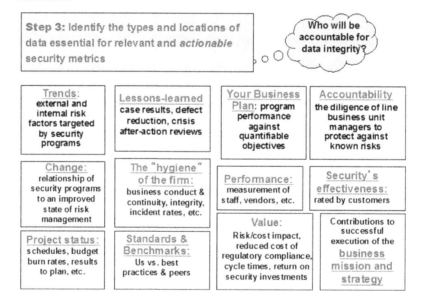

Actionable metrics require analysis, draw conclusions, and tell a story. The results they demonstrate provide direction for decisions, affirm actions taken, or provide clarity for next steps. Nonactionable metrics simply count things and have little value for influencing or finding causes of risk.

The above image represents a filing cabinet containing the various categories of metrics with an emphasis on making them actionable. Develop the contents of each drawer based on your constituents' needs as well as the need to maintain a library of measures consistent with the security organization's needs.

Putting the data to work: So, now I'm seeing a trend, a timeline on workplace violence. How do I get to the *meaningful, actionable* metrics? You employ the same process you'd follow to build a solution to the problem: What are the root causes, what specific steps or countermeasures should we employ to eliminate these vulner-abilities, and what performance measures would I evaluate to tell me if my proposed solutions were effective? This landscape looks something like this:

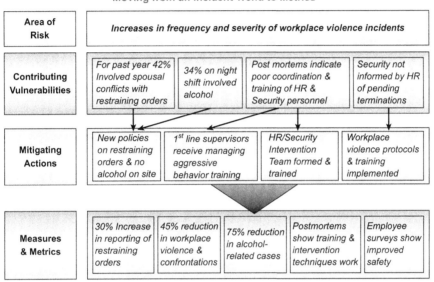

Moving from an Incident Trend to Metrics

Area of Risk	*Increases in frequency and severity of workplace violence incidents*			
Contributing Vulnerabilities	*For past year 42% Involved spousal conflicts with restraining orders*	*34% on night shift involved alcohol*	*Post mortems indicate poor coordination & training of HR & Security personnel*	*Security not informed by HR of pending terminations*
Mitigating Actions	*New policies on restraining orders & no alcohol on site*	*1st line supervisors receive managing aggressive behavior training*	*HR/Security Intervention Team formed & trained*	*Workplace violence protocols & training implemented*
Measures & Metrics	*30% Increase in reporting of restraining orders*	*45% reduction in workplace violence & confrontations*	*75% reduction in alcohol-related cases*	*Postmortems show training & intervention techniques work*	*Employee surveys show improved safety*

STEP 4: ESTABLISH RELEVANT RISK-RELATED METRICS

Relevant metrics clearly link to something you want to accomplish that has a direct benefit to the business. We can approach this step in a couple of ways: (1) establish metrics that demonstrate our role in enterprise risk management and (2) establish metrics that demonstrate our alignment with business strategy and objectives.

Risk-related metrics will allow you to determine and to demonstrate to management how security programs and services are impacting the business' risk. To develop these:

1. Prioritize the risks confronting your enterprise. What is the appetite for risk? Which are most important to the business, and which have the greatest potential consequences?
2. Determine which risks security has full or partial responsibility for managing (remember that security is a shared, delegated accountability in several key areas).
3. Inventory the products and services you have in place to address these risks.
4. Identify the results management wants to see from its investment in these products or services; how these products and services are impacting risk management (positively or negatively); and whether they're doing the job reliably and cost effectively.

Your focus on risk also provides an opportunity to demonstrate security's alignment with, and value contributions to, the business. Can you envision a metric that demonstrates the results of the steps you are taking to reduce or manage program costs while maintaining or improving the state of security in your company?

As you establish your metrics, focus on developing those that can serve the dual purposes of assessing risk and demonstrating value. Highlight metrics that show such benefits as increased protection and decreased cost, enhanced customer satisfaction or confidence due to security measures, increased recovery of losses, reduced risk to revenue-generating activities, reduced insurance costs, reduced risk of attack, and reduced notable audit findings attributable to security defects.

Below is a summary example.

Metrics are designed to facilitate decision making and accountability

* **Based on security** performance goals and objectives

* Quantifiable, **obtainable, feasible to measure**

* Repeatable, **provide relevant** performance trends over time

* **Useful in** tracking performance **and directing resources**

Adapted from Hash & Grance, National Institute of Standards & Technology

STEP 5: FOCUS YOUR METRICS ON DEMONSTRATING SECURITY'S MULTIPLE BENEFITS TO THE BUSINESS

Our metrics need to be focused on assuring measurable benefits to the business; some are indicators of enhanced levels of protection, and others indicate positive reductions in cost and risk exposure.

* They drive standard-setting and facilitate the critical assessment of program performance.
* They set expectations for owners and operators of risky business processes.
* They set objectives that result in improved response, faster recovery, and lower cost of business operations.
* They facilitate measurement of qualitative and quantitative results that may serve to support a variety of business objectives while providing measurable direction to program implementation.
* They enable measurement of the consequences of failed response and the benefits of above-standard performance.
* They force consideration of alternative approaches, thereby enabling cost avoidance and cost efficiency.

- They facilitate teamwork and management direction by setting visibly measurable objectives and program performance plans.

> Step 5: Focus development of a body of metrics to demonstrate
> Security's multiple benefits to the business

Additive Benefits	**Deductive Benefits**
• Increased level of protection with improved controls and less cost	• Reduced risk to revenue generating activities
•Increased engagement of employees in securing corporate assets	• Reduced cost of security related incidents
•Enhanced ability to satisfy customers with improved methods of protection	• Reduced cost of insurance
•Increased market penetration attributable to security measures	• Reduced notable audit findings attributable to security defects
•Increased recovery time to critical process interruption	• Decreased risk exposure from cost reducing outsourced activities
•Increased integrity to revenue generating activities	• Reduced risk to customers in sensitive transactions & relationship management
• Increased recovery of losses	• Reduced risk of attack through more measurably effective protective measures
•Increased confidence in effectiveness and need for security controls	• Reductions in employee interaction with time consuming security measures

Check the list to see where your programs may contain additive or deductive benefits you can track and report to management.

STEP 6: ESTABLISH INTERNAL CONTROLS TO ENSURE INTEGRITY OF ALL DATA, DATA ASSESSMENTS, AND PROTECTION OF CONFIDENTIALITY

There is an old saying that there are three types of lies: "lies, damn lies, and statistics." I won't dwell on the obvious downside of "lies" or "damn lies" in our job, but I will underscore the importance of accuracy and integrity in your use of data and statistics.

Assurance of accountability

You don't need a dedicated staff or individual to maintain a quality metrics program. If your scope includes the full range of security services, or if you are a sole practitioner overseeing the physical security program, specific individuals need to be held accountable for maintaining the administrative integrity related to those data that will be maintained for metrics and other elements of program management. If you rely heavily on vendors to provide the day-to-day security service delivery, do not fail to incorporate contractual standards on reporting and data administration.

Assurance of data integrity

Consider these two key objectives for our security measures and metrics: (1) positively influence action, attitude, and policy and (2) materially impact exposure to specific risks. The visibility of these objectives imposes the highest standards of data integrity. The ability to craft strategy and tactics that effectively target specific risks relies upon reliable data processed by competent, focused analysis. But imagine the potential consequences of drawing conclusions and formulating recommendations to management on inaccurate, unreliable data overseen by flawed, poorly supervised sources!

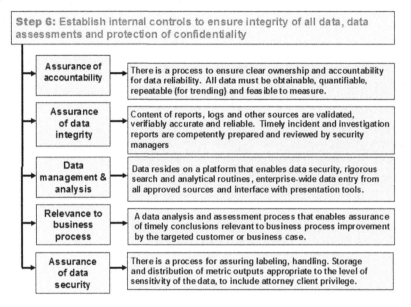

Step 6: Establish internal controls to ensure integrity of all data, data assessments and protection of confidentiality

Assurance of accountability	There is a process to ensure clear ownership and accountability for data reliability. All data must be obtainable, quantifiable, repeatable (for trending) and feasible to measure.
Assurance of data integrity	Content of reports, logs and other sources are validated, verifiably accurate and reliable. Timely incident and investigation reports are competently prepared and reviewed by security managers
Data management & analysis	Data resides on a platform that enables data security, rigorous search and analytical routines, enterprise-wide data entry from all approved sources and interface with presentation tools.
Relevance to business process	A data analysis and assessment process that enables assurance of timely conclusions relevant to business process improvement by the targeted customer or business case.
Assurance of data security	There is a process for assuring labeling, handling. Storage and distribution of metric outputs appropriate to the level of sensitivity of the data, to include attorney client privilege.

Data management and analysis

You can maintain a solid metrics program with standard desktop applications like Excel and PowerPoint. But scalable, commercially available incident reporting software is highly recommended to provide a more tailored and robust infrastructure for standardized reporting, facilitate customized administrative routines, and enable quantitative analysis and trending.

Relevance to business process

There are two perspectives with security metrics in my view. One involves the essential maintenance of data to support security program planning, management, and performance assessment. The other analyzes a variety of risk and program-specific data and draws conclusions of *measurable* relevance to business risk management. We seek to structure measures and metrics that inform (increase awareness) and assess the effectiveness of internal controls. Remember, we seek to influence policy and enable the business to more securely engage in business activities that might otherwise be too risky.

Metrics are the fuel of a corporate security communication strategy. The accuracy and reliability of your data and the conclusions you draw from them are directly tied to the reliability—the trust—of the security program and its leadership.

Assurance of data security

A measurably effective metrics program will be storing and generating a variety of outputs containing highly sensitive information. Reporting on risk is risky business—it may reflect on the reputation of the business. Think about a presentation to top management or the Board on investigative findings related to employee misconduct or the need to address significant vulnerabilities in the protection of customer information. This is potential stuff for the upper right hand corner of the *Wall Street Journal.*

As the need for such metrics is identified, you may want to discuss special protection of the files and outputs with General Counsel. They may want to apply Attorney Client Privilege for any material that may be generated on matters of high sensitivity. A classification scheme consistent with information protection policy should be applied and, if for some strange reason there is no such policy at your company, you are encouraged to seek guidance on confidentiality labeling, distribution, and secure storage. Remember, the data we cull from our logs, incident reports, storage media, and other sources we maintain are discoverable in litigation for negligent security or other legal matters.

This last step is primarily about quality assurance and housekeeping. Obviously, there are a lot of "devils in the details," but these six steps should serve to provide a solid foundation for a security metrics program and, along with the self-assessment, a quality check for what you have in place now. But, if you are going to put this solid program with attentive management to work, it still comes down to the few slides that you present to your audience of one or many. Below is some useful information to use as a guide in the delivery of your results.

A FEW CLOSING THOUGHTS

If you're not measuring, you're not managing. Measures and metrics are all about directly aiding the consideration of options, processes associated with making effective, defensible decisions and, as a significant benefit for embedded protection-supporting, an accountability model within our constituent business processes. Metrics reflect quantifiable progress toward goals and facilitate trending for performance navigation and tracking.

A qualitative security measures and metrics program is founded upon an established and clearly communicated set of internal controls focused on the integrity of the data that are gathered, the quality of the analysis and assessment applied to that data, and the assurance of data protection. The consequences of failing to embed these principles within your metrics program will go directly to the credibility of the security program and its management.

It is important for us as individual business leaders to develop metrics programs in our organizations, not just because it's good for business and security, but because outside forces will eventually step in to do it for you. Take the initiative. You will see the results in the quality of security's connection to the business.

GREAT DATA, GREAT OPPORTUNITY BUT *BAD* PRESENTATION!

So you've got good reliable data gained from a lot of outstanding work by your security team (or you), there is a great message to be delivered, and you're ready to build that presentation and then knock their socks off. But something went wrong on the way to the applause—to put it bluntly, your presentation (or your delivery) stunk.

> Do you really understand the audience you are trying to influence with your metrics and what buttons you need to push to connect your information with their desire and urgency to act upon it?

I've delivered hundreds of presentations over the past several decades and built the decks by the seat of my pants, flashy, with bullets galore spewing allegedly relevant data and pushing PowerPoint to the edge of its virtual limits. I've rehearsed until my delivery was worthy of one of those slick TV salesmen pushing you to put down 100 bucks for that thingamajig you don't need. Then I've watched the audience tune out, nod off, read the handouts before I've finished my intro or, worst of all, offer not one question when pushed for participation. I didn't appreciate the simple concepts you can see in the Extreme Presentation Method on the next page.[1]

If you think it's the PowerPoint slides that are the product of this metrics construction process, you're wrong! That's just the wrapper for your script. When you open PowerPoint you get choices: bullets, tables, graphs, and artsy stuff. Ditto with Excel; you're inputting lists of numbers and then leaping into a chart. Probe the literature on presentation skills and you will read about "death by PowerPoint" and sleep-inducing bullet or list talk. You may only have 5 min to deliver your important message. Look carefully at the circle in the Extreme Presentation Method and think about the decisions you have to make about what you want to achieve with your message.[2]

The purpose of your metrics is to advise, persuade, influence, sell, impress, and drive action. Security metrics should eliminate plausible denial by informing, recommending, and driving action. Our business is about the serious business of managing risk. If you follow the concepts in the following graphic, you will make your presentation persuasive and visually convincing, you will more likely make your case, and you will have the ability to measure the success of your story. That's a metric worth pursuing.

---

[1] *Advanced Presentations by Design: Creating Communication That Drives Action*, Dr Andrew Abela, Pfeiffer (2008).

[2] Every company has established presentation formats, available support for populating charts, and training on using various applications as well as on presentation skills. Find them and use them.

Extreme Presentation™ Method
Ten Steps to Persuasive Presentation

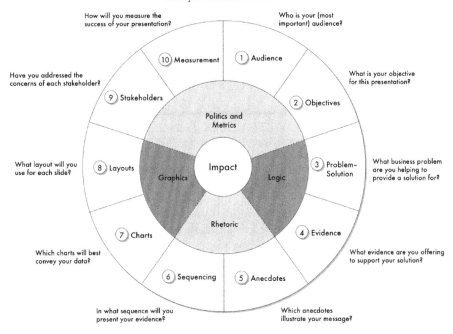

The Extreme Presentation method takes a marketing approach to presentation design: focusing on how to "sell" your ideas to your audience. The method consists of the five essential elements of an effective presentation and ten practical steps to put each of those elements into practice.

The circle in the center of the Extreme Presentation method diagram, with the word "impact" in it, indicates that the entire purpose of the method is to ensure that you have impact on your audience. Around that inner circle, the next ring contains the five essential elements of an effective presentation:

• **Logic**: we need to make sure that there is solid logic in our presentation and that our recommendations are robust;
• **Rhetoric**: we must tell an interesting story, in a compelling way. Logic is important, but of no use to you if everyone has tuned out because they are bored;
• **Graphics**: to make sure that you are using the most effective visual elements and overall layout;
• **Politics**: to apply effective influence in order to get your audience to take action; and
• **Metrics**: to be clear on what the specific objective is for the presentation, and how success will be measured.

There are two steps in each of the five elements, for a total of ten steps. These steps are shown in each section of the outer ring.

WHAT IS THE STATE OF THE ART IN CORPORATE SECURITY METRICS?

Hopefully, the self-assessment review earlier in this chapter has provided something of a status report on where you find your metrics program today. If you found your program short of where it should be using the measures provided or amended by your own standard (or that of your employer), you are not alone, as you will see in the following discussion.

It is a fact that far too many corporate security executives and managers have failed to understand the need to develop business-focused measures and metrics. This is in spite of the fact that their shareholders, executives, and internal business partners all manage from a foundation of performance metrics. It's gaps like this that have kept their security programs, and their knowledge of enterprise risk, out of executive and board-level visibility.

I previously discussed what you will find when you Google "security metrics": page after page of solid, established results...*on information security*. Infrastructure reliance, IT investment, and evolving threats over the past several decades have ramped up board-level perception of risk to a point that, were you to ask the average CEO what keeps him awake at night around the topic of security, you will likely get something about information protection. Our information security colleagues have done an outstanding job of understanding their universe of risk, developing detection and prevention tools, and building a body of standards and measures of security program performance. We, who protect their perimeters, vet their employees, investigate their transgressions, and watch often helplessly as they outsource the crown jewels, bumble along counting incidents and calling them *metrics*.

Contract security guards in the United States alone account for more than $16 billion and employ significantly more people than public law enforcement. Businesses spend billions on physical and logical security technology and tens of millions on background checks and an array of investigations. Yet, when you ask a source that should know about the total cost of security for their company, they typically don't know the answer because there are too many variables spread across multiple parts of the business.

So, given the expanse of the larger corporate security universe, where are the established standards, measures, metrics, and benchmarks to guide comparison and program performance assessment? Why did the American Society for Industrial Security (ASIS) struggle for so long before uttering the word "standard"? If the National Fire Protection Association (NFPA) and the U.S. Occupational Safety and Health Administration (OSHA) can issue codified standards on workplace safety, where are the statistics we can use to assess how we stand versus industry peers in workplace violence and other key risk indicators? How do my security program costs compare to others versus some measure like revenue, sales, or per employee? How about a measure of ethical health like the ratio of employees as subjects of investigation per 100 employees? I've got a few hundred of these but so would you if you really thought about it.

Why are these metrics important anyway? I think there are several reasons, but here are a few. (1) If you're not measuring, you're not managing. (2) You are in the risk management business; what impact are your security expenses having on your employer's exposure to risk? Are we "safer and more secure" than at this time last year? How are you measuring that, and what have the adjustments accomplished? (3) Management gets metrics from just about everybody else in the company and what are we to think if they aren't asking us for ours? What are they to think if you aren't advertising your department's performance metrics? (4) Your company's level of "security" depends on nonsecurity people engaging in a variety of actions to protect our assets. What are the metrics on their performance?

IS THIS THE STATE OF OUR ART?

Across our industry, there are Corporate Security Officers (CSOs) and security program managers who think this metrics business is a waste of time—nobody's asking so don't worry about it. As you will see in the benchmarking data that follow, we are seeing more who understand that their associates in the business (the ones competing for scarce resources) are maintaining and reporting upon performance indicators. But there are lots of others who we see too late in the game. They are the targets for outsourcing and reductions-in-force and their surrogates are seen quoted below.

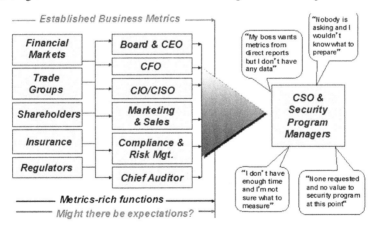

Look no further than your business partners!

Why do all those constituencies and colleagues around us understand that measuring business performance and the effectiveness of planned programs is a core management practice? Given the fact that our companies live and die on a host of well-established business metrics, why do so many of us in the business of security fail to understand and embrace the need? Look at the security-related regulations that have emerged over the past several years and the requirements for demonstrating compliance with defensible measurements. If you are a security manager looking across the table at your information security counterpart, he or she can drown you in the measures and metrics they use to assess the effectiveness of their safeguards. These are all metrics-rich functions led by managers who understand and depend on specific measures and associated metrics.

How do you stand versus your partners and stakeholders in effectively utilizing metrics for program development and measurement? What did your self-assessment say about this?

You don't need to get fancy or overfill the bucket with numbers and charts. Each of the constituencies you see here has a legitimate need for a targeted few metrics that are meaningful to them. Auditors need to track elimination of defects in internal controls, senior management needs to monitor key performance indicators (KPIs), your boss needs measures of your department's performance against specific objectives, and you need to keep watch over those key metrics you know are at the core of your enterprise protection mission.

In all honesty, there *are* real obstacles to building and managing an effective security metrics program. The quotes in the figure are real views held by many security managers on the value of metrics to them and their departments.

Real obstacles deserve real solutions

In a 2007 Security Executive Council survey, nearly 70% of respondents stated that they don't collect security program metrics for the purposes of presenting to senior management. This trend has continued, and in probing these and later findings, several themes emerged. The following examples provide an opportunity for discussion on building an effective metrics program.

Problem: "I don't have any data."

Solution: Open your file cabinet. The data are everywhere. You are counting things all over the place and working your tail off to fill tally sheets. Put the data to work! *There is no security program you own or share that fails to possess some associated metrics.* You have systems you monitor, incidents you count, funded projects that you have requested to meet some security objective, vulnerabilities and risks you have identified, crime trends in your area you track, the performance of your employees and vendors you direct, and false alarms you have prayed don't come from certain points. For the boss who hasn't asked, he or she does not appreciate the risks your programs address on a 24/7 basis. And who's fault is that?

If management isn't asking, surprise them. Go find the CFO or the chief metrics officer in your company. The data are waiting and you have important lessons to deliver and stories to tell.

Problem: Management hasn't requested security metrics.

Solution: Surprise them. In one way, you're lucky. You are flying so far below the radar that they don't even know you're there. Consider this: Does your management want to be able to clearly see whether you're conforming with corporate values and policies? Would they like to have a visual representation of the state of the company's risk, desirable or undesirable? Would they like to have measurements and data at hand that show whether the company is in compliance with applicable laws and regulations? Do they want to know whether past and current security investments have resulted in decreased risk or fewer incidents, so they can more easily determine the direction of future investment?

You can provide all this with security metrics. If management isn't asking for them, the best-case scenario is that they don't realize that metrics are the way to get these results. The worst-case scenario is that either they don't consider security an important part of the business or they don't know what security does. They're asking for metrics from nearly every other business unit. If they're not asking you, it might be because they aren't thinking about you at all. If that's the case, you've got big problems.

But when it all comes down, it doesn't matter why management isn't asking us for metrics. We should be providing them. As the security experts, it's our job to manage risk and to inform management on our status. We should be taking metrics to them; we shouldn't have to wait to be asked.

Problem: We don't have the money to create a security metrics program.

Solution: What money? Measuring your various programs is not something extra to do. It is a key element of management and an expectation of your position. Metrics are the outputs of the measuring process. The tools and data you need to create security metrics already exist. If you conduct after-action reviews, if you speak to your peers about trends and best practices, if you assess your risk on a regular basis, if you track project status or log incidents, you've already got the necessary data. If you have access to a computer with PowerPoint, you've already got the necessary tools and technology. Do you need to do some analysis to turn the data into metrics? Of course. You might not have the budget to dedicate a staff member to metrics creation, but who better to develop the necessary metrics than you? You know the program, the business, the risk, the needs—and you have the authority to collect and access all the information you need.

Problem: There is a lot of talk about performance metrics in my company but where does accountability lie for the maintenance of a measurements and metrics program for corporate security?

Solution: The answer, as shown in the graphic on the next page,[3] is that it is shared up and down the organization, but the CSO is the initiator who must design and sell the program up and down the chain of accountability.

Many security managers believe their executives don't clearly articulate what types of business-related security metrics they would like to see. However, in many instances, the same security managers fail to sell their own unique perspectives on enterprise risk to influence corporate risk perspective and policy. The responsibility for the failure or success of the metrics program rests with both these roles and with

---

[3]The chart has been adapted with permission from *IT Security Metrics Guidance*, Hash and Grance, National Institute of Standards and Technology.

other employees and executives in the chain. To ensure that metrics receive the support they require, both in development and in organizational acceptance, security must seek to institutionalize protocols and expectations for security risk awareness and shared responsibility for risk management.

The below graphic clearly implies that the hierarchy of responsibility commences and terminates with the security leader. Look at where the upward arrow establishes accountability. We are responsible for starting the process using our unique perspective and databases. We have the expertise to conduct an after-action review and determine how an event unfolded and where the gaps lie with regard to responsive internal controls. The real challenge lies in penetrating the higher levels of senior management and encouraging them to embrace our value-added services.

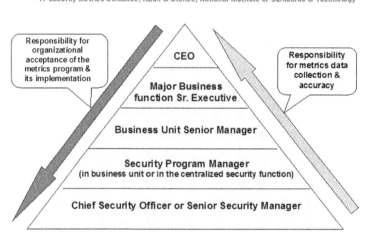

Metrics-Related Roles & Responsibilities*

* IT Security Metrics Guidance, Hash & Grance, National Institute of Standards & Technology

Let's look at the levels of responsibility, because they say a lot about real ownership and buy-in for security measures and metrics.

CSO or Senior Security Manager: This person has responsibility for metrics data collection and accuracy, and is the owner of the central warehouse where all security-related data are stored and analyzed. If you don't "own" the full spectrum of security data, you should think about establishing a Security Committee comprising representatives from internal organizations that own various pieces of the overall picture. Examples for membership include Internal Audit, the CIO's Chief Information Security Officer, Risk Management, Compliance, Legal Counsel, and business unit representation, with specific attention to a higher risk unit.

Line Security Manager: In many organizations, line business units staff a security function that relates specifically to the risks in that business process. Many corporations decentralize line security responsibility to appropriate line functions with a centralized CSO as the focal point for security policy and investigations. Other examples are found in fraud risk managers, contingency planners, and specialized risk management units.

Business Unit Leader: Senior management often fails to clarify the responsibility of this first line of defense. These are the custodians of the assets, and they set the expectations for integrity and corporate asset protection. The metrics program needs strong focus on this level of accountability.

CEO (or COO or Other Senior Executive): This person has responsibility for organizational acceptance and accuracy of the metrics program. The CSO's access to this level allows him or her to make senior management aware of the implications of various measures, and provides the platform for holding subordinates accountable.

Failure to build the metrics program around an accountability model like this can severely impact the potential benefits and effectiveness of the program. Metrics are designed to inform and impact policy and decisions. The reach of your work is critical.

Problem: You have the data but not enough time.

Solution: Sorry. It's your obligation to understand what it means and how to use it to get results. You may be one of the many sole practitioner CSOs overseeing a variety of outsourced security vendors and a small support staff. As difficult as it may be, you still have the obligation to understand the data being generated by your programs and routinely *informing* (*informing* is different than *reporting*) management on security-related activities and trends they need to know to perform their risk management responsibilities. "I don't have the time" is a logical conclusion in the face of limited resources; but how well will that work after something bad hits the fan that had a variety of leading indicators you were seeing out of the corner of your eye?

Let's say you maintain trend data on a small set of notable incident types that you bundle into your avoidable risk storyboard. You don't have time to do a deep dive on a few hundred incidents, but you should take the time to pick a few as indicative of notable trends. "Let me show you some facts around this case that are similar to 45 others we have investigated in the past quarter." The deeper dive on that one event can yield a host of concerns around avoidable risks. These short-term exercises move the department from a data warehouse to a business intelligence and risk management service. It also helps tell the story about what you could do if you had the resources to really dig into the data and report on a more formal basis.

Analysis enables metrics to tell a story, describe the root cause of a trend, and demonstrate how risk has been impacted by our collective efforts to mitigate.

Problem: You have the data, but what do they mean?

Solution: You are an experienced risk manager. Use that knowledge to understand what the data are telling you. A security metric is not a number plucked from a list of other numbers; it's simply not meaningful standing alone. Don't get me wrong—you need lists of numbers and their descriptive data. You also need a data management system to enable collation and analysis. Analysis enables metrics to tell a story, describe the root cause of a trend, and demonstrate how risk has been impacted by our collective efforts to mitigate.

Consider a CSO whose company is making a corporate-wide push for all business units to maintain a set of metrics to support a broader and deeper perspective on enterprise risk management. His self-assessment concluded that security was too focused on asking "how much" and counting things rather than developing actionable, risk-focused metrics that find real value in what lies behind the data. The security organization had organized its approach in several buckets of activity. Following are some conclusions from a few of the buckets.

- **Site Security Operations**. These are the first responders, the most customer-facing security entity, and the biggest budget item by far. These operations consume 1800 h/week across 10 locations, logging several hundred activities per site. Multiple spreadsheets enable drilling down into the numbers, but there is nothing about what they mean. What locations are demanding more resources or presenting greater risk than others? What performance measures with what results are being found for the contract guard service? What business units are the most and least attentive to following security protocols? What has been learned about alarms and their responses? What are the top five key performance indicators (KPI) for this set of activities, and what do they say about security's contribution to the protection of the company?
- **Site Risk Assessments**. Security has conducted 63 security surveys/assessments in the past 6 months, which should cast a spotlight on the effectiveness of safeguards as well as business unit risk and compliance. Where are the soft spots in the protection strategy? What common vulnerabilities or gaps were identified? What percent of those were found across the sample? How many recommendations were provided, and what percent have been implemented? Importantly, how were those recommendations addressed?
- **Security Project Involvement**. There are 237 projects underway or completed. How many targeted risks or locations of concern will be impacted? How much more secure are the locations that received equipment through these projects? Are any of these projects calculated to reduce the cost of security to the customer? What percent were completed on time and on or under budget? If I'm the boss, why should I be interested in these data?
- **Investigations by Business Unit and by Type**. Of 274 investigations, 62% were in business units with 15% of the headcount and 45% of the top 100 most critical business processes. Is this significant, and what does it say about the state of security at these locations? Are there any common denominators found across multiple investigations? What are the root cause findings from investigation post-mortems? If I'm the CEO or a member of the Board, what are these data telling me about the attention of managers to enterprise protection? When you connect the dots across investigations and incidents, what have you learned that needs to be passed on to influence and inform?
- **Hours to Customer Service**. The company has already paid for the hours. What has it received for that investment? For example, what is the ratio of hours of guard patrol to reduction or elimination of known risks?

- **Background Checks**. What has security learned from 14,254 background checks? Are there more derogatory findings in specific recruitment pools or vendor groups? The metric that your human resources (HR) group cares about is cycle time to completion. Are you delaying the business unnecessarily?

This CSO understood that counting incidents and transactions is an essential part of building our metrics. But standing alone and reporting to management, they totally fail to tell a story or prompt action. Management needs and should expect a deeper dive on risk. Consider how security's unique, almost singular, perspective on risk can engage, advise, and integrate its programs with the enterprise risk management strategy.

Problem: You have the metrics and they are going in the wrong direction.

Solution: Sorry, but metrics are bidirectional. If you are paying attention, the leading indicators are there to see and act upon. You have built a solid process around measuring security program performance and you have been reporting to the point that the boss or other authority figures are expecting them.

- Your objective to reduce a risk trend (with Board and CEO visibility) by 25% has gone up 22%,
- Those critical cycle times continue to move north when that temporary head-count was intended to move it south, or
- The results of your internal review on the next government inspection indicate that the results could impact award fee and endanger a critical schedule.

This is about measuring, after all, and that is precisely the point. Measuring guides direction and metrics provide the meters and dials to track what is being measured.

It's easy to see that the problem this security manager has is not the metrics—it's about how effectively resources are being managed to obtain the results sought. This is precisely why metrics are so important as an integral element of your program management scheme.

The dial on that expensive new initiative that has gone in the wrong direction didn't just spike like a blown radiator in your car. Incident data, monitoring directed to impact analysis, and risk assessment keyed to root cause reduction all would have provided actionable indicators. Cycle times are not quarterly snapshots; they comprise minute-by-minute, hourly, daily, or other finite measures of process execution recorded at a frequency that enables a manager to determine status and implement improvements on the run.

I defy you to find any authoritative discussion about planning and objective setting that does not include an absolute requirement for embedding measurements in the proposed work. The results, whatever the direction, are supposed to be visible to impose analysis and decision.

Problem: "I have the data but I'm not sure they are accurate."

Solution: Stop! Go no further until you are absolutely positive on data accuracy, the validity of your analysis, and the conclusions you have drawn from the data. If you are a sole practitioner with a handful of metrics or a CSO with a staff waiting to fill a library, both require the same commitment to integrity throughout the life cycle of your data. Metrics are the fuel of a corporate security communication strategy. The accuracy and reliability of your data and the conclusions you draw from them are directly tied to the reliability—the trust—of the security program and its leadership.

Problem: "I have lots of spreadsheets and all kinds of data on incidents and our responses, but I either get pushback or lack of interest when I show the results to management!"

Solution: Really? That's because you are just counting and not using the brains and experience they are paying you for to interpret the data and use the results to inform and educate. Look at this spreadsheet to see what I mean. Engage your team in digging for root causes and actionable results.

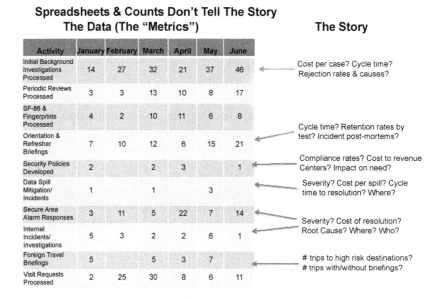

Spreadsheets & Counts Don't Tell The Story

The Data (The "Metrics")							The Story
Activity	January	February	March	April	May	June	
Initial Background Investigations Processed	14	27	32	21	37	46	Cost per case? Cycle time? Rejection rates & causes?
Periodic Reviews Processed	3	3	13	10	8	17	
SF-86 & Fingerprints Processed	4	2	10	11	6	8	
Orientation & Refresher Briefings	7	10	12	6	15	21	Cycle time? Retention rates by test? Incident post-mortems?
Security Policies Developed	2		2	3		1	Compliance rates? Cost to revenue Centers? Impact on need?
Data Spill Mitigation/ Incidents	1		1		3		Severity? Cost per spill? Cycle time to resolution? Where?
Secure Area Alarm Responses	3	11	5	22	7	14	Severity? Cost of resolution? Root Cause? Where? Who?
Internal Incidents/ Investigations	5	3	2	2	6	1	
Foreign Travel Briefings	5		5	3	7		# trips to high risk destinations? # trips with/without briefings?
Visit Requests Processed	2	25	30	8	6	11	

Problem: "I have the data but I'm not clear on how to use them most effectively."
Solution: Good, actionable metrics tell a story.

Next time you have a physical and they do the usual lab work, ask for a copy and see if you can determine your health quotient. Sure, there are a few we've all memorized like the bad this or the good that. But it's typically line after line of unintelligible gobbledygook—really important gobbledygook. A key measure of good data is their ability to inform and drive action in a specified direction. News organizations like the *Wall Street Journal* present reams of data that have to reveal their message to knowledgeable, time-challenged readers daily. Your senior management and Board members follow, absorb, and make crucial business decisions on a host of spreadsheets, graphs, and trend lines. What kind of decisions would they make from gobbledygook?

Good metrics demand a story. The story reveals the lesson, the learning from the conclusions drawn by analysis of the data. Like any good story, you have to know your audience to best select your theme to connect to its frame of reference.

As you can see in the spreadsheet notes, I've introduced the limitations of the singular focus on incidents per whatever factor you choose and how much time those activities have consumed. These are data we must maintain to plan and manage, but here we are just counting things rather than analyzing our hard-earned data so that we may inform and influence. To repeat: counts don't get action. What's your story with these data? We often forget that our typical customer doesn't see the data we present through anything remotely close to a level of informed judgment. Oh, they are disturbed by that trend that shows the 21% increase in workplace violence at Plant X but then do we leave them to draw their own conclusions on the root cause of these events? There has to be a story here that drives judgment and moves action.

In the Plant X workplace violence example, analysis revealed a prevalence of alcohol use on the night shift with an obvious lack of supervisory oversight. In drilling down, it became clear that shift supervisors, security, and HR were unclear on roles and reporting, and there was a general absence of policy and protocols around workplace behavior. The Security Director built a briefing around these well-founded conclusions and was able to engage HR, Legal, and plant management on solutions that subsequently reduced these incidents to near zero. The story told to top management not only demonstrated leadership in resolving a potentially serious set of risks but established security's role as an effective collaborator and business partner.

Good metrics must convey reliable information. We may be tempted to look at our data and make gut conclusions. The result may reveal symptoms and miss root causes. The story then is substantially fiction rather than fact. Fiction is not a good thing in our business. Effective, actionable risk management requires disciplined analysis. We have the knowledge to understand the data we have gathered and maintain the lists that need to be counted. This covers the "how much," but we have the obligation to probe the "what, where, why, and how" to construct those scripts that reliably inform and influence.

When you look at your incident data for the past several months, what theme emerges? Pick a trend and drill down. What are the common denominators? How many of these risk events were preventable? What vulnerabilities contributed to their occurrence? What few cost-effective actions will most impact improvements?

Now tell them the story.

Problem: I've got my data but management wants to know about how we compare.

Solution: So reach out and compare!

BENCHMARKING YOUR METRICS WITH PEERS

While it's clear that standalone metrics lead to significant internal benefits, their value increases exponentially when they're paired with the metrics of others. Comparing your metrics results with the results of other businesses in your sector and across sectors lets you rate your security program's performance, which could help you identify security gaps as well as gain funding and executive-level support. Unfortunately, the security industry has often shown itself unprepared and unwilling to develop a framework to accommodate benchmarking on a significant scale.

How is benchmarking useful? Comparing your security metrics results with those of others can give you insights beyond those you receive from studying your own metrics without context. Say, for instance, that you've established a metric to show security's cost as a percentage of the company's revenue. You've collected all the data and done your calculations. However, as you prepare to present the results to management, you realize that you have no way of proving to your CFO that the numbers you've arrived at are evidence of cost efficiency.

The percentage may look great to you, because you may have talked with peers about their overhead and heard some statistics at seminars that convince you that you're way ahead of the curve. But your CFO is a tough sell and is going to think your cost percentage looks awfully big sitting out there all by itself. Without solid data showing that your security program eats up a smaller percentage of revenue than those of your competitors, your numbers may be more of a hindrance to you than a help.

Without metrics results from other companies, you have no way of identifying what's missing from among your own security measures and programs. Your internal metrics may show that you're meeting your own and your management's standards in all your existing initiatives, but they can't tip you off that your standards are lower than the standards of 80% of the other companies in your sector.

Reliable benchmarking data also allow you to label your program "good," "better," or "best"—or "bad," "worse," or "worst"—and you can't honestly do that with only your internal metrics. If you could prove your program was good, better, or best, you may have an easier time securing support and funding for security initiatives, and you'd be able to easily show due diligence in case of a breach or lawsuit. If you could prove your program was bad, worse, or worst, you'd be able to see exactly where you needed improvement, and you'd again have an easier time convincing senior management of the need for funding and support.

FINDING VALUE IN SECURITY BENCHMARKING
INTRODUCTION

Benchmarking is frequently employed by security industry organizations and security executives to enable comparative analysis. The process can be highly disciplined and comprehensive or merely present a variety of organizational and demographic data, leaving the digging to the reader. Practitioners need to carefully evaluate published data to ensure reliable comparability and follow a disciplined approach when building their own benchmarking project. The following discussion summarizes the objectives of the more disciplined process and some suggested approaches to its limitations.

Benchmarking adds the most value when it reveals transferable best practices.

Benchmarking is the process of comparing one's business processes and performance metrics to industry "bests" or best practices from other companies. Dimensions typically measured are quality, time, and cost. In the process of best practice benchmarking, management identifies the best firms in its industry, or in another industry where similar processes exist, and compares the results and processes of those studied (the "targets") to one's own results and processes. In this way, they learn how well the targets perform and, more importantly, the business processes that explain why these firms are successful.

The following is an example of a typical benchmarking methodology:

- Identify problem areas
- Identify other industries that have similar processes
- Identify organizations that are leaders in these areas
- Survey companies for measures and practices
- Share the leading edge best practice data
- Implement new and improved business practices

Because benchmarking can be applied to any business process or function, a range of research techniques may be required. They include informal conversations with customers, employees, or suppliers; exploratory research techniques such as focus groups; or in-depth marketing research, quantitative research, surveys, questionnaires, reengineering analysis, process mapping, quality control variance reports, financial ratio analysis, or simply reviewing cycle times or other performance indicators.[4]

THE CHALLENGE

The initial challenge in a review of this topic is definitional. Much of the "benchmarking" that we so frequently see in the security management space tends more often to be one-to-one comparative surveying than the more rigorously analytical practice of examining business process performance such as that described above. This more collegial and less time-consuming approach is directed to merely compiling comparative data on targeted functions such as headcount, costs, and demographics across a sample of colleagues' organizations. In this approach, "a company will focus its benchmarking on a single function to improve the operation of that particular function. Complex functions such as HR, Finance and Accounting and Information and Communication Technology are unlikely to be directly comparable in cost and efficiency terms and may need to be disaggregated into processes to make valid comparison."[5] This finding can certainly be true for corporate security functions and, as we have repeatedly found from our extensive use of functional benchmarking,[6] the challenge is in making "apples-to-apples" sense of the resulting data.

---

[4] Wikipedia.

[5] ibid.

[6] OPaL with over 250 companies, multiple client-directed surveys, and specific functional groups with deep probes on Global Security Operations Centers (GSOCs), guard force utilization, metrics, and total cost of security.

ESTABLISHED MODELS OF BENCHMARKING COMPARISON

1. Internal: We in corporate security can admire our colleagues in environment, health and safety, and information security who have a host of risk and operational metrics that may be legitimately compared between organizations. Mature comparative models are also present within corporate HR and real estate/facilities organizations.

2. Public Sector: For risk benchmarking, we may find models within the FBI Uniform Crime Reports, National Criminal Justice Reference Service (NCJRS), Department of Homeland Security (DHS), Labor, and others. While often frustratingly dated, these sources publish trend data on crime and other information that enable some level of reliable comparison in areas of risk.

3. Industry Sources: International Security Management Association (ISMA) members are highly active in pursuing a variety of more functional/organizational comparison data and *Security Magazine* annually publishes its Security 500 data. Several industry-specific security groups also periodically engage in benchmarking. The data from these and other industry sources need to be carefully evaluated for source data reliability, as they may rely on open sources rather than attributed input for their results.

4. Security Executive Council (SEC) experience: The Council extensively benchmarks both among members and more broadly on their behalf. The OPaL process has polled over 250 companies on three categories that we have determined provide qualitative information on security program business impact and alignment: organizational readiness, program maturity, and leadership status. Several more specific probes have extensively documented contracted security officer performance measures, hospital security program metrics, total cost of security, security metrics practices, and best practices in global security operations centers.

This unique industry perspective and continuing experience with practitioners has provided a solid platform for assessing the current state of security program benchmarking. What has this experience taught us about various security functions that make actionable and reliable comparison and learning difficult?

CURRENT STATE OF SECURITY BENCHMARKING

There are a variety of factors that serve to confound comparison of security-related data, even within peers[7] that would seem to have directly comparable security missions:

1. Unless well understood, security benchmarks do not provide accurate cost comparisons and actionable conclusions. Companies aggregate costs differently, apply widely disparate methods of assigning security costs across revenue and cost centers, and have significant costs in purchased service accounts that can complicate one-to-one comparison.

---

[7] The Business Performance Improvement Resource (UK) found 50% of companies engaging in benchmarking had significant difficulties in comparing data.

2. Security programs vary widely due to organizational structure, scale, assets, regulatory needs, risk awareness, and risk tolerance. A company with regulatory requirements like those found in the defense sector has significant security program cost and operational drivers that are totally foreign to high-tech or manufacturing firms not engaged in those products or services—firms that might otherwise be seen as functional "peers."

3. Each of the following organizational factors and risk-based business drivers presents market, legal, financial, and reputational risk influences (appetite for risk) to executives and Boards of Directors. In turn, they can dramatically impact the ability to find comparability in benchmark data input.
   a. Differing exposure of personnel and assets to known crime and safety risks
   b. Differing threats and sensitivity within proprietary networks and data
   c. Differing legal/liability/regulatory risk exposure for absence of responsive measures
   d. Differing levels of criticality in business processes requiring unique or more intense levels of protection
   e. Differing perspectives on risk appetite and approaches to risk offset strategies
   f. Significant differences in cost accounting models that spread (bury) service costs in distributed revenue centers rather than centrally where they are far more visible
   g. Building configurations that require more or less consideration of cost-based security-related posts or activities
   h. More or less exposure to the threat of knowledgeable insiders
   i. Variability in lessor or lessee requirements that dictate costs or protection options
   j. Business models that favor internal versus external (outsourced) staffing

4. The immediacy of threat and risk. Another spin on risk appetite. A company that has specific, more recent, and severe experience with security threats will likely devote more resources to protection activities.[8]

5. Security as a business enabler. An increasing number of companies have found that security can be a market differentiator and deserves a suite of services and attendant costs that "peers" may not desire.

6. Cultural and shareholder-directed service expectations. For example, security services in a privately held company may be more reflective of and responsive to the owners' bias to their concept of "protection" than that of a publicly traded company.

As an example, the following table displays 13 current security benchmark partners in (nonbanking) insurance and financial services that are aligned annually in an established industry benchmarking initiative. While allegedly comparable, these firms possess an incalculable range of qualitative and quantitative risk and business drivers that influence their respective security program and

---

[8] As we saw a few years after 9/11, this trend has definable shelf life.

resources allocations. How are we to approach meaningful comparison among these security "partners"?

Revenue	Security Budget	# Employees	# Security	# Contract	# Proprietary	Total
100,000,000,000	26,000,000	80,000	120	270	0	270
81,000,000,000	61,000,000	50,000	65	450	0	450
40,000,000,000	17,500,000	9000	17	202	0	202
27,505,000,000	27,605,000	42,000	80	350	0	350
22,000,000,000	8,500,000	35,000	10	12	140	152
19,000,000,000	3,731,444	4500	6	16	50	66
13,600,000,000	58,000,000	43,200	151	24	132	156
9,649,000,000	27,723,100	29,660	41	216	0	216
8,000,000,000	2,408,000	5530	19	11	0	11
8,000,000,000	4,000,000	11,000	5	65	11	76
7,540,000,000	8,200,000	7700	33	80	33	113
7,500,000,000	5,100,000	9200	29	24	0	24
5,500,000,000	10,200,000	10,000	58	75	0	75

This underscores the challenge with functional benchmarks that tend to push simple quantitative comparisons like heads and budgets rather than qualitative measures like KPIs. The former lack critical context and simply yield apples and oranges, whereas the latter allows business, cultural, risk, and mission connection and comparison. You can leverage these data to compare security cost as a percent of revenue and security cost per employee. However, contrary to the primary objective of benchmarking—the transfer of qualitative, actionable knowledge—these numbers are too limited to provide any indication that they reflect best practices or are more or less cost efficient.

QUALITATIVE OR QUANTITATIVE?

What action should we take if we know that a benchmark partner in the same industry has 2X security cost as a percent of revenue versus our company? Are they that much more cost efficient, or simply experiencing less risk and, thus, less pressure for security spending? Or is their appetite for risk significantly greater? These are valid (and accepted) measures but, standing alone, are not *actionable*. At the end of the day, that is the primary value of the benchmarking process. Consideration needs to be given to KPIs and key risk indicators (KRIs).

KEY PERFORMANCE INDICATORS

The ability to obtain a few KPIs should be an objective of a benchmarking initiative that seeks to provide transferable value. For example, where might some best practices discovered in the following examples enable actionable consideration at the sponsoring company?

- Percent of services with a targeted cycle (or response) time that successfully meet that target over a given period. What is it about a security team's deployment strategy that enables consistent ability to meet an aggressive response time objective?
- Cost of background investigation as a percent of total onboarding (staffing) process or cost of physical security as a percent of occupancy rate. Given rationalized case costs, why and how are this partner's processes more cost efficient?
- Cost of protection as a percent of maximum foreseeable loss. This links known facility security cost to an established insurance metric for trending or comparative analysis.
- Total hours of security staff time directly assignable to security incident management as a percent of total hours available. Is it beneficial to learn how a peer is able to direct costly staff time to higher return/higher value activities?
- Percent of critical business process interruption incidents where process recovery was within the recovery time objective (RTO). Recovery on-time to plan=reduced cost of impact and is a critical success factor.
- Ratio of general security certifications to total security population. A measure of onboard competency that should reflect an increased likelihood of service excellence.
- Rates of performance by contract guard firms to similar areas of service level agreements. This is a potentially valuable indicator of comparative vendor performance.
- Annual cost of security-related regulations. This is a means to identify best practices in tested methods of compliance.
- Percent of security initiatives funded and incorporated in business unit plans at security's recommendation. This is a measure of security's alignment and influence with key customers.

KEY RISK INDICATORS

KRIs are admittedly more problematic for benchmarked sharing due to confidentiality concerns, but when respondents are masked in the results, KRIs provide useful comparisons for more trusted exploration.[9] Here are a few examples[10]:

- Workplace violence incidents per 1000 employees
- Internal misconduct incidents or security policy violations per 1000 employees
- Losses to crime and internal misconduct as a percent of revenue
- Percent of derogatory background findings for specific geographic areas and employee groups

---

[9] This can be the equivalent of the FBI's uniform crime rates and a seriously lacking body of comparative risk data for corporate security. Large, multisector comparative sources of data are stored and could be anonymously aggregated from established incident reporting programs like PPM 2000, Ethics Point, and others.

[10] These examples also have comparative industry data available from established sources like the National White Collar Crime Institute, SANS and Poneman Institutes, Bureau of Labor Statistics, and other respected sources.

- Ratio of cost of loss to cost of protection
- Percentage of identified security risks that have a defined mitigation plan against which status is reported in accordance with policy
- Square feet space of business operations in countries or locations outside security resources or oversight

BEST PRACTICES

KPIs often imply embedded best practices, and successful response to KRIs typically engage a level of performance that rises to KPI status. Consider those opportunities when addressing the design of the benchmarking instrument and the population to be solicited for participation.

MANAGING THE LIMITATIONS OF BENCHMARKS AND BENCHMARKING

There are multiple limitations that must be addressed if benchmarking can be effectively used to direct measurable security process improvements. Here are some of those limitations and some approaches to managing them.

1. **Definitional limitations**: Participating benchmarking partners often fail to establish clear standards regarding data definitions. Companies have unique business and organizational drivers, and significant misinterpretations can result when key data element definitions are not common across comparing companies.
   Compensatory measures and success factors: Develop prework to obtain agreement with all participants on key definitions. Ensure consistent collection and coding of raw data to align with the definition.
2. **Limitation on data specificity**: The benchmark data request is too general to provide actionable data or too specific to obtain comparable data.
   Compensatory measures and success factors: Prework definitions can minimize data defects. A process for follow-up clarification and repair can address faulty responses.
3. **Size limitations**: The number of companies targeted for participation is too small to compensate for the probability of lack of responses. A limited response results in too small a sample to provide useful data or to be statistically relevant.
   Compensatory measures and success factors: Prework to (1) include a large enough sample to accommodate some percent of opt-outs and (2) gain assurance on participation to minimize nonresponse.
4. **Confidentiality limitations**: Relevant participants opt out. The data requested have high value for response quality but are deemed not available for sharing by key participants.
   Compensatory measures and success factors: It is essential that prework be done to identify areas of potential resistance and develop trusted areas of response. If

sample size is sufficient, nonattribution can mask identification and trusted relationships can enable actionable discussion of best practices in risk mitigation.

5. **Sector limitations**: There is a tendency in targeting to stay within one's backyard where more collegial engagement and relationships are known. This is particularly true with security practitioners and typically extends to remaining within one's own area of practice. This tendency defies the more established purpose of benchmarking, which is to identify best practices in business process and learn from them.
   Compensatory measures and success factors: Virtually every security process has an identifiable surrogate outside of security that may offer transferable best practices, and exploring "out of the box" should be seriously considered. We know that we can apply best-in-class practices from call centers to GSOCs, from audit processes to investigations and from just-in-time studies to security-related cycle and response times.[11]

6. **Organizational variability limitations**: The table on page 32 displays a host of obvious variables among security organizations within the same sector. Consider service delivery options of a CSO serving as "an army of one" versus a company that commits significant headcount and resources to security services. Property protection costs (guard services, physical security operations, and technology deployment/management, etc.) typically are the major cost drivers of corporate security budgets and tend to be common fields of benchmark targeting. Several points of service departure need to be taken into account where such configurations of service delivery differ. For example:
   a. Cost, headcount, and service quality between comparators with proprietary versus contract officers.
   b. Cost, headcount/full-time equivalents (FTEs) between comparators with closed versus open-access environments. Visitor controls and outsider access tend to be far more labor intensive.
   c. Cost and headcount between comparators employing internal versus outsourced investigations, background vetting, and other on-demand services.
   Compensatory measures and success factors: This is similar to the steps taken to address definitional limitations, but requires deeper analysis in participant selection to ensure that notable differences are rationalized or there are sufficient points among key areas of inquiry to provide transferable data. For example, a participant with a proprietary security operations team comparing to one with contract services may find data comparability in a hybrid model where select services, such as GSOC or EP, are employees.

7. **Limitations in process cost, time, and effort**: Large areas of inquiry with potentially complex or time-consuming response requirements, particularly when directed to security executives with limited staff resources, will encourage nonresponsiveness.

---

[11] Several security departments engaged in operational excellence and Six Sigma practices have learned from nonsecurity business processes.

Compensatory measures and success factors: Again, prework and advance selling of participation to targeted peers is essential. Phasing a broader, multitopic instrument over an extended schedule can enable a deeper dive and help ensure improved response; however, where specific participants with limited resources are desired for assured response, a more focused design with known areas of data availability may be advisable.

GETTING THE MOST OUT OF VALUABLE RESPONSES

After evaluating responses and finding potential gold, there is tremendous value in visiting the target to delve more deeply into their operations and establish a continuing relationship. The SEC's GSOC Best Practices team visited 10 participant sites and was able to see and learn far more than what can be learned from a one-dimensional survey response. We now have over 50 global companies involved in our GSOC working group that enables ongoing best practices assessment and member engagement.

CONCLUSION

Simply gathering a variety of business and organizational data in a collaborative, collegial setting is a perfectly appropriate area of comparative analysis. But it leaves significant voids in relevance and actionability, many of which have been noted above. Data such as these demand legitimate context: What are we to take away from a result that shows a markedly lower cost-per-whatever or the possibility that a peer is twice as efficient in some measure as we are?

As demonstrated in the discussion on limitations, there are an imposing number of variables in the structure and delivery of corporate security services. Selecting a methodology that is clear on the objectives of the proposed project for the sponsor and for each participant is essential. Prework (one-to-one contact) to ensure that definitions and survey questions are understood takes more time but will pay dividends in quality of responses.

Security executives seriously interested in learning best-in-class business and security practices should plan on deeper dives into a well-planned survey that has been presold with targeted participants. The notion of "collaborative" should be an incentive for partners to learn as well.

BENCHMARKING SECURITY METRICS PROGRAMS

In 2009,[12] the SEC initiated a benchmark survey to gather information on the current status of security metrics programs within 27 well-established corporate security organizations serving companies with a global business portfolio. While admittedly a small sample, these companies represented a solid cross section of industry sectors, and all had mature and multiservice corporate security programs, several engaging in use of best practices. The survey provided a detailed view of the status and focus

---

[12] Later benchmarking and individual program review results by the author up to the date of this book are consistent with these findings.

of metrics initiatives in the member companies. This effort was later expanded in a series of monthly Security Metrics Working Group sessions to explore the topic in greater detail. Several highlights from the initial benchmarking exercise are summarized here. Perhaps you will find these results supportive—or at least instructive—of a direction for your own program. I would also encourage you to return to the metrics self-assessment tool at the front of this book to provide a sanity check on the discipline currently being employed in your data management.

WHO IS DRIVING THE NEED FROM ABOVE?

The general consensus of need was about one-third driven by higher corporate management, a third self-driven, and a third with both as drivers. In spite of this range of prompts, about 75% of participants indicated that metrics were an accepted element of other business operations and that this influenced their interest.

WHAT BUSINESS DRIVERS ARE PUSHING THE NEED FOR IMPROVED METRICS FROM WITHIN THE SECURITY ORGANIZATION?

Some common themes emerged to provide a focus for the working group's efforts:

- Benchmarking, program efficiency/effectiveness, and security's return on investment (ROI).
- The desire to leverage metrics to improve alignment with the business, and let them make more informed decisions about accepting or remediating security risks.
- Using the data helps establish required business KRIs and KPIs.
- The ability to demonstrate to senior management the current state of security at each site, performance targets, and show improvements to our service delivery; clearly articulate the security risk to the business at a higher level.
- Our company is analyst driven and data focused. As such, we have always had to use grounded data and benchmarking to demonstrate program results and effectiveness.
- We would like to measurably demonstrate risk reduction, improve risk assessment, and communicate these factors to senior leadership.

WHAT HAVE BEEN THE ROADBLOCKS TO METRICS DEVELOPMENT?

Our assessment that there was a limited body of work in general security measures and metrics was affirmed with broad consensus on what our members saw as the biggest roadblocks to developing the kind of metrics program they believe would be of the greatest benefit to their department:

- Lack of standardized, industry-wide metrics.
- Lack of standard metrics and techniques and the willingness to share.
- The biggest roadblocks are lack of agreement on which activities and incidents measured against each other define effectiveness, the definition of the thresholds

or triggers that would constitute an alert, and the multiple databases that have to be mined longhand rather than automatically.
- Lack of systems across the organization to capture the necessary data, staff understanding of the importance of metrics, and the lack of executive focus on security metrics; the focus is on operations.
- Not being able to get our arms around the proactive/preemptive facets of security that cannot be measured, and not looking outside the security team for the total dollar impact to the company.
- Time and lack of peer data. The ability to demonstrate hard benefits that justify security spending.
- Program maturity, lack of transparency, and data spread out among too many business areas and repositories.

OBSERVATION

While it was not stated directly with this sample of security executives, it should be noted that a significant roadblock for many security organizations is with a general lack of effective incident reporting and data management systems—obvious keys to development and maintenance of timely and meaningful measures and metrics.[13] Another spin on this analytical constraint to a consolidated view of risk is the dispersal of security functions under various departments (CIO, Legal, Audit, HR, Risk, Compliance, etc.), often resulting in multiple, disconnected repositories of data.

WHAT SECURITY PROGRAMS ARE THE FOCUS OF YOUR METRICS?

It is not surprising, given the data seen in the following chart, that a clear majority of survey respondents indicated multiple mission-related points of interest for their metrics programs.[14] An interesting sidebar to these discussions unfolded during the latter sessions: security's ability to align and influence their business unit clientele appeared to take on more interest.

Session agendas tended to use the six topical categories seen in the program focus column in the following chart as a guide for content discussions, and various members have provided high-quality information on their metrics initiatives within these categories. Understandably, these contributors are among the participants having more mature metrics, as seen in the top two bars in the left column, below. It is also noted that the more experienced practitioners in these black arts are from among those with an information security portfolio—another indicator of the maturity and richer inventory of data in this discipline.

---

[13] Note your self-assessment results. Perhaps you are not alone?
[14] The chart displays higher totals due to respondent selection of multiple program interests.

WHAT BEST DESCRIBES THE CURRENT STATUS OF YOUR SECURITY METRICS PROGRAM?

While all group members acknowledged the need, the figure (given below) shows that more than 75% described a relatively mature current state, with the balance in a fairly early developmental status in their program evolution.

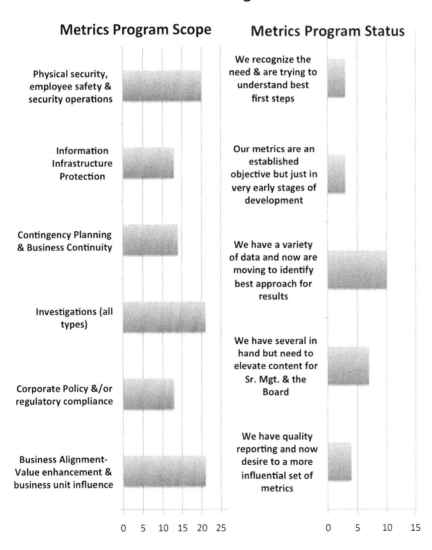

How 27 Global Companies See Their Security Metrics Program

One of the principal objectives of the Security Metrics Working Group was to fill the void in cross-sector metrics useful for benchmarking and internal performance measurement. Our initial steps included identifying a number of (hopefully) transferable measures, surveying the participant companies to seek consensus on a sample of different types, identifying data availability constraints, and testing utility by populating the data.

Assemble a combination of high-tech, manufacturing, retail, consumer products, health care, communications, and aerospace sectors in the room and find a few security metrics that would work within their companies and diverse portfolio of security services. Needless to say, interesting debates unfolded, and we ultimately arrived at the dozen metrics as shown in the figure given below. Follow-up polling focused on ranking each metric on a 1 (highest) to 5 (lowest) scale of importance and, for the purposes of this discussion, only those selected in the top two were tallied.

I'd leave it to the polling experts to do the deeper dives into the motivation of these findings, but suffice to say that three-quarters of those selected for their sample are directed to financial performance indicators and the polling was conducted in the midst of a major recession. It is also a universal desire of CSOs to seek metrics that can be used to deliver evidence of security's value ("justification of security spending") to the enterprise.

As for *security cost as a percent of revenue*, be aware that should you use a metric like this, plan on top management asking "how do we compare on that score with our competitors or peers?" Also be alert that knowledgeable pushback will underscore the fact that, even among peer group companies in the same sector, security departments typically differ in potentially significant ways. As underscored in the earlier discussion on benchmarking challenges, what is "security cost" if the respondents' suite of security services are not reasonably comparable? These are issues that can be addressed, but you need to carefully establish defensible points of comparison. Other accepted examples in this realm are security cost per square foot (again, define what is included) and one I like better, security cost per employee. Other examples, like the ratio of workplace violence per 100 employees or employees as subjects of internal investigations per 100 employees, are more accepted by disciplined risk surveys and offer measures of potentially significant operational and reputational risk.

Metrics Poll–Utility/Importance

1 = Most Important to us / 2 = Extremely Important

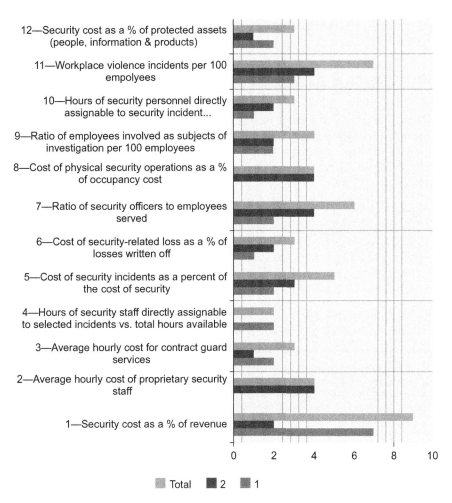

The working group security leaders tended to reflect a strong connection to the challenges confronting their businesses such as global expansion, cyber risk, outsourcing (the expansion of insider risk), and cost optimization. There was an evident need to leverage metrics to more effectively communicate security's value proposition and demonstrate the relationship of security programs to business objectives. Due to the diversity of the companies represented and the service portfolio of the members, the risk portfolio was expansive with few, rather than more numerous, common drivers.

This benchmarking initiative demonstrated the relevance of a small but diverse set of measures to a multisector group of security executives. A key finding, in my view, was the universal acceptance of the need and value of security metrics to their internal management objectives and, more importantly, to their obligation for risk and value-based executive communication.

SINGLE VERSUS MULTISECTOR BENCHMARKING

Given the diversity of this multisector working group, the SEC's opportunity to support the International Association of Hospital Safety and Security (IAHSS) in a similar metrics working group presented the prospect of identifying a body of measures appropriate to what appeared to be a more homogeneous sector. Hospitals are all about risk and represent a unique, physically demarked environment from which to view a security mission:

- Typically at the top tier of workplace violence statistics
- Risky patients: psychiatric, infants, dementia, felons under guard
- Risky environments: parking lots, regulated information and controlled substances, perpetrators and victims mixed in emergency waiting rooms, higher crime in city center facilities
- Intense financial pressure on service costs

Given a choice among a diverse selection of three dozen metrics, it is not surprising that this organization's members prioritized its top 10 as follows:

1. Aggressive incidents resulting in need for physical intervention or restraints by security
2. Security incident and event demographics
3. Security service (or other specific type) calls per daily guard hour
4. Percent of security incidents resulting from patient mental health/aggressive behavior
5. Aggressive incidents per daily guard hour
6. Workplace violence incidents per 1000 employees
7. Reported theft per 1000 inpatient days
8. IAHSS or other standards, guidelines, or peer-established performance criteria adopted and accepted as compliant
9. Ratio of security officers (first responders) to employees served
10. Security exercises and drills indicate acceptable levels of knowledge of response procedures consistent with potential risk exposure

While focusing on response to these risky work settings, this list also demonstrates an undercurrent of pressure on cost containment and the ongoing need to inform and gain support from management. With this group and others I've evaluated, I also sense frustration—a need to remind their customers that security is only a part of the solution and residents need to own a role in protection.

Since each sector has its set of unique risks, requirements, and controls, benchmarking within your sector allows you to make specific comparisons without having to account for the significant security-centric differences between industries.[15] Yet, with security becoming increasingly sophisticated and branching out in new directions yearly, should sector-specific benchmarking be the highest level of commonality we seek to achieve?

If we aspire only to benchmark within sectors, we will end up with hundreds of different sets of metrics that can't be easily translated across industry lines. While that would be preferable to what we have today—which is very little benchmarking (in this metrics area at least) at all—it isn't optimal. Ideally, there should be a single, common set of metrics that could be used across all markets or sectors that would apply to security at any company of any size, regardless of what business it conducts. Then, those common metrics could be modified within individual sectors to accommodate the peculiarities of the given market.

In other words, perhaps we're doing this backwards. The security industry has begun by developing metrics at the company level, then attempting to find commonalities within a sector, and we're not even seriously considering cross-sector benchmarking because by the time we get to that level our metrics have become so specific and complex that it's difficult to find shared elements to compare. I think that was a major takeaway from our initial Security Metrics Working Group.

Shouldn't we be trying to develop a baseline of security metrics that apply in every sector, and then moving down the chain from there? This would allow us to engage in meaningful benchmarking at a national and global level. It would also provide an easier entry into the metrics and benchmarking scene for sectors that currently don't engage in these activities to any great extent, because they could work from the baseline to develop sector-specific metrics instead of having to begin from scratch. For this type of high-level benchmarking to take place in security, some entity or a partnership of entities must first take the initiative to identify a set of measures that can be commonly used across sectors. So far, and aside from our limited SEC initiatives noted here, no such entity has emerged in either the public or the private sector.

SUMMARY

In these past few pages, I've summarized my view on why I believe measuring is so important in our enterprise protection business and provided a fairly straightforward self-assessment tool that should help to establish where your program stands and what incremental improvements may be appropriate to a more mature content and approach. If you seek to build a program from scratch or simply want to follow up on your assessment, a six-step process for building or renovating a security metrics

---

[15] Having said that, the IAHSS displayed some significant differences in service populations (urban/rural, public/private, specialty care vs general population, research, etc.) that tended to drive the risk management mission somewhat significantly.

program is outlined. Because I so often hear reasons that security practitioners have problems with their metrics, I've listed the more common concerns with some ideas on how to resolve or move past them. Finally, in sharing the feedback from some knowledgeable colleagues on how they are approaching their metrics, we provide some benchmarks that readers may find useful for calibrating their own directions. My earlier book, *Measures and Metrics in Corporate Security: Communicating Business Value*, provides a more detailed discussion of these program-building concepts and their (to me) undeniable relationship to the essence of security management.

In Chapter 2, my focus is on building your program on a foundation of the unique and rich pool of data derived from security activities. I believe that the value proposition for a metrics program may be measured by the extent to which we can effectively communicate what we have learned from the data, and then how well we craft the messages to have an impact on an improved state of business risk management.

Risk, after all, is why we have a job here. What's your story?

Quantifying & Communicating on Enterprise Risk

INTRODUCTION

In launching a comprehensive metrics development program, a chief security officer (CSO) from a Fortune 500 corporation who leads a very solid and comprehensive corporate security program communicated to his staff:

> *As an organization, we have generally struggled with enterprise metrics that truly show our value proposition to the company. I also want to be able to represent our program more effectively from a risk perspective during budget reduction times. Having effective, compelling metrics allow our senior leaders to make better educated funding decisions.*

Risk-related metrics not only direct security resource planning and performance measurement but become essential ingredients in the CSO's communication and influencing strategy. They recognize that senior executives need to be able to understand the unique perspective on risk, and metrics can speak the language of the boardroom. Good metrics drive action.

This chapter begins with an excellent article authored by several of my Security Executive Council (SEC) colleagues that originally appeared in the March 2010 issue of *Corporate Secretary* magazine.[1] Increasingly, regulations make board members accountable for risk awareness and subsequent management. They look to each function of the organization to address board-level risks and assurances that each element of the business is doing its part. Clearly, a process to ensure Unified Risk Oversight™ is needed.

When developed to its full scope and capability, corporate security serves solidly as an integrated element of corporate governance and enterprise risk management.[2] Security executives directing these functions build their programs around probing

---

[1] This content cannot be copied or distributed without written permission from The Security Executive Council.

[2] Unfortunately, this statement cannot be made for far too many companies who possess a variety of threats and avoidable risks. The emphasis denotes the fact that "full scope and capability" implies acceptance by top management for their place at the table.

risk assessments. Their programs are grounded on objectives that measurably serve to protect shareholder interests and enterprise assets.

You have a job because there are risks that management believes require unique competencies and dedicated resources. In our business, we see risk through an educated lens and bring special tools to the challenges of enterprise protection. But how will you measure your performance in addressing these risks? Will your metrics accurately specify real progress in the elimination of hazards or merely deliver statistics that fail to nail a relationship between your plan and the result sought? Security's contribution to the measurable management of risk depends absolutely on an understanding of root causes. Otherwise we suffer the consequences of wasting precious resources and reputation on attacking symptoms. We saw this relationship earlier in step 3 of the metrics program building process, and a variety of perspectives follow on the role of metrics in contributing to avoidable risk. The other selections in this chapter provide a few ideas and different perspectives on the reporting of security programs' contribution to risk targeting and enterprise risk management.

MANAGING ENTERPRISE-WIDE BOARD RISK

Sometimes great ideas come with big consequences. The continued business trends toward globalization, advantages of economic scale, and strategic partnering are multiplying corporations' opportunities, but they are also acting to multiply the impact of risk failure. One risk failure at a single point in a company or its supplier network—particularly one picked up by the media—can now have a profound effect across the entire enterprise, placing a company in jeopardy far beyond traditional measurements. It is clear, for example, that the failure to properly design a gas pedal can create repercussions beyond the scope and imagination of an automobile company's engineering department.

Risks occur in all size and shapes; most can be and are responded to correctly, but the failure to recognize the potential consequences of a risk failure beyond the initial report can bring serious damage to companies. Add to that the scandal-induced requirements for greater accountability and oversight, and it is clear why we have seen an increased push from the board of directors and senior management to conduct enterprise risk assessments and follow through with robust risk management.

Traditionally, only a few business units of an organization have coordinated risk management. This may make sense for some industries, but for most, an approach coordinated across the enterprise will yield better risk mitigation strategies and tactics.

A CONCEPTUAL RISK PICTURE

As management and the board strive to develop a clearer picture of risk in their organizations, they should endeavor to look across all functional groups to review, organize, and monitor the company's diverse collection of risks. The SEC, a problem-solving research and services organization that involves a wide range of risk mitigation leaders, has analyzed many corporate enterprise risk assessment plans and strategies to identify common concerns and opportunities to create a more consistent risk oversight process. The work was part of a research initiative to create a baseline corporate risk landscape that shows security's involvement in risk management.

The focus of the study was to identify risks that had security-related consequences and areas in which security mitigation strategies would add value to overall enterprise risk reduction. However, this process of risk identification and classification could be applicable to any function of the company.

After analyzing numerous and diverse enterprise risk assessments, the SEC identified common risks that faced corporations. These were organized into eight descriptive categories (left column of graphic on page 49). Next, they identified activities under each category that had related security risks (second column). This list represents many of the risks the SEC community has typically encountered, but is not meant to be an exhaustive list. Lastly, they drew on the successful practices and experience of its large faculty of former security and risk professionals (coined "Collective Knowledge™") to match security mitigation strategies to each "floor" of the corporation (third column).

The purpose of the research output was to provide a direct link between the business category and the potential use of a security program to mitigate the risks identified. Why security? Most security programs are designed to cross all business units; that puts the security function in a strategic position to help provide enterprise-wide protection against an array of risks. Security protection programs do not by their nature have to belong to the corporate security department. Instead, they are often shared programs in which a team comprising several business units collaborates to provide risk mitigation. Coordination with human resources (HR) for new employee background verification process is a classic example, usually employing HR, security, and legal departments.

SEC's constituency uses this tool to map how the security function can add value through risk-mitigation strategies across the enterprise. They report that displaying the risks in line with the values of the board helps them gain support and move initiatives through the organization.

ENTERPRISE RISK COUNCIL

To enhance their focus on the risks confronting their organizations, more companies are moving to establish enterprise risk councils (ERCs) composed of key business leaders who offer broader perspectives on the various risk concerns. This ERC format is designed to provide the same holistic approach to risk mitigation that the board provides for identifying and understanding risk. The ERC carries out its duties by allocating resources, analyzing cost benefits of mitigation solutions, and providing report card information to senior management for review with the board of directors. In this model, an audit committee reviews and analyzes the ERC's success in accomplishing its duties. The audit committee reports are used in part to determine executive compensation in connection with risk management and mitigation. The simple absence of a risk event does not guarantee bonus compensation, but the board's compensation decision should be driven by management's attention to identifying and managing risks.

SECURITY'S ROLE IN RISK MANAGEMENT

Many companies have found that some proactive security programs must be considered during, and integrated into, planning for new product and business program introduction. However, risk losses are too often considered to be one time variable expenses for which planning cannot be justified. The opposite is true. Events such as fraud and criminal attacks are normal in the global marketplace. Determining the extent of those risks, examining the cost of mitigation, and including that cost as part of the fixed cost is necessary for product launch.

A recent global supply chain study conducted by Stanford University demonstrated that a security program's inclusion in the basic movement of goods in the supply chain not only reduced shrinkage, but also enhanced productivity, lowered costs, and increased the speed of shipments involved in the study. Imagine a security program enhancing operating margin, speeding delivery, and enhancing customer relationships while also mitigating risks.

NEXT STEPS

It is critical that all functions play a role in understanding the new risk landscape. The corporate secretary has the opportunity and possibly the obligation to promote and govern board-level risk analysis. The research and conceptual graphic provided here was intended for security leaders, but this same process could be used with all staff groups and revisited regularly within the company. Having a common "picture" to help create a risk-aware enterprise and a model of Unified Risk Oversight™[3] can be a useful exercise.

---

[3] The concept of unified risk management focuses on the inter-relationship of policy and standards, threat and risk assessment, vulnerability mitigation, and risk-based defense-in-depth. Metrics are key to building effectiveness measures into both inputs and outputs of these processes.

BOARD LEVEL RISK & SECURITY PROGRAM ELEMENTS*

Board Level Risk Categories	Business Areas with Security-related Risk	Security Department Security Program Strategies/Mitigation	
Brand Reputation & Ethics	• Customer Relationship Data • Community Relations • Corporate Governance	• Privacy policies & compliance • Law enforcement liaison	• Regulatory security adherence • Allegation response
New or Emerging Markets for Business	• Global/International • Mergers & Acquisitions • Competition	• Intelligence analysis & mitigation • Country business risk assessment	• Information safeguards • Due diligence investigations • Business intelligence gathering
Financial	• Assets Management • Accounting & Reporting • Market Fluctuations	• Asset protection • Exceptions management • Violation detection & reporting	• Allegations of manipulation investigations • Regulatory inquiries
Information	• Information & Privacy • Intellectual Property • Networks • Applications • Hardware • New Technologies	• Data classification • Intrusion detection • Authentication & access control	• Physical access controls • Digital I.D. management
Human Capital	• Misconduct • Environmental Hazards • Turnover • Employee Skills & Performance • Compensation & Benefits • Labor Union Issues • Services	• Background checks • Awareness & training • Code of conduct • Drug testing	• Benefits loss prevention • Labor disruption planning • Intellectual property protection
Legal Regulation/ Compliance & Liability	• Antitrust Violation • Noncompliance • Audits • Accreditation • Third-party Vendors • Supply Chain • Liability • Litigation • Partnerships & Service Providers • Sales & Marketing • Procurement	• Regulatory controls • Risk assessment • Security programs certification • Partner due diligence • Records retention policy	• Investigations • Program Integrity • Regulatory compliance • Vendor contracts/code of ethics & regulations
Business Continuity & Resiliency	• R&D & Manufacturing • Logistics • Environment/Safety • Distribution • Business Continuity • Outsourcing • Branding	• Information safeguards and intellectual property protection • Disruption detection	• Mitigation management • Emergency response • Disaster recovery plans
Physical/Premises & Product	• Inventory & Products • Unauthorized Access • Partnerships/Services	• Warehouse facility protection • Product protection program	• Property protection program • Facility access policy

*Representative list, derived from enterprise risk assessments research.

OPERATING THE RADAR AND THE RELEVANCE OF "WHAT IF"

I believe it is totally logical that our employers expect security management to anticipate known risk and dig to understand what could happen given certain conditions or circumstances. It is totally reasonable for senior management to see us operating the radar and probing what those blips might be on the screen. To that end, I think there is great value and learning that comes from security managers engaging their teams and their business clients in "what if," a discussion that leverages our intelligence and incident data and then moves to connect the dots.

Board-level risk assessment sets the stage. Process-specific risk assessment details the defects and gaps in protection. These provide more fact-based evidence of risk with greater clarity of connection between the defect and likelihood or potential for consequences. A radar image is less defined and is more of an alert that requires tracking and analysis. A couple of examples of security's blips on the screen are found in understanding how leading and lagging indicators can provide relevance to "what if" analysis while providing more detailed direction to formal risk assessments.

LEADING INDICATORS

Can we predict future risk events? Could a high frequency of unaddressed nuisance alarms contribute to your responders not responding and thereby create an increased risk of loss? When we have the intelligence to install a reliable preventive measure and then fail to follow the rules, are we way off base to say the resulting risk event was predictable and thereby avoidable? In economics, a leading indicator signals future events and lagging indicators follow events. If you fail to test your business continuity plans, do you multiply the probability that your company may suffer a more severe impact when an interruption event occurs?

Our incident reports, investigations, risk assessments, tests, and other sources of risk-related data are replete with leading and lagging indicators. As a security manager who hopes to continue to be gainfully employed, I would opt for effectively working the leading indicators and really dig to avoid the lagging ones.

In this simple example, we can see the relationship to three types of security events. Now imagine yourself on a team engaged in a post-event lessons-learned examination. Do you think that data on alarm histories that were simply logged as "nothing found" or not logged at all now are telling a different story? How about the pushback you got from the business unit executive on his lack of scheduled testing of their plans or that "we've got other priorities right now" response to your risk assessment findings?

Let us consider a slightly different spin on six fairly obvious examples of leading indicators appropriate to related management objectives. If you do not like my examples, try to plug your own potential leading indicators into six objectives relevant to your security mission.

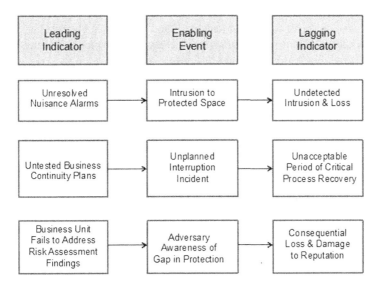

ADDRESSING THE OBVIOUS

You have a host of risks on your watch that you have classified as preventable, and (I hope) you have established a set of approaches to mitigate them. Here we have a trend in both frequency and severity of infractions that are indicative of a pattern of: (1) clear intent, (2) ignorance of policy, or (3) failure to communicate. You need to understand where the breakdown(s) are occurring across this spectrum and reset some switches quickly and competently.

MANAGING COMPETENCY

Speaking of competence, all corporate security programs rely on a host of inter-related competencies: first responders, business contingency planners, information security administrators, investigators, and business unit personnel who are custodians of internal controls. Where we fail to assure competence in key positions, we should anticipate something going bump in the night.

PROTECTING THE SUPPLY CHAIN

Virtually every business today relies on a supply chain, and a significant portion is operated under the umbrella of regulatory standards. Convince me that the failure to impose contractual security requirements appropriate to the risk profile of the product or service provided is not a potential leading indicator of downstream risk.

MANAGING "WHAT IF?"

The answer to this essential question is why we have crisis, business continuity, and contingency plans associated with our critical business processes. Do we develop detailed plans, pre-position backup resources, and wait to see how well we perform as the crisis unfolds? Untrained planners and responders coupled with untested plans are a highly reliable leading indicator of future risk.

MANAGING ACCOUNTABILITY

Increases in unresolved risk assessment or internal audit findings related to security vulnerabilities are about as good a set of leading indicators as you will find in our business. The facts are on the table, the owners of the risky processes are identified, and the schedule for response is set. Or is it? Your ability to deliver a quality risk assessment that drives responsive corrective action is a test of your influence and your competence.

MANAGING SYSTEM RELIABILITY

Even the most casual skimming of this work underscores the incredible array of technology we may use in our efforts to secure our sensitive business asset and operations. However, that investment in technology can become a liability when routine maintenance and testing procedures go wanting for lack of priority. How do you affirm the reliability of your protection strategy in the face of untested security measures? What happens to owner and responder confidence when poor maintenance results in a pattern of nuisance alarms?

SUMMARY

Look at your metrics for some key leading indicators that you can track and use to influence corporate policy, business awareness, and knowledge. You have a unique set of meters and dials that can offer alerts to the business that speak volumes on the value of the security program.

If you have appropriately structured your ongoing measures and planned your risk assessment processes to provide comparative metrics, you will have:

- Results of tests that yield a percentage of protection system or process failures and successes,
- Training records showing awareness and preparedness of key players,
- Documented frequency and results of prior tests,
- Downtimes of critical systems or business processes, and
- Specific benchmarks of protection system performance.

IDENTIFYING EXPLOITABLE SECURITY DEFECTS IN BUSINESS PROCESSES

When they shine a light on exploitable security defects, leading indicators show how you are moving from "what if" to "highly likely."

It is essential to make the connection between the vulnerabilities our risk assessments have prospectively identified and some level of likelihood or probability of consequence. The data enable a focused communication with the business unit(s) and engagement with management in essential areas of risk ownership and accountability. We can debate the likely consequences, but leaving the door open is a clear invitation to loss.

Look at these four examples. Finding one or more of them in any 24-hour period is far too easy in most workplaces. That is the point of exploitable, avoidable risk! Sloppy business practices create opportunities for those who seek to exploit them. Using our data to reinforce simple compliance with basic security practices is a fundamental responsibility of the security organization and its leadership.

Exploitability* of Selected Security Defects

(* each calculated from 10 consecutive penetration tests conducted xx/yy/zz)

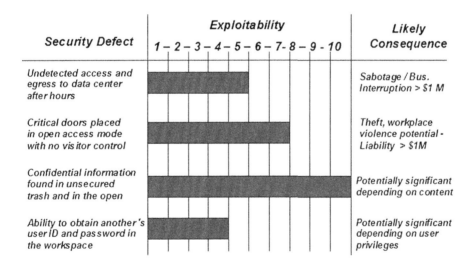

Security Defect	Exploitability 1 – 2 – 3 – 4 – 5 – 6 – 7- 8 – 9 - 10	Likely Consequence
Undetected access and egress to data center after hours		Sabotage / Bus. Interruption > $1 M
Critical doors placed in open access mode with no visitor control		Theft, workplace violence potential - Liability > $1M
Confidential information found in unsecured trash and in the open		Potentially significant depending on content
Ability to obtain another's user ID and password in the workspace		Potentially significant depending on user privileges

RISK MANAGEMENT STRATEGY

Security has examined the lessons learned from several incidents and reviewed the results of security operations' tours and inspections over the past several months. They noted that four security defects were frequently encountered across the range of corporate facilities:

- Undetected access to the 24/7 data center after business hours,
- Critical doors placed in open access mode with no visitor control,
- Confidential information found in unsecured trash in the open, and
- The ability to obtain another's user ID and password in the workspace.

These defects, if exploited, would have varying degrees of consequence. To quantify the exploitability of each vulnerability, the security team conducted 10 penetration tests over a two-week period during business and nonbusiness hours, within spaces that management acknowledged to be sensitive. The results were as follows:

1. Five of ten attempts to gain access and egress to the 24/7 data center after hours went undetected or unchallenged.
2. Seven of ten tests found critical doors placed in open access mode with no visitor control.
3. Ten of ten tests found confidential information in unsecured trash in the open within the C-suite.
4. Four of ten tests discovered examples of the ability to obtain another's user ID and password in the workspace, typically involving a note left in the open on or about a workstation.

Security's plan is to take these four fairly simple and straightforward examples of exploitable security defects first to the "owners" of the various spaces where penetration was achieved. They want not only to make these owners aware of the defects but to acknowledge where they affirmed the effectiveness of security practices. When pointing out deficiencies, they especially want to avoid accusation or surprise attacks. The goal is to use this data as a strong security awareness tool with the management team.

WHERE ARE THE DATA?

These data are the product of routine risk assessments and the daily tours performed by security officers, particularly after normal business hours. The "rules" that specify the standards for protection at key locations and within routine business operations establish the procedures and expectations for accountability, but it is essential to examine the adequacy of these protection measures to uncover gaps in the quality of internal controls around critical assets and business processes. This exercise also underscores the value of postincident lessons-learned examinations that reveal basic vulnerabilities in security measures. As far as potential consequences are concerned, security can speculate on impact of the noted defect or they can obtain specific impact data from the business unit.

A CAUTION ON LIKELIHOOD

Can you prove that an undetected access to the data center by an individual intent on doing harm would cost more than a million dollars? If you have done your homework, proving it is possible is fairly straightforward. But there are a host of factors that could change the likelihood of detection and quality of response to mitigate the potential damage. The penetration tests should be sold as supporting a "what if" scenario that has far more credibility than one lacking in prior demonstration.

FOCUS YOUR METRICS ON AVOIDABLE RISK

Any discussion on risk prevention and avoidability in our business will invariably find us headed for the slippery slope argument around proof that we (our efforts, programs, or specific safeguards) have, in fact, prevented a crime or security incident from occurring. I have heard some pretty powerful people push back on my proposed evidence, but I can usually wear them down with a common sense example. "If you drive fast on a curvy road in the rain with bad brakes and no seat belt, is there an increased probability that you may get into an accident and likely get seriously injured?" So, what if I remove all these risk-inducing factors? Have I taken steps to avoid that accident? Use smoking at a fuel spill or bungee jumping with twine or whatever scenario you like. You get the picture.

The business risk environment is directly comparable in my opinion. People do stupid things and are tempted to break the rules. Bob Simon at Harvard Business School likes to introduce the need for good internal controls with the example that we have brakes on our car not so we can stop, but so we can go faster with the assurance we can stop. If we have done our job, our security measures have been designed and vetted to address what we believe are credible threats or hazards. We know the desire is out there (or in here) with the bad guys and what they scope out is the opportunity. Measurably reducing that perceived opportunity is grounded in the notion of prevention and avoidance.

If we fail to act on well-established red flags around fraud, workplace violence, or industrial accidents, we contribute to opportunity and the metrics of probability. When we test for gaps in internal controls and defects in security measures and then communicate the what, where, and how of these exposures to the right people, we are providing the foreknowledge of prevention.

So, can I absolutely prove that that door you keep propping open will result in a security incident? No. But when it does happen, I am not going to be the one for whom the lawyers are looking.

Of course it is avoidable. And therein lies a key measure of the effectiveness of a well-communicated security metric. Good security programs and internal controls are built with the objective of preventing and thereby avoiding risk. Think about how you view a trend and then assemble the data you have available in a way that reveals an exploitable gap in a security measure. Now you have the opportunity—the obligation—to leverage that data to point out the accountability for mitigation. You have put your work product in motion to enable future risk avoidance. While you consider this, think about how you might make a clear connection between a risk avoided and the return on the security investment that enabled that result.

The next several examples focus on various opportunities to leverage security data from different programs targeting the prevention and avoidance of risk.

MEASURING THE IMPACT OF BACKGROUND INVESTIGATIONS

If you do not hire liars and felons, are you avoiding risk?

We have all seen the headlines about a workplace violence incident in which the company discovers too late it had a convicted felon with a history of violence on its payroll. The worst-case scenario: the active shooter, the predator, or the thief who steals the knowledge that defined our success is one of us.

Are background investigations predictors of potential future behavior? When we prospectively identify an employee candidate with a verifiable criminal history, what is the probability of a risk to our company should we hire him? Typically, it is not this history that determines the outcome of this hiring decision, it is the action of the candidate in failing to reveal or lying about the facts.

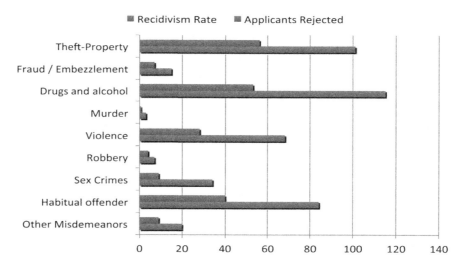

Employment suitability standards will specify the rules and considerations left to hiring managers when presented with alarm bells like these. But when the potential for risk is one of those considerations, an applicant's past weighs heavily on a hiring decision and for good reason. The US Department of Justice, Bureau of Justice Statistics, and many of the states maintain recidivism statistics for several of the more serious crimes. We see those data in the chart above for a manufacturing company's background investigation results in which more than 12,000 screens yielded rejections in each of these categories of criminal histories.

Is there a value story around what background investigations bring to the risk avoidance discussion? If the process was managed in accordance with clearly advertised requirements and defined legal standards and 447 individuals were not hired due to security scrutiny, is it possible that a problem was avoided?

What is not on this chart is a bar indicating the number of applicants who failed to indicate the fact that they had a prior arrest and conviction. They lied, and this "material discrepancy" was sufficient to eliminate the applicant. This failure to be truthful on prior employment history is a potential avoidable risk gold mine, particularly when prior job descriptions and compensation are effectively vetted. "Liars need not apply" should be part of employment advertising.

TRACKING PREVENTABLE RISK

In our business, bad things happen for a variety of reasons. If we can show how they could have been avoided, we contribute to learning and underscore accountability.

When you track the results of your incident postmortems to identify root causes of incidents and risk assessments to prospectively document vulnerabilities, you have the data to impress management on the consequences of failure to follow policy, procedures, or other elements of your internal controls that contribute to risk exposure. You document how the event could have been prevented or, at a minimum, the consequences minimized.

A significant percentage of security events are preventable. Use your metrics to influence behavior and fundamental corrective action.

RISK MANAGEMENT STRATEGY

In the following example, the CSO understands that it takes more than the open-ended "what if" to nail management's attention and obtain results. This security team knows that documenting "preventable losses" is likely to have far more impact than a spreadsheet full of incident statistics that may get lost in the roll-up of quarterly or annual risk reporting.

Rate of change for frequency and severity of security <u>preventable</u> risk events

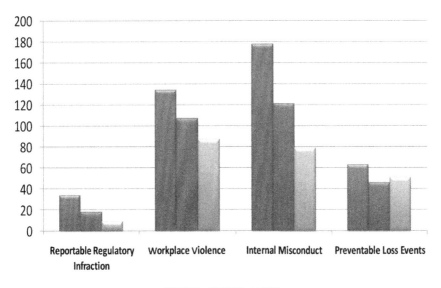

■ 2009   ■ 2010   ◾ YTD

If you check in with your risk management group (the insurance side), you can have a fascinating discussion on fortuitous loss and preventable loss. The former is deemed unavoidable, owing to accident and chance, while the latter is avoidable and therefore, but for someone's misfeasance, malfeasance, or nonfeasance, took away from the bottom line in more, shall we say, interesting ways.

When we conduct risk assessments that prospectively identify hazards and vulnerabilities that could be exploited by a knowledgeable insider or studious bad guy, we log an avoidable risk. The same may be said for incident postmortems that flesh out the root causes of security events.

Not all of these lessons uncover known exposures for which we have installed a countermeasure that has been breached or somehow failed. Discovering that which was previously unknown is, after all, the real gem in a risk assessment process. But this is about what best use you can put to the unique knowledge you have on business process risk. This is about using that unique perch we have to see risk in ways that no other part of the business has.

This CSO understood that well-documented and reliable metrics can tell a powerful story and push results far more effectively than simply counting things and publishing spreadsheets that fail to inform and demand action. In 2008, he saw the risk of not sounding the alarm on risks he could prove were preventable. The trend was confirmed in 2009, and the decision to track several categories of risk events with this focus was affirmed. Four are displayed above.

- Reportable regulatory infractions run the gamut of consequences but it is the notion of "reportable" that makes this group of preventable findings potentially more severe. Avoidance of sanctions through compliance activities is the focus of significant internal controls and often significant expense. Failure has potentially considerable reputational risk.
- When its cause is admittedly preventable, a notable workplace violence event can have devastating impact on victims and employees, not to mention a company's psyche and bottom line.
- I could make a case that all internal misconduct is preventable if accountable people paid attention, but never mind. Think about market share, the value of trade secrets, reputation, and how much the press loves stories about the well-placed insider gone bad.
- Preventable loss events are just that—they speak for themselves as examples of internal controls not followed, managers not paying attention, good systems operated badly, low bid vendors not effectively supervised, and failure of top management to care enough.

After spirited discussion, the chief executive officer (CEO), requiring board-level awareness and a commitment to targeted reductions, selected these four. The results speak for themselves, with significant reductions in three critical categories.

This is an example of how simple trending of data generated by a security organization committed to measuring program performance and proactive engagement with management can achieve an improved state of enterprise protection. Corporate security here is a change agent capable of influencing corporate strategy while also increasing its visibility as a contributor to the company's success.

COST ASSIGNMENT TO PREVENTABLE SECURITY INCIDENTS

A significant number of security events are clearly avoidable and preventable, and by sampling incident reports or engaging in after-action reviews, we gain actionable data on such events. While developing a reliable cost estimate may appear to be daunting, this metric has significant impact with management and enables security management to use lessons-learned examination to modify behavior and reinforce critical policy and procedure. This analysis can also provide a valuable view of incident (type) cost as a percent of (1) revenue, (2) occupancy, or (3) cost of operation.

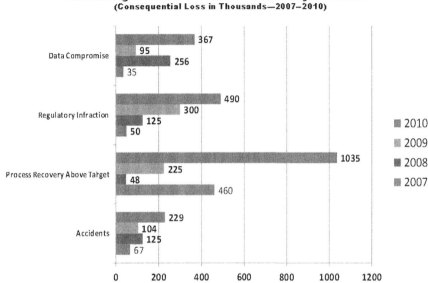

Cost Assignment to Preventable Security Breaches
(Consequential Loss in Thousands—2007–2010)

IDENTIFY AND ADVERTISE THE CAUSES OF LOSS

This is about avoidable risk and accountability.

Assigning cost to prior risk events, especially those that are repeating themselves despite advertised caution signs, speaks a very clear language to management and board members. While the objective here is to inform key constituents of the causes of loss in key areas, the events tell volumes with regard to avoidable risk. Losses occurred not because the company was in the dark on security-related risk. They happened because those accountable for ensuring established security measures failed to execute those responsibilities. Some loss may have resulted regardless, but they were far more severe due to individual and collective malfeasance and nonfeasance. We seek to increase management's awareness of the actions and situations that contribute to security-related incidents and boost the business units' accountability for improved risk management. You want this presentation to lead to some tangible demonstration that we have learned from our mistakes and that business units are taking ownership of the protection of corporate assets. If you look carefully, corporate security owns some accountability in some of these events as well.

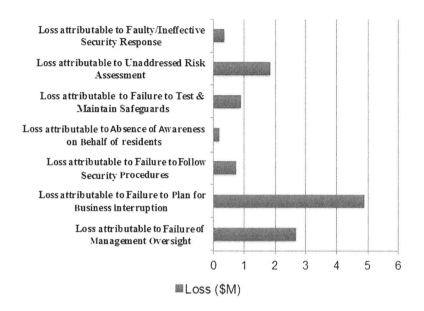

RISK MANAGEMENT STRATEGY

You report on losses due to various incidents. What have we learned from these incidents? How and why did they occur? How can we reduce our loss experience? If you have an ongoing program of incident postmortems or lessons-learned analysis, you should already have the useful, actionable data needed to create this chart. If you do not have such a program, now is the time to launch one.

Charting security-related losses is a bland exercise. Instead, this chart attempts to plot some of the knowledge we gain from events, to make the point that lack of security and inattention to policy have consequences. The five categories in our sample graph could easily consume a half-hour- to hour-long presentation on what has occurred, what we have learned as a result, and what is being done to address the problem. For example, in "Loss due to failure to address known vulnerability," the key word is "known." The risk had been previously identified, but corrective action obviously was not taken. Who failed to follow up? What process should be in place to better ensure attention to known risk? If the CSO had pushed all the right buttons, would the picture have been as consequential?

This is not about taking prisoners; it is about learning to avoid future risk.

MEASURING THE ELEMENTS OF EFFECTIVE ACCESS MANAGEMENT

If there is a cornerstone of a measurably effective enterprise security program, flawless access management has to be high on the list of candidates. If you do not know who is in your space or on your "trusted" systems, how can you say your enterprise is "secure"?

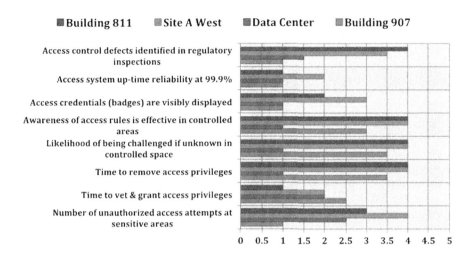

Corporations spend millions of dollars on access control, from manned security posts to a variety of manual and electronic access systems. Having made that investment, the state of this core safeguard is far too often poor to absurdly open to the most unsophisticated adversary. Why? Corporate cultures tend to expect employees to be respectful and polite. Holding the door for someone behind you is a sign of that value. In many work environments, doors designated as "secure" are routinely propped or bypassed with the open support of management. Manned posts may be incompetently or inattentively staffed. Key systems are totally outdated and uncontrolled, and too often employees are terminated and their means of access is not removed for a return trip. Unfortunately, access integrity is too often overridden by the desire for convenience and a lack of common sense ownership of this basic security measure by those who live within the "protected" space.

We can debate the pros and cons of various elements of a physical security program, but there is general agreement of the central role played by flawless access control to measurably effective enterprise security. Defective access management and control is a common denominator in threats of workplace violence, insider misconduct, negligent security litigation, and a host of loss events. On the other hand, it is a core enabler of safe and secure workplaces, regulatory compliance, information and data protection, and the human factors side of facility emergency management.

This organization recognizes these risks and is commencing a program of increased assurance regarding access integrity and program management. The strategy reflected in this chart represents eight key risk and performance measures they use to track this core safeguard. Note the connection between risk and performance indicators—the former is a measure of the effectiveness of the latter.

- *Number of unauthorized access attempts within sensitive areas*—If the objective of the program is to control access to authorized individuals, it makes sense to track attempts by unauthorized people to gain access.

- *Time to vet and grant access privileges*—This is a key onboarding cycle time measure that is typically laid on by HR and reflects the need to get employees in their seats and productive as quickly as possible.
- *Time to remove access privileges*—A combined risk and performance measure linked to the HR termination process.
- *Awareness of access rules is effective within controlled spaces*—Access management is a local process that relies on diligence regarding knowledge of who belongs and ownership of designated space.
- *Access credentials are visibly displayed within controlled space*—The dynamics of controlled space assignments and other factors impact resident knowledge of the legitimately authorized population. Visible badge/credential display mitigates this risk.
- *Likelihood of being challenged if unknown within controlled spaces*—Similarly, residents need to challenge those who they do not recognize and report suspicious behavior to security.
- *Tested reliability of access control system and critical subsystem components are sustained at 99.9%*—These systems are part of the company's critical infrastructure and need to be maintained at the highest level of confirmed reliability.
- *Access control defects are identified within regulatory agency inspections*—Virtually all security regulations contain a variety of access management and control standards. In many regulated environments, compliance is independently inspected, and violations have to be self-documented and reported. Maintaining an ongoing compliance program that includes routine performance metrics such as these is essential to compliance management and avoidance of costly penalties. The wording of this measurement focuses on the fact that inspections during the period being reported have noted noncompliance.

This company sees physical access control as an enabler of a safe, secure, and compliant enterprise and uses its metrics to affirm this commitment.

As is clearly evident in the above discussion, defective access control is a common vulnerability found in inspections, investigations, risk assessments, and after-action reviews. Measurably effective access management is a core safeguard, but there are a variety of ways to achieve that goal and a variety of user perspectives on how it could best work. Great policy and procedure backed up by well-designed barriers and technology is quickly defeated by a resident decision to prop a door or leave an attended control post unattended. Simple tests like those seen here yield results.

Let us look at another example of measurement around this critical area of security management, the testing of physical access management in several company departments.

STRATEGY

If we are serious about our mission, we test safeguards on a regular basis. But we also test them to measure how well they are working and to find soft spots in our strategy. There is no security manager reading this that has not had to deal with a business unit that pushes back and demands "an inviting space and convenience"—translation: unrestricted access involving disablement of electronic or staffed entry controls.

Why does it take a workplace violence event to dramatize the need for effective access control?

How well have we considered the business culture as we have dealt with this "difficult" client? You can bet that for every person openly complaining about security controls, there are more out there who are simply looking the other way when those controls are purposefully bypassed to make life easier for the employees or residents. Any good patrol plan and a cadre of engaged security officers would have already told you which business functions would be targets of opportunity because of such bypasses. In the example shown in the graphic below, security went a step further and conducted 10 unannounced access attempts for each business unit.

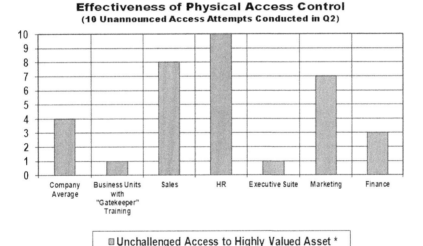

Effectiveness of Physical Access Control
(10 Unannounced Access Attempts Conducted in Q2)

▨ Unchallenged Access to Highly Valued Asset *

(* Customer lists, unsecured CFO Laptop, desktop access via posted password, computer room, etc.

If we look at the results of these penetration tests, what might we speculate are the biases of the three bad guys here: marketing, HR, and sales? I do not think I am generalizing when I state that these functions are typically hard sells for the kind of controls we tend to like. They want convenience and freedom, and we either post someone who challenges entry or install things that impose restrictions.

What should we do with these results? First, let us understand that the findings of these tests revealed access to customer lists, an unsecured chief financial officer (CFO) laptop, desktop access via posted password, and piggybacking into the computer room by unknown individuals, so it is clear we have to find ways to improve. We could run to the CEO, or we could approach each of these managers, discuss what we found, and then find solutions that serve a common ground of enterprise risk management.

A Different Spin on Access Management Effectiveness—The example above focuses on a simple test that revealed defects in basic access control measures in several critical business units. A more instructive example is seen below, in which seven key elements of (physical) access management are displayed with a general overview of compliance for a single business unit or facility. Brief descriptors are offered for each of the control elements selected for review.

Access Control Dashboard

Access lists and updated authorizations are reviewed monthly in accordance with policy	●○○○○
All persons authorized for on-going physical & logical access are background vetted	○○○○●
Access spaces are configured and protected in accordance with security policy and standards	○○○○○
Visitors are escorted and Receptionists are trained for applicable access procedures in their spaces	○●○○○
Periodic security tests confirm resident awareness of access oversight responsibilities	○○○○○
Cleaning crews are supervised consistent with contract and trash inspected nightly	○○○○●
The access control system meets the 99.5% uptime reliability standard	○○○○●

1. *Access lists and updated authorizations are reviewed monthly in accordance with policy.* This data is typically found in online logging and storage of access authorizations and associated lists. Automated reviews to identify outdated authorizations enable audit and reporting. It is essential to have links to HR and purchasing to purge access immediately when employees and contractors are terminated.

2. *All persons authorized for ongoing physical and logical access are background vetted.* This data may be easily assembled when completed background investigations are required for granting logical and physical access.

3. *Access spaces are configured and protected in accordance with security policy and standards.* All spaces are probably not created equal. Periodic security audits will yield data on those more sensitive spaces that fail to meet physical security guidelines.

4. *Visitors are escorted and receptionists are trained for applicable access procedures in their spaces.* In many organizations, receptionists are the gatekeepers of business sites. Sign-in and badge procedures may be audited for compliance with this basic safeguard.

5. *Periodic security tests confirm resident awareness of access oversight responsibilities.* Security personnel without badges can stroll into controlled spaces and collect data on the frequency of challenges by residents. If the personnel without badges can access more secure areas unchallenged, this should be brought to management's attention immediately.

6. *Cleaning crews are supervised consistent with contract and trash is inspected nightly.* Cleaning crews are often the weak link in physical access management. Service contracts should specify standards of oversight and operations. Daily, random security checks on access and trash collection will provide data on conformance with these requirements.

7. *The access control system meets the 99.5% uptime reliability standard.* Uptime of critical security systems should be set in vendor specifications and routinely logged and audited for reporting purposes.

The notion of access management effectiveness is particularly critical in this consideration of preventable and avoidable risk. It would not be overdone to suggest that the maintenance of access integrity is the key to physical security program effectiveness, and when compromised, risk prevention is impossible and the doors are open to the full range of internal and external adversary objectives.

MEASURING SECURITY AWARENESS

We cannot avoid risk if those responsible for maintaining the procedures that ensure it are unaware of their responsibilities. The absence of awareness is a key contributor to risk. Two key measures of the effectiveness of a security program are: (1) how well security communicates the responsibilities it expects employees to meet, and (2) the affirmation that those expectations are being met.

Security awareness is a centerpiece of a measurably effective corporate security program. That principle requires us to craft and effectively communicate specific guidance to address potential areas of risk. I use "guidance" because many organizations abhor the term "policy." Use whatever description for your expectations you feel appropriate to your culture, but do not fail to identify critical expectations and advertise them. Logical and physical access control integrity is a fundamental security principle that touches virtually every employee, and it is too easy to allow an unknown tailgater to go unchallenged or to write off a simple computer security procedure because it is inconvenient.

We are paid to anticipate risk. That expectation drives our multiple efforts to identify vulnerability through a variety of means including risk assessments, countermeasure tests, and incident postmortems. When we use probes like these to better understand what happened and why, we may find that those in the best position to prevent or act responsibly were not aware or were negligent of their role in enterprise protection. We need to test and affirm employee awareness of security responsibilities, and periodic surveys of targeted populations are an effective way to accomplish this.

Survey: Awareness of Logical & Physical Access Responsibilities

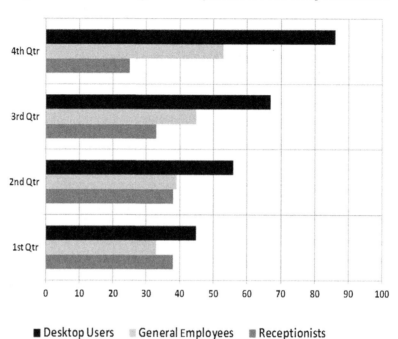

■ Desktop Users   ▨ General Employees   ■ Receptionists

In this example, our security organization has focused on a simple testing of awareness of access control responsibilities by targeted receptionists and desktop users and a sample of the general employee population. Receptionists are gatekeepers and should be empowered to maintain access integrity while welcoming visitors. In a more process-oriented way, the myriad of desktop users must follow established authorization procedures to gain access to preapproved business applications. The corporate intranet offers a variety of user-friendly means to quiz and reacquaint specific employee categories with security policy while identifying soft spots in awareness. Security officers on tours have frequent contact with receptionists and employees at access points and can preadvertise an "access awareness day" with a simple quiz and handouts like badge reels or small reminder cards. Similarly, information security teams can engage desktop users at logon or other times to test awareness of security procedures.

SURVEYS DELIVER THE DATA

The data you need to understand levels of awareness are in planned or random surveys of targeted employees or other stakeholders (like vendors in possession of proprietary information or processes), risk assessments and postincident analysis. Your various business environments may offer a variety of means to gather and reaffirm awareness data on security policy. Be creative; engage employees in the process. If this is done well, it will also help you build good public relations for the security organization.

TESTING DELIVERS THE DATA

In the example above, security has used a logical access password cracking tool to test the strength of this key safeguard. The story here reinforces the importance of training to an engaged and aware population. We know that training and awareness programs have a shelf life, so for critical components in the delegation of security accountability, testing and performance feedback play a key role in the maintenance of employee commitment.

Let us look at this from another perspective: the principle that awareness of risk assures the preparedness to respond.

RISK AWARENESS ASSURES PREPAREDNESS

We can quantify the level of our clientele's engagement in their role in enterprise protection, we can measure preparedness for crisis, and we can test personnel in their assigned roles in security plans and procedures. The degree to which we can reliably estimate our ability to respond well to a risk event can be the difference between a managed result or an unmanaged cascade of consequences.

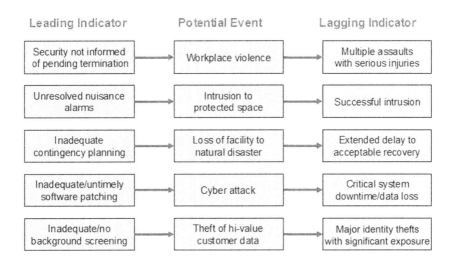

Security practitioners often equate security awareness programs with posters in break rooms, intranet alerts, and informative brochures on the risk of the month. While these media serve a useful purpose, security's risk awareness strategy must be significantly more disciplined and structured than a periodic communication exercise. Our metrics provide the quantitative measures for delivering the most actionable messages.

The test of sufficient awareness is found in the midst of crisis. We are paid to anticipate. We must proactively identify what could go bump in the night and determine how to prevent, detect, and respond to it. Risk awareness is the result of planful action involving multiple steps. As we saw in several aspects of the measures maps, the lack of knowledge, engagement, and accountability were at the root of the examples overviewed.

1. **Planning**: A risk-aware organization has an established, enterprise-wide risk assessment process that provides qualitative information on the vulnerabilities of enterprise assets and mission-critical business processes. It tests the resilience of safeguards and eliminates plausible denial through focused analysis with up, down, and sideways reporting. It addresses the concept of likelihood by understanding the degree of exposure gleaned from testing, incident postmortems, and intelligence. It understands how combinations and multiples of risks can interact and thereby increase exposure.

2. **Preparedness**: The risk-aware organization operates the radar on high strength but carefully avoids what we may call the Chicken Little syndrome. It looks for the cues, but exercises caution by testing and qualifying the data being received. It uses metrics as detective indicators that serve to inform and alert on changed risk conditions. It has pushed accountability for risk awareness down and out within the enterprise and set clear expectations on timely escalation of concern. Business processes are prioritized, risk tolerances set, and responsibilities assigned. Plans that address the range of consequential events are developed and tested.

The degree to which we can reliably estimate our ability to respond well to a risk event can be the difference between a managed result or an unmanaged cascade of consequences.

---

3. **Training of response resources**: Awareness has to be ingrained at the beginning and tested over time. Both general and business-specific orientations of new employees and resident contractors incorporate a fundamental understanding of risk and obligations of response. Because this is a learning organization with educated, knowledgeable players in key positions, awareness is reinforced through training exercises that dissect incidents to identify root causes and test to affirm that the players know the plays.

4. **Incident response**: The risk-aware organization is proactive. This is about the interdiction of risk due to foreknowledge. If our awareness efforts enable someone to identify and report or respond to conditions that will likely lead to an incident, we have a powerful measure of security program effectiveness.

But we are here because the business recognizes that bad things *will* occur, and the organization has to be prepared to take definitive steps to minimize the consequences. Risk awareness provides the foundation of our ability to react with timely competence. This is a key performance measure of our preparedness to minimize the consequences of the risky event.

5. **Consequence analysis and follow-up**: Measureable reductions in risk exposure may be found in a disciplined lessons-learned or after-action analysis. This is a key element of maintaining a responsive risk awareness program. It is about learning. Through this process, we identify the gaps in our protective measures and the competence of our response.

Awareness is synonymous with watchfulness, vigilance, responsiveness, and alertness. These terms work well within our security mission. When we enable our clients to be knowledgeable of risk and their responsibilities to prevent and respond to the indicators, we have an incredibly powerful multiplier effect in the ability to deliver measurable value to the enterprise we serve.

The risk aware organization has the radar working on leading indicators of future risk rather than the lagging indicators of current crises.

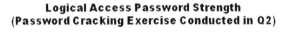

**Logical Access Password Strength
(Password Cracking Exercise Conducted in Q2)**

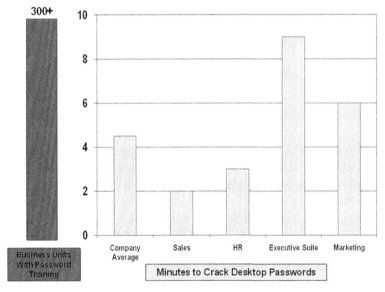

WORKPLACE VIOLENCE

Workplace violence is avoidable. If you disagree, do your homework. Far too many incident postmortems discover the red flags that were in front of those who should have seen and understood them. A good metrics program has these leading indicators on the radar.

The potential for workplace violence is a constant concern and foundation of crisis plans for every security executive. Scenarios are built collaboratively with law enforcement, actual cases are exhaustively analyzed, and exercises involving active shooters to hostile terminations are conducted. We live in fear of a horrific event such as those too often seen on the evening news. Understanding "what if" in this threat arena is an imperative.

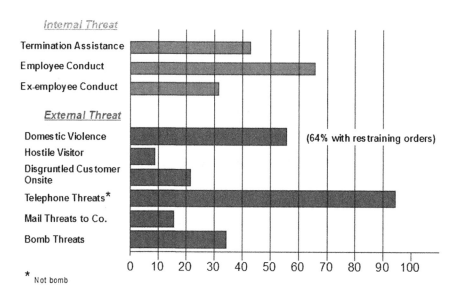

Workplace Violence: 2011

I have tried on a few occasions to work with groups of security organizations to develop a benchmark for workplace violence incidents per 1,000 employees.[4] Despite a variety of sources reporting on this area of business risk, we always seem to stumble over definitions. What constitutes "violence," how is victimization measured, and who is maintaining the data?

There may be institutional reluctance to acknowledge that hostile workplace factors are present but unaccounted for. It is unfortunate that too often, HR fails to engage security in those initial incidents that later escalate to far more serious events. They are the likely first responder in these situations, and when a linked partnership exists with security, root causes can be more accurately defined and appropriate safeguards addressed.

Incident postmortems too often demonstrate that the red flags for a workplace violence event were obvious.

The above chart presents data for a large manufacturing company for which these incidents tend to be a more frequent occurrence and tracking is the delivery

---

[4] This is the metric used by the US Department of Labor, National Institute of Occupational Health & Safety (NIOSH) in their 2004 and 2010 reports.

mechanism for the red flags. This is an example of counting providing the alert.[5] These data present the need for a strong relationship among security, HR, and legal departments is fundamental, and active awareness of potential/emerging problems at the business unit level is essential. Investigative postmortems are especially effective in a learning and briefing on this topic.

- What cues should supervisors and co-workers have seen?
- How effectively and well was the response managed?
- What was learned, and what are we doing to prevent similar occurrences in the future?
- What were the outcomes for victims, employees, and perpetrators?

In terms of risk awareness and avoidance, it is noted that in 64% of the domestic violence cases restraining orders were found in the victim's profile. Inasmuch as these orders typically apply to the workplace, should there be a discussion on confidential reporting of such orders to better alert appropriate parties to the potential for confrontation? Privacy is a legitimate concern, but collateral damage from a hostile confrontation is as well, as hindsight indicates.

This chart just scratches the surface and begs for a deeper dive from collaborative after-action reviews involving HR, security, and counsel. Social media review programs may offer some valuable insights on the source and nature of the external threats.

ADVERTISING THE FAILURE TO ACT

What is more avoidable than the overt failure to act on known threats and vulnerabilities?

Do you routinely dig into your incidents to identify the root causes and pass on the learning to those who need to know? If not, plan on logging more of the same and documenting allegedly smart people repeating their mistakes (or worse). Root cause analysis (RCA) is an established process in quality management, engineering, and risk management. It may take other forms in our business, such as lessons-learned examinations, incident postmortems, and after-action reviews (AAR). The objective is the same: to objectively, relentlessly identify the factors that created a failure of a control or set of controls so that those conditions may be prevented in the future. This is about nailing the real cause, not the lightly assumed symptom. Communication is the critical step to record the process and close the accountability loop.

In the following example, we see a corporate security organization that has formalized a process (or combination of analytical processes) focusing on continuous improvement in security risk management. Their approach seeks to understand the degree to which known threats and vulnerabilities are a factor in this company's security incident experience. The idea is that when we can confirm that the threat is known and the vulnerability that was exploited by this source is known, we had

---

[5] This event history also demonstrates the need for a well-planned active shooter program.

the essential elements to avoid or prevent this incident. But it is the notion that so many of the defects in protection that are implied here are repetitive that drives the relevance of this summary analysis. Moreover, from a perspective of consequential risk, these may be events that contribute to personal injury, litigation for defective security, embarrassment to brand, and likely targets for a board inquiry.

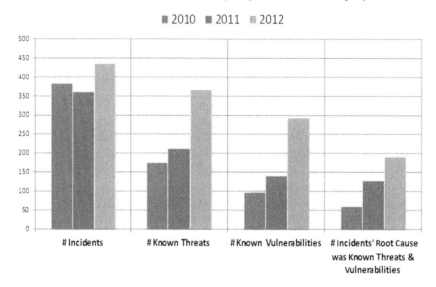

RCA is focused on identifying what factors verifiably contributed to the magnitude, timing, and location of a risk incident. It forces a broad consideration of multiple sources of incident causation. A variety of human, physical, technical, or other factors may contribute to the exploitability of asset vulnerability. What are they? If accidental, what conditions led to the breach? If manmade, how does it appear they were discovered and exploited by the adversary?

Success in this process is changed behavior, tested elimination of process defects, increased awareness of individual accountability, and eventual reduction or elimination in recurrence of like events. When there may be multiple causes, an advantage of RCA is in the identification of a single solution that closes down more than one exposure or isolates a simple, low-cost approach.

Unfortunately (or fortunately as the case may be), the learning frequently focuses on the adequacy of some element of the security program. The absence of awareness often lies in the lack of an established or properly directed program. The failure to address leading indicators like nuisance alarms, inadequately trained personnel, poor planning or execution in incident response, and lack of maintenance of critical security components or program elements are all found in well-executed AARs and RCAs.

LEVERAGING THE LEARNING

I have often heard a colleague say "what we need around here every once in a while is a well-managed incident that grabs management's attention." The emphasis is obviously on the "well-managed," but the notion is sound. Risk is inevitable, and the degree to which we are prepared typically tells the tale of the degree of consequence. Engaging a team from the affected business unit, security, and others in corporate governance speaks more to avoiding future risk than taking prisoners. Success can be celebrated and best practices identified, or we can learn together what could have been done better.

MEASURING COMPLIANCE RISK

How serious is the notion of compliance in your company? Is your reputation in the marketplace linked to conformance to an established set of laws, rules, or standards? Are there protection mandates in the contracts you have with your customers and key suppliers? How are you measuring compliance to established security standards? What are the implications of inadequate security with regard to your insurance?

We are a key player in the governance of these internal controls, and measuring compliance is a core metrics process. The objective is to track, analyze, and report on risk-related conditions and events that are subject to mandated or self-imposed compliance and additionally, to identify root causes so as to eliminate defects in safeguards and establish accountability for corrective actions.

RISK MANAGEMENT STRATEGY

Every organization experiences serious events or conditions that must be escalated to a designated individual or authority for notification and remedial follow-up. These are the incidents that make it to the board's risk management or audit committee. They may require regulatory or customer notification. They are likely to have note-worthy financial impact. You do not want them on your watch, especially if the failed control belongs in security's portfolio.

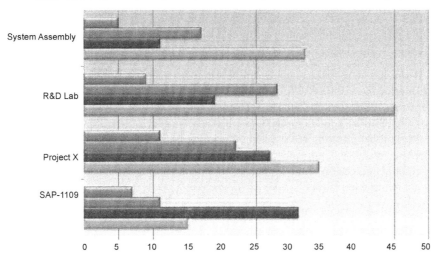

Reportable Security Violations: 2010

Unauthorized Disclosure Delayed Response Alarm System Defects Failure to Properly Secure

To add insult to injury, most are avoidable. The rules and responsibilities are—or should be—known. This chart is typical of security's normal approach to metrics: We maintain counts of what and how much. The essential next step is what security management does with this data. If you accept the fact that what you see here indicates avoidable risks, the next step is to dig deep and uncover the root causes.

Compliance standards all possess embedded measures for monitoring conformance. For example, if certain types of information must be protected to a specific standard, inspections will reveal the status of safeguards, and automated tools and protective systems can monitor for and alert to attempts to compromise protection. Processes to ensure or verify personnel reliability may be measured, as can response to potential threats to protected assets. In sum, there is a diverse inventory of sources for actionable metrics.

In the best of circumstances, an internally directed compliance review or risk assessment identifies the internal control defect or security vulnerability, nails the cause, and addresses the exposure before an event occurs. Your value metric is the number of vulnerabilities you have proactively discovered and fixed. In the worst-case scenario, the defective control that you knew about somehow never got fixed. Somewhere between best and worst is the case in which a previously unidentified defect directly contributes to a notable event. Both of these metrics also need to be tracked—at least, while you are around to track them.

Look at the four indicators being tracked by the department in this graphic.

- **Unauthorized disclosure** relates to proprietary information that has been transmitted by any means in violation of standards of protection.
- **Delayed response**: We can all envision certain types of incidents, alarms, or calls for service that establish standards for first-responders. Time from dispatch to arrival is logged for verification of adequate response time.
- **Alarm system defects**: Alarms installed to monitor sensitive areas or assets must meet specific standards of reliability. Standards for tracking faulty, false, or nuisance-induced annunciations are checks on system reliability and responder confidence.
- **Failure to properly secure** relates to the missteps of persons accountable for following established protection standards, whether the cause is malicious intent, negligence, or a flawed understanding of their responsibility.

If you live in a business environment where regulatory compliance is a critical measure for the viability of the company or simply need to better understand your obligations under various legislative standards, I strongly encourage your examination of the SEC's Regulations and Compliance Management (RoCM) tool. Although a work in progress, it represents a significant body of researchable information on security-related legislation and regulations.

In further extension of the few examples offered above, here are some additional key compliance indicators:

- Pass/fail rate from government-conducted security inspections (keyed to program life cycle),

- Response time to special access area alarms in excess of mandated threshold,
- Percent of personnel submitted for clearance found to have material derogatory backgrounds,
- Percent of programs with tested conformance of safeguards and internal controls,
- Number of reportable security defects found in outsourced suppliers per audit or inspection,
- Percentage of control deficiencies identified as a percent of total controls in the safeguard process,
- Elimination of sanctionable penalties associated with frequency and severity of compliance deviations,
- Number of unauthorized persons found in controlled space per period,
- Cost of investigation and resolution of data breaches by business unit per period,
- Security cost as a percent of total regulated program revenue,
- Number of unaccounted laptops with encryption disabled,
- Number of defective or unsecure physical access controls found by tours per 24-hour period,
- Number of false or nuisance alarms per protected area per 24-hour period,
- Average time to clear identified control deficiencies,
- Number of information protection violations per 100 employees,
- Percent of controlled access areas with fully tested business continuity plans,
- Percent of unused access credentials for on-board personnel per reporting period,
- Percentage of tested population having accurate awareness of security procedures,
- Number of security violations by personnel with approved access as a percent of total approved population,
- Incident post mortems involving compromise of specific types of internal controls having regulatory implications,
- Fines or enforcement actions avoided by timely identification and corrective action,
- Security-related award fees achieved compared to total fee potential,
- Number of notice of corrective actions required by regulators.

Think about what is reportable in your company and what protocols are in place to ensure reporting compliance. The rules are clear if you are in a regulated business environment, but may not be in a less formalized setting.

WHEN DOES AN *AVOIDABLE* RISK BECOME *INEVITABLE*?
THE IDEA

There is a line across which we move from a risk that is avoidable due to the effectiveness of the safeguards we have in play to one in which risk is virtually inevitable. In this increased state of risk, we have either disabled or failed to enable our essential security measures.

THE BUSINESS RISK PROFILE

Let us consider a large retail chain that for several years has been aggressively acquiring smaller regional competitors while shedding internal business units in favor of outsourced service vendors and suppliers. Every effort is being taken to cut cost and increase profitability to position the company for acquisition. Over the past 24 months, the company has been experiencing increasingly serious inventory losses across their distribution facilities and a notable increase in internal fraud and misconduct. The security program is assigned to the facilities manager, who has totally outsourced what he sees as security to multiple guard force vendors assigned to local cost centers.

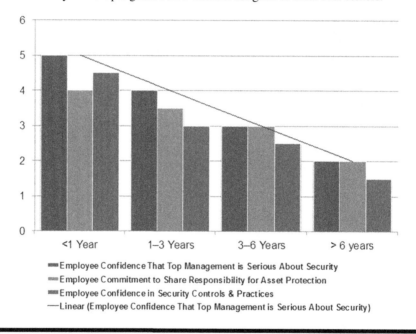

- Employee Confidence That Top Management is Serious About Security
- Employee Commitment to Share Responsibility for Asset Protection
- Employee Confidence in Security Controls & Practices
- Linear (Employee Confidence That Top Management is Serious About Security)

The assurance of preventable risk is on management's watch. The switches are set and expectations are affirmed here. The results need to be monitored and communicated.

THE RISK MANAGEMENT STRATEGY

At board urging, the CEO has tasked the chief risk officer to probe and identify what factors are contributing to these loss trends. He has engaged an outside firm to conduct a risk assessment that has incorporated an employee survey, which, among other loss prevention issues, has sought out perceptions of security policy and practices. This survey obtained responses from more than 2200 employees at all levels and all shifts across the company's North American operations. The answers noted here were organized on a scale in which 1=disagree to 5=strong agreement. A few key results are seen in the chart above, but it is what is behind these numbers that is compelling.

First, it is not surprising that those respondents with less than a year's tenure have the highest levels of confidence and lowest perceptions of problems. After all, that

HR and loss prevention pitch on how seriously the company takes its security procedures and the consequence of wrongdoing is still fresh in their minds. But look what happens as the veterans influence behavior and learning sets in. Cost-cutting, performance pressure, and rule-bending combine to create an environment where looking the other way while looking out for number one is the chosen course.

Take the question on employee commitment to share responsibility for asset protection. In a more controlled setting, this is a question that typically focuses on security awareness and related ownership. But in this environment, it is merely a reflection of what is seen as the way the company behaves. Why should employees share in a process that they clearly see management failing to articulate and acknowledge as an expectation? The trend line sums it up beautifully: "the longer I've worked here, the more clearly I see that our bosses couldn't care less so I'll be darned if I'm going to do my part!" Actually, the problem runs much deeper than that. It is so clear that management is disengaged and the controls are so turned off that, given the motive, the opportunity to take what I want is almost advertised on the break-room walls. Not only is management not seen as welcoming suggestions for improved security, management is viewed as not even caring if anything is secured! Thus, no surprise at the fairly quick failure of confidence in security controls and practices. What few security procedures we do have are virtually meaningless.

Ethics and expectations are not visible on management's slate of commitments. The few indicators we see here are likely just the first level of darker issues bubbling in the offices along mahogany row.

TRACKING NUISANCE AND FALSE ALARMS

Nuisance alarms are more than a nuisance.

The reliability of our programs is an essential ingredient of executive confidence and support. If you are looking for a place to focus your quality assurance, shine it consistently on alarm system reliability and response. Whether they are experienced or uninitiated, your customers find frequent invalid alarms unacceptable, and they make your responders distrust the validity of calls. As you will see in the second example below, when they occur at offsite facilities dependent on law enforcement response, false alarms often cost the company in fines.

Anyone who has spent any time in a command center has heard the dispatched officer's radio response "checked area, negative results." The alarm came in from a point that deserved monitoring, but there was no apparent cause. If we assume the officer did his due diligence, what set of conditions contributed to alarm activation? On the dark side, an adversary may be testing response time and quality. On the maintenance side, that alarm point may be improperly installed or directed. On the risk assessment side, that alarm point may now be in an area where the activity, environmental, or risk profile has changed and is impacting detection reliability.

Are nuisance alarms leading indicators? Is it possible that these conditions could somehow contribute to an avoidable risk event?

A large campus or a geographically distributed complex of facilities may have thousands of alarm points with disparate protection objectives. A prioritization scheme for this dispersed array is essential, and the simple chart here displays six focal points that may be found in a typical company.

In this example, we are tracking anomalies: 6 months of alarm events requiring a manned response resulting in no known cause. Our standard of alarm reliability is a 95% confidence level, so generally speaking, we are in pretty good shape for this period of analysis. Depending on the value you attach to the assets being protected by this set of physical security elements, you may elect to increase or decrease this confidence level. But for some select portion of your alarm system configuration, it is essential that a standard of reliability and responsiveness be established and maintained.

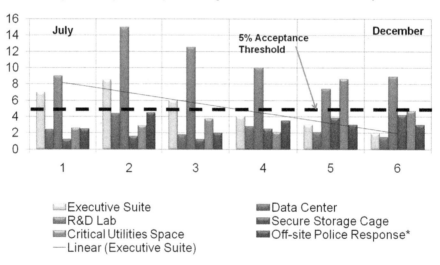

Percent of Invalid Alarms for Top 5 Critical Spaces: 6 Months Ending 12/31/10

(Invalid alarm = Dispatched response confirms no verifiable cause)
(* Off-site police response subject to false alarm ordinances)

It should be obvious to any security professional why we have elected to track the rate of nuisance alarms associated with executive spaces. Any of these may represent a significant area of risk exposure for the company. But as noted earlier, the most damaging impact of invalid alarms may be in the developed lack of confidence your first responders will have when that all-too-frequent address is dispatched. Security officer training should include procedures for checking alarm device operation, and alarm responses need to be appropriately documented in logs or incident reports[6] to clearly indicate the validity of the alarm after an informed investigation of cause. Do

---

[6] I too often hear that there is no simple way to document an invalid alarm due to limitations of reporting systems. I reject that excuse. The inability to track alarm system reliability is a significant risk.

not miss the implication of user-caused alarm events. This is a frequent root cause and has clear implications for wasted security time and loss of first-responder confidence. Too often we find propped doors, ignorance of equipment procedures, and poor facilities maintenance causing properly functioning alarm systems to send the right signal for the wrong reasons. Use your data for attitude adjustment.

Any experienced security manager can tell stories of the consequences of nuisance alarms at executive residences or office spaces. In the best of circumstances, it is not pretty. In the worst, significant risks are the potential consequences. As for our fictitious facility in this example, we see an average of a 3% false alarm rate for facilities where no security presence is available. If you are fortunate enough to have police response available and willing, that figure likely represents a frequency of fines from responding municipalities or, worse, notification that response will no longer be provided.

REDUCING NUISANCE ALARMS

Nuisance alarms are measurable, and qualified personnel may easily determine causes. Alarm annunciation should be accompanied by the utmost degree of confidence that the activation is due to the risk for which it was installed and monitored. When that argument fails, take a hard look at what false and nuisance alarms are costing the company. On that financial metric, the following chart shows what one company can do to really impact the cost and implications of false alarms when they attack it systematically.

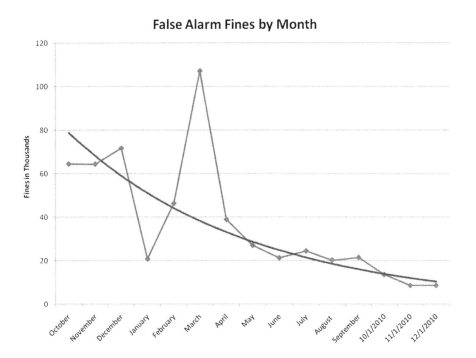

SUMMARIZING AVOIDABLE RISK

These examples have been offered as opportunities to leverage security's unique perspective to influence accountability and sponsor risk avoidance. The strategy is gained from its analysis of the data gathered in the routine tasks of incident response and investigation and/or as a postevent examination of lessons learned. The message underscores the value of metrics as a source of fuel for telling stories that can get results far more effectively than the simple presentation of counts of things. There will be many other examples throughout the remainder of this book, but if you are a security manager armed with your own data, go find some stories about avoidable risk you can tell to some people who need to hear them.

METERS AND DIALS—TRACKING AND MONITORING KEY RISK INDICATORS

Just as we use the gauges on our car to monitor the status of critical components, security's metrics may be organized to provide a selectable variety of indicators to support our ability to anticipate and avoid hazards and risk. This next discussion provides multiple examples of how we can build and present our information for internal tracking and security program management while also delivering some essential reports to management.

> *Take special note of the critical importance of an established, reliable incident reporting and information management process to developing and communicating on risk. Ensure that any sensitive data receive the level of protection established by policy or as directed by counsel.*

I believe one of the most important objectives of a corporate security organization is to maintain a variety of processes calculated to provide the enterprise with timely, actionable, and reliable information on the full range of security-related threats and risks confronting the enterprise. Key risk indicators are the metrics that enable management to gauge its appetite for risk, measure performance of its safeguards, and address gaps in protection.

KEY RISK INDICATORS AT THE ENTERPRISE LEVEL

How connected is your security organization to senior management's business and risk management strategies? How connected are they to your programs and their shared responsibilities for enterprise protection? Probing the quality of these connections should be a core element of the security executive's risk management agenda. Consider the following approach to support this probe.

An interesting and often revealing conversation takes place when a security leader sits down with his or her boss or a senior executive from a business unit and asks them to rank on a scale on which 1 = low to 5 = high questions like the following:

- What is management's appetite for security risk?
- What is management's level of knowledge and understanding of the security mission?
- How well do you think we in security understand the business?

- To what extent do you see business units taking ownership for security risk and controls within their areas of operations?
- To what extent does management see security contributing to the success of the business?
- What is your perception of the maturity and acceptance of the security program here?
- Do you believe security risk issues are appropriately identified and escalated from the business units to security?

The quality of our communication and the metrics that accompany and support the messages are key players in influencing and informing management's appetite for risk. What we see in the following chart is a failure to communice at a critical level. There is a fairly significant disconnect between the parties on where the business sees risk and the perception of security management. It appears that the lack of a shared strategy is at the heart of some real problems here. Management's risk appetite is higher than it should be, and the business in not appropriately engaged in ownership of risk controls because it really does not understand what security does or how it can contribute to enterprise success. Nor does management see security effectively understanding the business, so how can they talk the same language? At this point, it is not possible that this security organization can effectively drive security policy, impact risky business practices, or build a collaborative relationship with their key business clients.

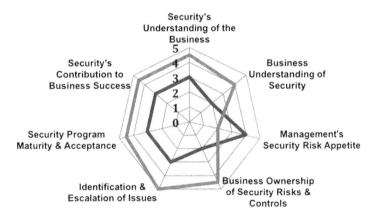

━━Where You Are   ━━Where you Want To Be

This is a conversation that every security executive should have with their business leaders. These are fundamental questions that have answers that not only drive a strategic and measurably effective relationship. They are the essence of enterprise risk management.

SUMMARY

A chart like this provides an excellent opportunity to discuss the relevance and resilience of key business relationships with the security program and the template is easily found in your PowerPoint application. This is an example of how key risk indicators (KRIs) might be illustrated in assessing where you are at a point in time against where your organization's security program aspires to be. I have found this little drill to yield interesting discussions between security managers and their boss or others in senior leadership. The idea is simple: you pick several key risk indicators at the enterprise level and then score where you believe the company lies on a scale on which 1=low/bad to 5=high/best. Then get the scores from your top executives. I bet you end up with some interesting differences of opinion from different sources.

The bottom line is that KRIs should be "key" risk indicators—macro level and focused on the enterprise. There are no magic indicators, but there are some (tone, appetite, transparency, ownership of controls, etc.) that line up with what others in audit, legal, risk management, etc. may be conveying. Try this out on a colleague there to refine your selection.

In this example, we are using several indicators that are keyed to reflect how security is seen as an element in the governance infrastructure and to elicit some honest opinions on security's role and level of alignment with the business. How you resolve where you think you are versus where your CEO quantifies these factors is your problem. I guarantee that it is a discussion worth having. Think about how that conversation might go in your organization.

Now, let us take a more detailed look at key risk indicators.

KEY RISK INDICATORS AT THE CSO LEVEL

Does a CSO have a *legal* obligation to inform management about risk? Is there a fiduciary obligation? Ask your legal counsel. This is an important consideration in metrics reporting by members of the corporate governance team.

Regardless of the legality and without question, we have an obligation to inform, educate, and advise. Our scope and lens on risk is unique within the governance infrastructure. Our programs reveal volumes on business unit attentiveness to enterprise protection—a window to broader issues of risk management. I believe one of the most critical, value-centered, and influential management reporting obligations security managers have is to provide relevant KRIs to their corporate management and, through appropriate gates, to the board.

An excellent research paper commissioned by the Committee of Sponsoring Organizations of the Treadway Commission[7] (COSO) entitled "How Key Risk Indicators can Sharpen Focus on Emerging Risks" summarizes the purpose and value of these metrics as follows:

> *"The development of KRIs can provide relevant and timely information to both the board and senior management, which is significant to effective risk oversight. Effective KRIs can provide value to the organization in a variety of ways. Potential value may be derived from each of the following contributions:*

---

[7] "How Key Risk Indicators can Sharpen Focus on Emerging Risks", Mark S. Beasley, Bruce C. Branson, Bonnie V. Hancock, Committee of Sponsoring Organizations of the Treadway Commission, December 2010.

Risk appetite—KRIs require the determination of appropriate thresholds for action at different levels within the organization. By mapping KRI measures to identified risk appetite and tolerance levels, KRIs can be a useful tool for better articulating the risk appetite that best represents the organizational mindset.

Risk and opportunity identification—KRIs can be designed to alert management to trends that may adversely affect the achievement of organizational objectives or may indicate the presence of new opportunities.

Risk treatment—KRIs can initiate action to mitigate developing risks by serving as triggering mechanisms for organizational units charged with monitoring particular KRIs. As well, KRIs can serve as controls by defining limits to certain actions.

Risk reporting—By design, KRIs can provide measurable data conducive to aggregation. Summary reports can be quickly communicated to appropriate senior managers and board members with oversight responsibilities.

Compliance efforts—For organizations subject to regulatory oversight, KRIs may be useful in demonstrating compliance with established requirements.

KRIs designed to assist the board and executive management in anticipating trends in potential risk-related events can add considerable value to enterprise-wide risk oversight efforts by positioning the board and management so that they can proactively adjust strategies in advance of or in response to risk events. The design and roll-out of a set of KRIs is an important element of an organization's enterprise risk management process."

Key risk indicators are your tracking tools for avoidable risk management and security awareness.

I have found that establishing a linkage between key performance indicators (KPIs; discussed later in this book) and KRIs to be a highly effective means of communicating what we know about the root causes of risk and how well accountable parties (including security) are doing in meeting risk reduction objectives. KRIs, after all, impose a defined set of actions.

In the following example, the CSO has selected a variety of KRIs for quarterly management reporting. He might choose to focus on the relationship of a couple of trends like untrained information security administrators and network penetration attempts or regulatory infractions and internal misconduct. There is program performance progress visible here, as well as disturbing leading indicators that have gone ineffectively addressed. This example may better serve as a summary display given the diversity and amount of data presented. What it does offer is a dashboard that provides longer-term trend data to contribute to program performance assessment and focus targeted audiences on areas requiring increased engagement. There are likely linkages between several of the internal risk trends seen here that should be driving analysis and collaborative efforts across the corporate governance team. The correlation of the timing of economic recession on this company is also a potential contributor that deserves probing.

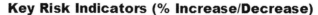

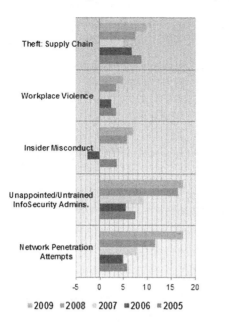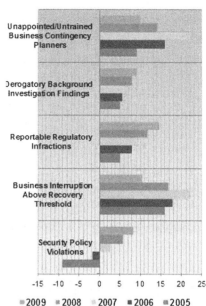

In the graphic below, the CSO is focusing more specifically on four business units, thus enabling a more pointed discussion on the stewardship of local management for basic security responsibilities. Here, KRIs are not being used as a sharp stick in the eye, but should serve to demand far greater accountability.

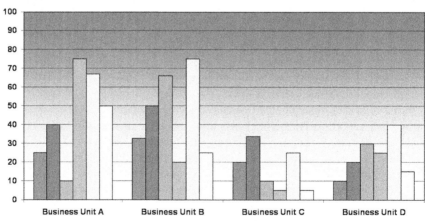

Remember that KRIs are critical leading indicators that may signal emerging internal or external risks and that our data are often the singular lens to interpret and provide insight to boards and top management. This is particularly true when that lens is effectively focused and aligned with corporate business objectives. This is an example of ability to enable the business to engage in prospective risk management and another key value indicator for security's programs.

TAKE A DEEPER DIVE ON MULTIYEAR TRENDS TO HIGHLIGHT RISK

In the following chart, you can see use of trend lines to focus management on three areas of loss, which obviously deserve more attention. This is where just counting does serve to shine a light on a variety of internal control failures that must be acknowledged, strategized, and mitigated. This is the use of reliable, collated data to eliminate plausible denial and force a discussion on the acceptability of notable categories of risk.

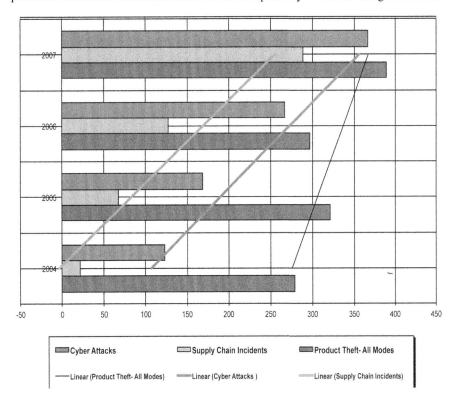

But the real story behind this chart is the absence of attention and accountability. The data have been there, increasingly flying these red flags for four years! One has to wonder where security management was looking and seriously question the condition of the company's risk management program. Cyber attacks are up 188%, and there has been a 56% increase in product thefts and a 13-fold increase in supply chain security incidents. This dramatic supply chain statistic was later found to have its root causes in the total lack of risk assessment and controls associated with extensive outsourcing initiatives in Southeast Asia and Mexico.

Would an established program of tracking and reporting on these areas of business risk have arrested these avoidable losses? Not without access and engagement of management. If you are appropriately investigating and documenting incident findings, having the right data is the easy part. The ability to influence policy and action is the test of security management's use of its information and the metrics that flow from it.

BUILD A RISK INDICATOR DASHBOARD

We need to find responsive ways to display and communicate the key information a manager needs to monitor a set of measures and effectively communicate the status of those measures. You are busy, and so are those you seek to inform. Immediate comprehension of business information is essential. The data in a risk indicator dashboard are presented in such a way as to maximize understanding with a minimum of explanation. You also reinforce basic security policy with periodic updates like this.

Organizational Integrity Dashboard: Our Critical Business Processes

	This Year	Last Year
CRITICAL BUSINESS PROCESS RISK ASSESSMENTS WITH APPROVED RESOLUTIONS	98 of 112	64 of 106
% UPDATED & TESTED BUSINESS CONTINUITY PLANS WITH ASSOCIATED REMEDIAL ACTIONS	77%	58%
% OF SECURITY INCIDENTS THAT EXPLOITED EXISTING VULNERABILITIES WITH KNOWN SOLUTIONS	9%	29%
% OF INFORMATION SECURITY POLICY COMPLIANCE REVIEWS WITH NO POLICY VIOLATIONS	31%	85%
% AUDITED COMPLIANCE WITH APPLICABLE BUSINESS INTEGRITY REGULATIONS	97%	78%

RISK MANAGEMENT STRATEGY

With an increased focus on transparency, regulatory compliance and board-level reporting, directors, CEOs, and CFOs have been increasingly open to immediate, proactive, and glaringly obvious warning lights. Your corporate security program can use this type of traffic light image in dashboard dials to present information to management on risk indicators. This next graphic provides a simple set of risk indicators that have been selected for a senior management briefing. The comparative data reflect several business processes the risk management team has selected under the heading of organizational integrity. The significance and tone is set by the fact that the data are based on confirmed results—risk assessments, compliance reviews, and incident postmortems.

It is also clear that this organization maintains an aggressive, ongoing program of risk assessment, the results providing high-level visibility and influence to the security team. If I were briefing this chart, I would be ready for some interesting discussion around the percent of incidents that exploited existing vulnerabilities with known solutions. What five critical business process risks are you tracking and reporting? What are the implications for top management and owners of the business process? What do you propose that security will do, and what are your recommendations for the process owners? How will progress be measured?

MEASURING RISK ASSESSMENT PROGRAM EFFECTIVENESS

It may be said that the absence of an effective risk assessment program should be at the top of the key risk indicator checklist.

Look at the continuum in the three metrics reported on the chart below. First, we are doing risk assessments; second, the results are driving remedial action; third, security is leveraging its role in enterprise risk management; and fourth, there is a clear trend of business unit engagement. But are we seeing good news or bad in this chart?

Is there is a lack of apparent maturity in this risk assessment program? The advertisement is for "3 key divisions," all of which clearly possess critical business processes. However, on average only half of these critical processes have been engaged in basic risk assessment.

Look at business division B as an example.

- Half their critical processes have been risk assessed, but which half?
- Of that half, only a third have approved remedial actions. So do we feel satisfied with understanding this level of exposure around only 17% of this unit's critical processes?
- 100% of our recommendations have been accepted and implemented for this portion of B's critical processes. Was this acceptance driven by the potential for consequences, influencing by security or something else?

If you were the CEO looking at this chart, what questions would you ask and why? If you were the CSO presenting, what story would you tell if you only had a 5-min slot? Or, as the CSO, how would you have delivered a heads-up alert to the executives of these three divisions that you were going to brief this to the CEO? You are looking for responsive collaboration around change and building bridges. But if they take the wrong turn, you still have the evidence on your side.

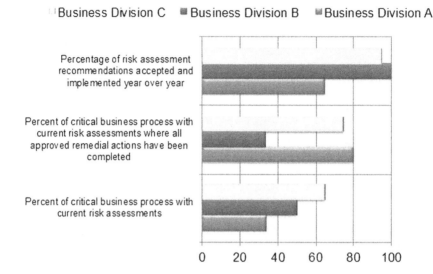

**Status of Risk Assessment Processes
in 3 Key Divisions of the Company**

Business Division C   Business Division B   Business Division A

Here is another view of how focusing what we learn from our risk assessments in the right places with the right information can be a powerful incentive for improved risk management.

In this example, we see a security program that has effectively tracked losses and critical process downtime attributable to defective internal controls, pushed deeper and more focused risk assessments and deployed a variety of tools for proactively identifying risky behavior.

Coupling solid risk assessment results with key risk indicators that are supported by root cause analysis offers up headlines that get management attention. Our objective is to eliminate plausible denial. But we have an obligation to probe and inform and targeting those risks that can threaten the franchise provides an incredible opportunity to put the security program positively in front of senior management and the board.

IDENTIFYING THE THRESHOLD OF "ACCEPTABLE" RISK

What is an "acceptable" risk in your world of exposure to security risk management? How much loss can be tolerated before some threshold of damage is breached? We know that zero risk is as unachievable as 100% protection, but without somehow pushing a consensus notion around some baseline target, we cannot get a handle on how much resource to devote to protection activities. Essentially, we are probing the company's tolerance for risk, and this is a critical discussion that too few security managers are prepared to have with senior management.

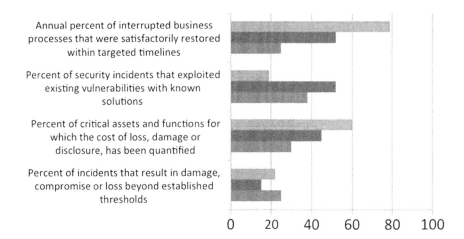

What factors help define an appropriate level of acceptance or tolerance? Here are a few:

- From our history, it is not probable and below what we can accept as intolerable.
- The consequences of occurrence are reasonably deemed to be minimal and manageable.
- The cost of protection is likely more than what we can estimate for total impact cost.
- Our insurers, regulators, and authorities say it is acceptable.
- The benefits outweigh the potential risks (for example, we will do business in a risky region with significantly lower costs and higher payoff).

The four measures seen in the above chart are linked to the need to identify potential, probable, and known impact from security-related events. But, of importance to a business-centered security manager, each one contributes to considerations around return on security investments, assessment of cost effectiveness, and program performance measurement.

Percent of critical assets for which a cost of loss, damage or disclosure has been quantified

This is absolutely key to protection planning and program management. Our whole risk management scheme relies on the ability to understand, in real economic terms, what the consequences of compromise could be given a set of rational—not absurd—scenarios. This is why linking what is learned from business continuity planning about recovery timing and cost is relevant to security resource management. All security planning should reside on a foundation of delivering the requisite level of protection at the lowest possible cost. "Requisite" means measurably consistent with criticality and consequences of loss.

Percent of incidents that result in damage, compromise, or loss beyond established thresholds

This is a KRI that clearly implies concern for the quality of detective, preventive, and response activities. Here, we have taken the quantified estimate of loss noted above and tracked those incidents that exceed that threshold. Obviously, our goal is to see that no incident has an impact beyond that standard and that can help define protection plans and safeguard capabilities. A simple example is a 5-min standard for response to certain types of calls or alarms.

Annual percent of interrupted business processes that were restored within targeted timelines

This is the counterpoint to the one immediately above, at least as it applies to business continuity risk. But you could extend to "percent of theft incidents with acceptable levels of recovery" or "investigations completed within planned cost" or any number of similar measures. These are important key performance indicators.

Percent of security incidents that exploited existing vulnerabilities with known solutions

I hope and trust that you are doing risk assessments. This should be a compulsory metric in every security presentation because it tells a number of compelling stories about security's proactive diligence and business unit accountability.

If you are not tracking metrics like these, I would recommend that you have a discussion with your corporate risk management or finance team. They can advise on how they are approaching larger business process risk tolerance considerations and factors they deem appropriate to impact measurement.

CREATING A BUSINESS UNIT SCORECARD
OBJECTIVE

To assess the security of various business units and effectively communicate our findings and recommendations to business leaders. We are using metrics to engage in positive change. We want local management to be more focused on their responsibilities for reducing risk, rather than leaving it to us as the inspector of last resort.

RISK MANAGEMENT STRATEGY

There are two ways to deal with business units' security trouble spots. One way is to bring them directly to the attention of the CEO and the audit committee. If we go this route, we may gain points for a "gotcha" that makes security look good in the eyes of upper management, but we will probably gain an enemy in the ranks who may remain a powerful thorn in the side of our objectives. A second way is to prospectively work with the business unit to assess and report on several key areas of risk exposure and collaborate on solutions.

The scorecard process is risky from an internal business relations perspective. No line manager wants headlines highlighting his or her failure to protect the enterprise. This process must be a preadvertised, coordinated, and accepted part of the corporate risk management strategy. When appropriately planned, incorporated as a consolidated part of the periodic metrics reporting process, and sold to participating line managers, it will be a powerful tool for addressing business units' perceived shortfalls in attention to specific areas of vulnerability.

We are not the corporate cops who get our headlines from nailing idiots who should know better. We are resident experts who have a unique perspective on operational risk and need to see ourselves as change agents intelligently using this unique knowledge. By informing the manager of this proposed assessment process and working with designated individuals in the business unit, we can create and present an honest report of past performance while still achieving a positive response from the manager.

Annual Business Unit Security Scorecard

Business Unit: Administrative Services   Accountable Executive: Paul A Jones
Risk Manager: Charles Brown   Scope: Corporate-wide

Maintaining an Ethical Environment	Excellent awareness & support for business conduct policy throughout the mgt. team.
Protecting Private Information	Repeated notable audit findings. Frequent source of network virus. Poor laptop controls Management insufficiently engaged in risk.
Maintaining Safe & Secure Workplaces	Propped doors & disabled access controls. Improvement in timely notification of emerging Issues having workplace violence potential.
Plan/Prepare for Business Continuity	65% compliance with full plan testing for critical business processes needs improvement.
Employee Vetting	No hires of candidates or vendors with notable adverse backgrounds in the past year.
Vetting 3rd Party Business Relationships	80% of all engagements past 2 years failed to conduct adequate risk-based due diligence.
Response to Security Incidents	Management's response to multiple incidents has been collaborative with good follow-up to address noted vulnerabilities.

Issue Resolution: All issues identified within this review have been addressed within a Risk Mitigation Plan scheduled for completion by the end of Q2.

This is not unlike the process used by internal auditors: We are coming; here is the focus; we will work with you to identify deficiencies and help you correct them, all on the record. If you do not want to play, we will do our job and let the chips fall where they may. Few intelligent managers will refuse to participate when it is put to them that way.

WHERE ARE THE DATA?

Look at the categories of review of a fictional administrative services unit in the nearby chart. Each one can point to a record to support the conclusions.

- *Maintaining an ethical environment*: In the example in the chart, there have been internal investigations that provide evidence that management has a low tolerance for misconduct and supports doing the right thing. Administrative services has been proactive in working with security as allegations have emerged, and they have supported sanctions when evidence supported them.
- *Protecting private information*: Periodic inspections and audits have shown poor controls in this area, according to security's and internal audit's records.
- *Maintaining safe and secure workplaces*: Security has advised administrative services of propped doors and disabled controls and the potential for workplace violence this vulnerable position creates. They are getting the point, so the scorecard acknowledges improvement with a yellow.
- *Plan/prepare for business continuity*: Security can find no record of contingency plan testing for one third of this unit's critical business operations, and this raises concerns.
- *Employee vetting*: Security gives administrative services the results of background investigation findings, and hiring records show they are not hiring the bad guys security has identified.
- *Vetting third-party business relationships*: Security can find no record that more than one in five third-party relationships has been vetted for security or business risk.
- *Response to security incidents*: Where incidents have occurred, the business unit has responded well.

TRACKING RISK IN OUTSOURCING

Outsourcing has become a fundamental business strategy for most major corporations. Ideally, it is a marriage of core competencies, leveraging expertise and focused on reducing the cost of operations. It is also about an inextricable link of corporate reputations.

This process is about those business activities that are at the core of the business and shareholder confidence. These relationships may provide external entities with virtually free access to proprietary business methods, trade secrets, or sensitive customer information. They may be in high-risk locations with notoriously unreliable infrastructures. The list of risks is directly proportionate to the criticality of the product or service sought in the proposed relationship. The awareness of those risks is directly proportionate to the degree to which qualified sources are engaged to proactively identify them. Security needs to be an integrated member of the due diligence team. The results we seek will provide senior management with an additional set of potentially important inputs to the engagement decision.

INFORMATION TECHNOLOGY CONTRACTOR RISK

In the following example, the CSO has been tracking in increasing number of investigative issues related to information technology (IT)-related contractors. His concerns have been reinforced by post-award control reviews by the audit team, and these data have been assembled to explore the need for a more risk-based due diligence program.

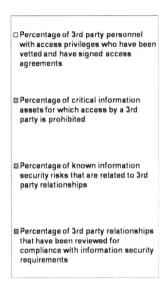
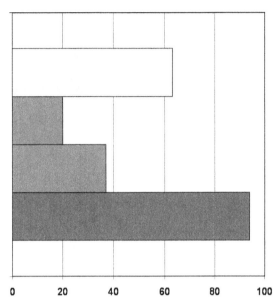

On one hand, this chart shows that the security strategy has been effective in driving requirements for background vetting (often resisted by suppliers), setting parameters on access to information assets, and performing risk reviews. On the other hand, the chart shows that more than a third of those with access have neither been vetted nor signed access agreements. Of greater concern are the findings that 80% of information assets allow third-party access and 37% of the known information security risks are related to outsourced partners.

Using this metric, the CSO can point out the known risks related to third-party relationships that are assignable to prior incidents and current risk assessments and can highlight particular findings of most immediate concern. For example, which of those unvetted nonsignatories have access to the company's most sensitive data or critical elements of the infrastructure? Similarly, which of the company's most essential platforms, applications or data sets have failed to limit access, and what are the potential consequences of these vulnerabilities? Engaging business unit heads who "own" these relationships and determining answers to these questions will enable improved oversight and required mitigation tactics.

WHERE ARE THE DATA?

As shown on the green bar, fully 94% of the company's outsourced relationships have been risk assessed, providing a rich and timely database for determining the scope and nature of risk in this aspect of the corporate outsourcing program. The

CSO can also gain useful information if the security organization maintains an effective incident reporting and cyber investigation program that yields data related to risks assignable to third-party relationships. Engaging accountable business units in the results of these assessments will also yield data on the potential risks associated with these findings.

Corporate security must play a key role in the avoidance of risk in outsourcing.

Companies engage in heavy-duty business process and financial due diligence prior to signing on the dotted line. Security has real substance to offer in this pre-engagement vetting of a relationship that may be missed by a less comprehensive and knowledgeable examination.

TRACKING KEY RISK INDICATORS IN BUSINESS CONTINUITY

If risk quantification and avoidance is the objective, there are few activities found in many corporate security portfolios that can beat contingency planning for proactive risk management. Here are five business units that own the top 10 most critical business processes in this company. Policy requires the test regimen you see here on an annual basis. This particular status report for the risk management committee of the board of directors is a midyear assessment. Call testing and walkthrough are the easy bits. There is a lot remaining to be accomplished on the more strenuous areas of plan testing.

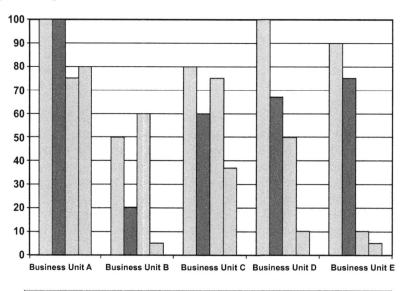

BUSINESS INTEGRITY AND REPUTATIONAL RISK

In an increasing variety of ways, security managers are in the business of reputational risk management. But how would you define a reputational risk for your organization? To what extent is it even on the corporate risk management agenda?

In a *Harvard Business Review* article in February 2007, the authors lamented the fact that established enterprise risk management (ERM) frameworks such as COSO fail to even address reputational risk. They summarized as follows:

> *"Executives know the importance of their companies' reputations. Firms with strong positive reputations attract better people. They are perceived as providing more value, which often allows them to charge a premium. Their customers are more loyal and buy broader ranges of products and services. Because the market believes that such companies will deliver sustained earnings and future growth, they have higher price-earnings multiples and market values and lower costs of capital. Moreover, in an economy where 70% to 80% of market value comes from hard-to-assess intangible assets such as brand equity, intellectual capital, and goodwill, organizations are especially vulnerable to anything that damages their reputations. Most companies, however, do an inadequate job of managing their reputations in general and the risks to their reputations in particular. They tend to focus their energies on handling the threats to their reputations that have already surfaced. This is not risk management; it is crisis management—a reactive approach whose purpose is to limit the damage."[8]*

We readily accept the notion of a security-based risk assessment. But what about a reputational risk assessment? What kind and likelihood of events could occur to your organization? What would be the potential impact on the business? To what extent are these scenarios a part of your crisis management and business continuity planning?

Cannot happen here? The truth is that some organizations will not admit that it *could* happen here. If this happens—and this is the really important bit—judgments about an organization are made not on the fact that a crisis has occurred, but on how well the company has managed it. A failure to consider "what if" will only increase the likelihood of this judgment being unfavorable.

But because we are talking metrics, how should we measure these risks and their controls? The most important is likely to attack it head on with the risk assessment process noted above because that forces a thorough consideration of the risk scope, likelihood, and effectiveness of safeguards. Several potential measures are discussed in this book.

CSOs and ethics and compliance officers alike are all aware of the ramifications of reputational risk. It has multiple implications for security programs, perhaps none more potentially damaging than what the well-placed insider may bring to public and shareholder view.

Let me share a short story to capsulize my concern, and then I will discuss some metrics that I hope will demonstrate how we can communicate and influence behavior.

---

[8] Reputation and its risks, Eccles RG, Newquist SC, Schatz R.; Harvard Business Review, February, 2007.

BROKEN WINDOWS IN THE BOARDROOM

For many years social scientists and public safety practitioners have debated the relevance of the theory that if a broken window in a building is left unrepaired, the rest of the windows will soon be broken as well. In other words, neglect is a signal that no one cares and will ultimately only invite more vandalism and disorder.

In the 1980s and 1990s, a number of big city mayors and police executives celebrated significant reductions in crime guided by the theory of "order maintenance" that had driven scores of smaller community policing efforts for nearly two decades. They sent loud and clear message that even seemingly innocuous misdeeds would not go unpunished and their police forces were never too busy fighting "real crime" to ignore toll jumpers, pickpockets, or graffiti artists.

Could the notion of order maintenance apply to the way we manage conduct in our businesses? But instead of broken glass or graffiti, is it possible that our private sector indicators are unclear expectations, defective accountability, and a willingness to simply look the other way? Is it safe to say that shareholder and employee "residents" have the right to expect a safe, predictable environment that malfeasance and poor ethical hygiene sometimes threaten?

Imagine, if you will, a particularly talented software engineer engaged in a high-visibility project that has CEO interest and strong financial support. A routine audit of his travel reveals several months of false expense claims involving entertaining fellow employees at bars and adult clubs. For fear of derailing the project, his manager tells the audit department, "it's been taken care of," and merely scolds the employee. Or what if an investigation confirms a clear case of embezzlement by a high-level finance employee who eventually admits to years of theft involving a million dollars? Management declines to prosecute to avoid adverse press and merely fires the employee after partial restitution. Unintended consequences emerge when the employee is hired by another company in a similar position shortly thereafter.

What is the big deal, you ask? Compared to those really big rip-offs we have watched unfold, these are not instances of great corporate crime or front-page scandal. Neither the shareholders' nor the company's standing in the market has been damaged, and the result is lost in the rounding. Has anyone really been hurt? This is kind of like comparing a bank robbery with stealing books from the library, right?

I think these stories of shame started with broken windows and little acts of corporate vandalism. In my business of corporate security, these are unswerving leading indicators. Put simply, I believe that there's no greater risk than that of the knowledgeable, empowered insider motivated to do the wrong thing.

We hope that a corporate culture that is anchored in doing the right thing is rewarded in the marketplace, but, conversely, it has been reported that market values fall one-for-one with losses caused by external events, but fall by over twice the loss percentage in cases involving internal fraud.[9]

---

[9] Measuring Reputational Risk: The Market Reaction to Operational Loss Announcements, Jason Perry & Patrick DeFontnouvelle, October 30, 2005, Social Science Electronic Publishing Company.

Do you think the bad guys go for the big score out of the box? No, they start with the little stuff. For those who think mandatory two week vacations are unnecessary, consider minimally communicated business conduct policies, little or no background vetting, a standards-absent virtual office, a passion for outsourcing our most sensitive business processes to companies (in countries) we know precious little about and that have no stake or buy-in to our notion of corporate integrity. That is just the easy ones.

Because the implications of shareholder and public perception of corporate ethical lapses are increasingly obvious, reputational risk is front and center on the minds of many directors and nervous shareholders.

State and federal legislation followed up by criminal and regulatory sanctions have incrementally raised the bar on consequences. Capital markets, shareholders, and the public are rightfully demanding accountability. Board members, directors, and some corporate officers apparently are responding to the increased limelight and potential for personal liability with a harder line on assurances that the organizations they serve have safeguards and controls in place that will identify prospective problems. Previously held norms of corporate governance are being tested for adequacy to their shareholders. Corporate ethics and a culture of doing the right thing are very much "in" topics. Investor confidence, already hammered by a significant downturn in the economy, now wonders aloud how to vet trust in a company's integrity in addition to its financial opportunity.

One way to do that is to have a comprehensive security program, grounded in accepted policy, visibly supported by senior management and led by a highly competent CSO who is connected to the business by effective relationship management. Within that charter is a clear mandate to manage a system of controls and safeguards that measurably contribute to the ethical hygiene of the organization. The CSO can be a key player in the corporate governance team and in the reputational risk management of the organization. But how do we build the program to make that connection? The devil is in the details.

Let us assume you and I are on a team to review and recommend a business conduct policy framework for our organization. We have been asked to build the framework within an established set of corporate values that has integrity as its centerpiece. The chairman and the board have made it clear that we are an ethical company in which our shareholders and employees can be assured that we will do "the right thing." Having been on that team, I will tell you that you do not start by thinking about felonies and misdemeanors. You do not ask the difference between naughty misconduct and outright bad behavior. At its core, it is about good hygiene and individual accountability. Companies are selective in deciding what is right or wrong. If a top executive pads his expenses once in a while, it might be overlooked, but if a temporary employee or some hourly worker did it, I bet she would be gone in a heartbeat. Yet it should not be about big shots and blue collars, plaques on the wall, and speeches about values. It is about a culture where accountability for doing the right thing is the way things are done. Period. Of course, it makes a great sound bite, and it is easy to say. But it is very, very difficult to implement. To make integrity a cornerstone of a company's culture, you need to make a clear business case. That starts with a common sense acceptance that, without the trust of the shareholder, the customer, and the employee, there is no business. In other words, trust has an economic, as well as an altruistic, value.

Who ya gonna call? Ultimately, who is responsible for setting the standard of ethical behavior? For looking for the broken panes in the various corporate windows? First and foremost, of course, are the board and CEO, who together set the tone and reinforce the values at every opportunity. They demonstrate the commitment to integrity in daily business conduct. The policy infrastructure becomes a constant reference point for business conduct. My company has more than 30 core business conduct policies published on its intranet and scores of related, more technical policies within various elements of the company. A critical element in the program is a module in the various manager training and development programs.

The local business executive, preferably the first-line manager, is also paid to know the neighborhood and work the streets. He becomes the agent of the culture and the behavior model. Show me a manager who demonstrates the wrong values, and I will guarantee his work group has other problems that would interest security and others. After the first-line manager comes a team of governance, oversight, and administrative resources, security, audit, ethics, compliance, legal, human resources, finance, and others who are in unique positions to see anomalies, failures or flaws in controls, lessons from various incidents, opportunities for improvement, and feedback to management. Once employees see management's commitment to a system of processes, procedures, and safeguards that ensure their concerns will be protected, you will start to see order restored. Security, legal, and HR departments are keys to that element of the integrity infrastructure. Once you connect the dots, you start to realize that it is not that you have a bad guy in production, it is that he has a bad manager who set a bad behavior standard that created a problem in the first place. And it does not stop there. Why did that manager's manager not realize the emerging issue? Where was HR in the exit interviews, in the daily interactions? What about the internal audits? After a significant internal incident, when you peel the layers back, you find evidence everywhere. The postmortem has to find the root causes so that you are not destined to repeat those mistakes.

If the CSO has unique linkages to his governance peers and proper access to the top, he can put the disparate pieces from the multidepartment findings together and end up with a picture of internal risk dynamics that is not available elsewhere. You might say that CSOs have the means to eliminate plausible denial. Effectively connected CSOs have a bird's-eye view of those and other disparate pieces of data on corporate hygiene. They connect the dots that others do not even see. As such, they are critical to corporate integrity. CEOs and other senior executives need to make room for this perspective if they hope to positively *affect* corporate strategy.

RISK PERSONIFIED—THE KNOWLEDGEABLE INSIDER

Given that short story I have just shared, I have often walked away shaking my head from discussions with supposedly knowledgeable business executives and security managers who insist on an almost exclusive focus on the bad guy outside their walls while they give virtually uncontrolled access to the crown jewels to their "trusted" employees. Over the past couple of decades, this incredulous view has been stretched to a near breaking point with our headlong dive into the outsourced, "lean" business model. What we may not know about our "partners" and their commitment to the protection of our reputation and shareholder assets boggles the mind. And I have not even mentioned our very own bad guys within our very own mahogany walls.

This portrayal of insider threat only scratches the surface, but I hope it prompts some questions for discussion among the corporate governance team. You want a meaningful metric? How many of these can be honestly answered in the affirmative? How many do you think it takes before you have the ingredients for high-probability insider risk?

Insider Threat Landscape
How many of these are answered in the affirmative?

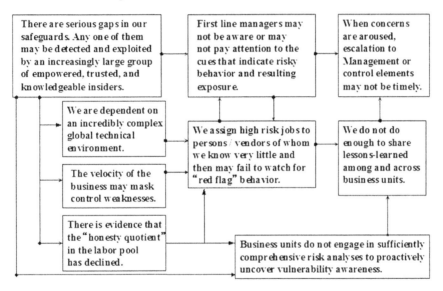

An honest focus on the threat from the knowledgeable insider requires a commitment to really pushing the envelope on "what if." Getting the right people around the table and asking that question around a potential franchise-threatening scenario is a lot more difficult than the annual business continuity test in which an event like a natural disaster can be somewhat more easily visualized and the implications posed. This exercise requires the suspension of belief about the integrity of one's co-workers, people whom you have vetted and who accept your vision of "doing the right thing." Or do they, and what if they do not? This little graphic tosses a variety of "facts" on the table. Is it possible that the velocity of the business could mask weaknesses in your internal controls? When we have had an incident with an insider, did we dig deep enough to understand what was broken and then really fix it?

There are several interesting aspects to the insider threat in business. At the end of the day, they all boil down to motive, opportunity, and desire. Visibly effective security programs and internal controls will work to significantly reduce opportunity and contribute to turning desire into fear of being caught. Motive remains, perhaps learning and waiting. Protection against insider wrongdoing requires a labor-intensive array of linked safeguards that begin with really knowing who we are letting into our trust and following that trust with a variety of checks tied to the assurance of effective controls.

The management (and magnitude) of insider risk requires top-down commitment to owning a host of integrated, moving parts. This is not about uncaring management and the lack of trust. It is about a risk-based, well-planned, and executed set of intelligent internal controls. These controls are measurable and need to be tested. That is where well-focused metrics can make a difference. Eliminating plausible denial in this space is not nearly good enough. They have to nail what actions are required and by whom.

> Security enjoys a unique perch from which to view the resilience of the ethical framework—the hygiene—of the organization. We need to send up red flags when internal investigations and incident postmortems indicate trends in sloppy internal controls and lack of management engagement. Metrics define the messages to be flown on those flags.

However "security" is scoped and defined within your company, its programs are critical elements in advertising the effectiveness of measures to mitigate the risk of the knowledgeable insider. Corporate security enjoys a unique perch from which to observe enterprise commitment to integrity-based business operations. That lens can focus on a variety of conditions, metrics, trends, and cues that present areas of concern for insider risk. Here is a short list:

- Percentage of platforms and applications without adequate identification, authentication, authorization and/or data integrity;
- Percent of business unit hiring of individuals with material derogatory background findings;
- Percent of risk assessment findings related to defects in internal controls accepted, implemented, and confirmed as operational by independent testing;
- HR or business unit management reluctance to engage qualified security investigation of allegations of criminal activity or serious misconduct;
- Failure to address anonymous reports of misconduct from established employee hotline mechanisms;
- Failure to perform appropriate precontract risk assessments of vendors whose services and access may present reputational risk to the company;
  - Failure to conduct periodic postaward reviews of contractual requirements related to personnel and process integrity;
- Failure to conduct postmortem examinations of internal investigations to identify vulnerabilities within internal controls and root causes of incidents involving trusted insiders;
  - Failure to act on appropriately vetted findings;
  - Evidence of business unit reluctance to inform or escalate concerns on integrity or misconduct;

- The percentage of subjects of internal investigations who indicate a lack of knowledge of the policy they are accused of violating;
- Failure to establish clearance requirements and report on internal or external audit findings pertaining to personnel and process integrity;
  - Percent of findings of inadequate internal controls from surprise audits of risk-prone processes;
- The number of terminations for cause as a percentage of the employee population;
- The number of employees involved as subjects of investigation as a percent of the employee population;
- Failure to exercise effective oversight of employee relationships with contracted vendors;
- Percent of HR and business unit supervisors with training in red flag behavior appropriate to business process risk.

Regardless of what scope your security function delivers, understanding your company's exposure to insider risk is an essential part of the mission. A trained and aware security officer manning an access/egress point is just as likely a resource for observing insider red flag indicators as an auditor. Clearly, the best observer is the trained first line supervisor who is empowered to set the tone for integrity. Security's relationship of trust with this clientele is absolutely essential.

INCIDENT ANALYSIS IDENTIFIES EVOLVING INSIDER THREATS

Investigations and incident postmortems enable us to identify attributes of perpetrators to aid in the formulation of preventive strategies and contribute to actionable management reporting. The CSO possesses a unique risk-focused database that should be used to track key risk trends. This basic metric is used to alert management to ensure awareness and support for corrective actions and their effectiveness over an extended period.

Risk Management Strategy

The metric seen below was developed by security to highlight concern for the number of incidents attributable to insider employees. In partnership with HR and legal, the CSO developed and applied a focused effort to develop, communicate, and apply a business conduct policy that has had a positive impact on employee misconduct. In 2002, the company implemented a large-scale outsourced contractor program that has resulted in a significant increase in inventory losses, systems abuse, and customer privacy violations. The solution involved more stringent precontract security reviews, periodic inspections, and procurement oversight. The trend now appears to be measurably reducing the number of incidents attributable to "trusted" vendors.

Where Are the Data?

Effective tracking of data on these three incident types requires much more than security's investigative reports. Our internal business partners in HR, procurement, audit, and various managers overseeing outsourced programs all have data that

represent the more complete picture and partnering with them gives us solid opportunities to influence policy and strategy.

KEY TRENDS IN
ORGANIZATIONAL INTEGRITY CASES

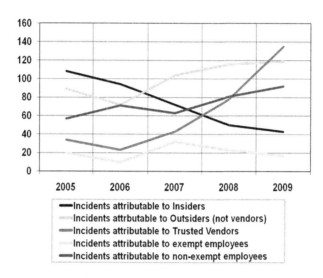

What do you want to achieve with this information?

This CSO understands the unique risk management perch the security role provides,
what metrics are important, and how to track it and use it to successfully engage and
influence senior management. The CSO understands that security is only a piece
of the solution and is anxious to collaborate and partner with other members of the
corporate governance team.

These trends reflect very significant (and sensitive) data on the source of
threats to the reputation and well-being of the company. The knowledgeable
insider is always the most serious threat because they live inside the protective
measures and have unique understanding of where the soft spots in protection—
vulnerabilities—are located and how to use them to advantage. With outsourcing
we have brought a whole new population into this "trusted" realm: contractors
and third-party business partners. You can bet that individual business units do
not go around briefing senior management when they have insider misconduct,
so it is important that security maintain the radar. Also, it is the multiple incident
trends that tell the story in this reputational risk area much more severely than
individual cases.

These metrics require action and go to the fundamental measures of business reputation.

What we want to achieve here is change. We need to eliminate plausible denial. Success is new or revised policy, more security-aware business operations that contain the controls essential to these new ways of doing business.

WHAT IS THE COST OF A BAD EMPLOYEE?

The knowledgeable insider is at the top of the list of threats to any organization, public or private. Part of our job is to make business leaders aware of the seriousness of this threat by using metrics that catch their attention. The following simplified time line measures one small aspect of reputational risk: the time involved in resolving an insider misconduct case resulting in termination for cause.

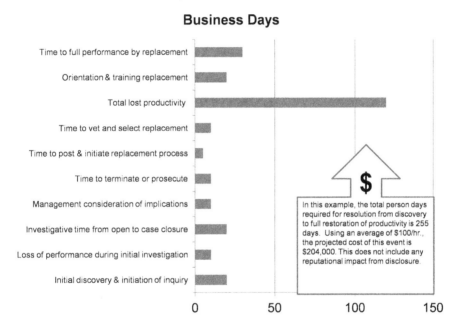

Business Days

In this example, the total person days required for resolution from discovery to full restoration of productivity is 255 days. Using an average of $100/hr., the projected cost of this event is $204,000. This does not include any reputational impact from disclosure.

Objective

1. To obtain and track data that documents the financial impact of identifying, investigating, and adjudicating an employee who is the subject of alleged misconduct rising to the level of termination or prosecution.
2. To use this data to sensitize business unit and HR leaders to the necessity of setting expectations and monitoring questionable business conduct.

Considerations

What is the value of a company's reputation to its shareholders and the marketplace? Ask British Petroleum. Where are Enron and Arthur Andersen? Sure, these are really big deals compared to one insider going bad, but even a single insider incident too often rises to the level of a serious crisis. Assessing the steps in a case like this (or any investigation for that matter) provides one of several potential views of incident consequences.

In this simplified case, let us say the employee's manager was suspicious of several items in two prior travel and entertainment claims and confronted him. He denied any wrongdoing, and an argument ensued. Over the next few weeks, security performed audits of several prior claim forms, and the investigation confirmed multiple fraudulent entries. In subsequent interviews, the subject admitted to the false claims and was terminated.

In all, 255 person days were required to go through the steps from identification of the potential problem to resolution of the case and replacement of the employee. Moreover, there were 120 days of lost productivity by the incumbent. Plug in your burdened labor rates for each category of employee or contractor working this resolution and calculate your cost. Keep in mind that if this were a more consequential, high-profile fraud, this cost would not account for the financial impact to the bottom line or the potential damage to the brand when the case was highlighted in the upper right-hand corner of *The Wall Street Journal*.

Measuring reputational risk

While our graph focuses only on the potential financial impact of an investigation and termination for questionable conduct, this area of operational risk really centers on the market's perception of the trustworthiness of the business and the potential impact of lapses of corporate integrity on shareholder value. Think about the potential for internal misconduct or criminal activity by insiders at your company. What events could cause significant financial impact or longer-term loss of market share?

To repeat myself, we enjoy a unique perch from which to view the resilience of the ethical framework—the hygiene—of the organization. We need to send up red flags when incident postmortems indicate trends in sloppy internal controls and lack of management engagement. We need to seek common denominators across multiple types of internal investigations. We need to share our well thought-out and documented concerns with our corporate governance colleagues in audit, risk, legal, and HR and work together to connect the dots.

Security incidents offer unique opportunities to drill down and identify a finding or two that can be used to demonstrate to management that we are not simply responding, but digging for root causes of business risk. The message in this simple example is not the cost of one employee gone bad, but the need to set clear expectations for doing the right thing and to use commonsense controls to test for conformance.

USE YOUR METRICS TO INFLUENCE POLICY

1 + 1 + 3 is a metric I like to envision when we can look across a set of data from different buckets of incidents and then have those few common denominators—root causes—leap off the page. Now I have the opportunity to attack a variety of risks with more clarity and less cost.

This next chart is one of my favorites. I can sell lessons to multiple audiences with this single slide. Examples like this taken from multiple investigative postmortems and after-action and root cause analyses can be incredibly revealing when you cull out the common denominators and connect the dots. It can make for a powerful visual presentation when you have the verifiable historical data to identify the root causes and business process vulnerabilities.

In this particular array, I am focusing directly on insider risk. In our business of internal investigations, we tend to inform management on individual cases and the factors that contributed to the subject's wrongdoing. That single incident then gets lost in the institutional memory. Using incident severity and frequency on each axis, I am able to demonstrate that these multiple insider cases present a clear picture of a few KRIs. Their persistence in our investigative findings demand action by management.

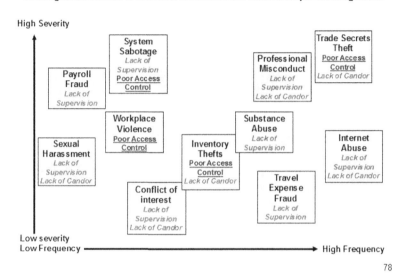

Using Metrics to Influence Policy & Behavior
Seeking Root Causes & Common Denominators From Multiple Investigations

A graphic like this uses a wide lens to focus the audience on the linkage between root causes and actionable solutions.

I doubt there is an experienced security practitioner who has not had to scold some business unit on sloppy access control, perhaps after a laptop or handbag theft or more frequently as a result of continuing alarms from propped doors. This example demonstrates how a more pervasive security defect like this can contribute to higher consequence and higher frequency exposures.

On this single page, we see scores of cases rolled up to 11 categories with verified root causes. Each group is actionable with one or more of your key constituents. HR has a stake in "lack of supervision" with regard to manager training and risk awareness; they also need to know that certain groups represented by the "lack of candor" finding may have cultural, inadequate background investigation, or supervisory inadequacies. "Poor access control" can be local decisions overriding security policy or bad physical security planning and implementation.[10]

---

[10] Insider risk also involves actions on behalf of business unit management or other accountable parties to delay reporting of suspicious activity, allegations of misconduct or other required matters that demand timely escalation. Such failures not only impact the probability of successful resolution but likely indicate deeper issues of integrity within the tardy business units and their management.

In my experience, a presentation like this can demonstrate and communicate a deeper understanding of internal control defects and illuminate the benefits of improved controls that offer a multiplier effect. But we also need to put our numbers in context that permits comparative analysis across business units (or trusted peers) as well as trending. Here is an example.

MEASURING IMPACT OF SECURITY INCIDENTS ON BUSINESS PRODUCTIVITY

When we talk to the business about the impact of security events on productivity, we are connecting to the value proposition. But from a bottom line perspective, loss of productivity is a key risk indicator, and it can come from an increasingly disturbing array of security events.

When we talk about metrics, it is easy to think of our work along the lines of cost of loss less recovery, response times, time to recover, incident trends over time, etc. But what are the impacts to the business in terms of lost time and productivity? These are real impact costs and are often lost in the otherwise valuable discussions about vulnerabilities, perpetrators, and investigative results. Metrics like these put another perspective on the true cost of safety or security breaches.

Strategy

This security manager understands the need to take his metrics beyond common workload and incident reporting. This company has the benefit of a multidepartmental security committee that meets quarterly to input each participant's unique perspective on risk, analyzes lessons learned, and seeks a 360° view of root causes. Working hand-in-hand with HR and affected business units, the security manager's team has smartly built and maintained a data file on the time spent by business unit and other nonsecurity personnel on selected incidents involving security intervention. While it is not seen here, security rounds out the perspective with a companion set of metrics that tracks investigative costs as well as documenting the root causes and other relevant results from investigative postmortems.

This approach provides a far more comprehensive and instructive picture on the implications of various incidents and enables a more constructive process of corrective action.

In the following example, we see three years worth of data on four incident categories: termination, malicious incidents, workplace violence, and workplace accidents. For the sake of this example, we will use an admittedly low melded labor rate of $52 per hour.[11]

---

[11] This rate considers the combined average hourly rate of individuals impacted by the events, plus all benefits, divided by 2080.

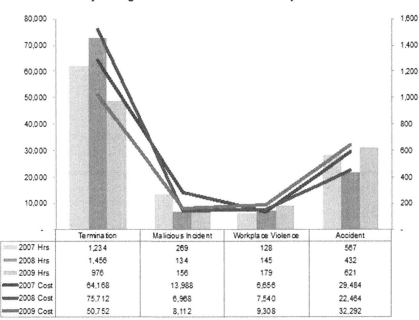

Productivity Impacts:
Hours Directly Assignable to Selected Security Incidents 2007–09

	Termination	Malicious Incident	Workplace Violence	Accident
2007 Hrs	1,234	269	128	567
2008 Hrs	1,456	134	145	432
2009 Hrs	976	156	179	621
2007 Cost	64,168	13,988	6,656	29,484
2008 Cost	75,712	6,968	7,540	22,464
2009 Cost	50,752	8,112	9,308	32,292

Termination

This refers to the time required to address an employee termination for cause once the line manager and HR have made the decision to terminate.[12] Factors include risk assessment, HR and business unit time involved in the replacement process, productivity lost from the termed employee, and the time necessary to get the replacement fully functional in the job.

Malicious incidents

These events typically impact or otherwise interrupt business processes and could range from vandalism caused by labor unrest or a disgruntled employee, actions of our about-to-be or just terminated employee, outsiders linked to employees, or more likely the impact of virus and malware on the information infrastructure and business processes. Many incidents in this latter category have dramatic postevent productivity impacts involving business outages and extensive restoral times at process-critical workstations.

Workplace violence

We often focus on the time required by victims and security personnel in dealing with violence in the workplace. But these cases often have preceding and ongoing incident

---

[12] A far bigger hourly and cost number may be seen when you consider time lost dealing with the evaluative and corrective actions that have to be taken prior to the termination decision.

management and productivity implications. Victims of domestic violence, often with restraining orders, have more days lost at work, and their functioning on the job, as well as that of their colleagues and supervisors, may frequently be impacted. This latter example is especially true where on-the-job workers are the adversaries.

Workplace accidents

This security manager has safety in his portfolio, and the company employs day workers and temps in addition to regular employees. He recognizes that this population comes with high turnover and individuals who may not be familiar with or attentive to safety rules and procedures. He is also sensitive to the fact that while productivity implications are clear for the affected individual and their part in the business process, perhaps the longer-term impacts are found in escalating insurance rates and regulatory sanctions.

When you build your key risk indicators, think about what metrics will best resonate with the business and drive the changes you believe will have the greatest impact on the factors that contribute to risk exposure.

Summary

This security manager did not build a complex database requiring hours of input and analysis. In each event category, data estimates on productivity impacts were gathered as part of investigative findings on financial impact/loss or as a component of incident postmortems. When we take metric snapshots on one factor alone, we may lose the opportunity to effectively connect these risk events to improved business knowledge. The value is in the ability to provide management with a more complete picture of security's view of enterprise risk management.

TRACKING INTERNAL INVESTIGATIONS

In the following chart, we see a CSO using a tracking metric on the ratio of internal investigation subjects per 100 employees in four business units with continuing high rates of employee misconduct. By working closely in a joint security/HR team and digging into multiple internal investigations, they have found that deficient or failed first-line supervision was a critical contributor to higher rates of employee subjects within these units. Supervisors were too close with subordinates, expense reporting was inappropriately monitored, and work environments were often out of control. Management had failed to set and manage expectations around appropriate behavior and basic compliance, and several employees and supervisors were disciplined and others terminated.

The governance team has made the business case to develop and roll out a business conduct policy training program for first-line supervisors, jointly presented by security, HR, and general counsel. The takeaway is that commencing at the end of Q3/2006 and through 2007, there were significant reductions in internal cases within these units attributable to clearly communicated expectations and policy coupled with more aware and accountable supervisors. This program is now an established component of management training and reinforced in supervisory performance evaluations.

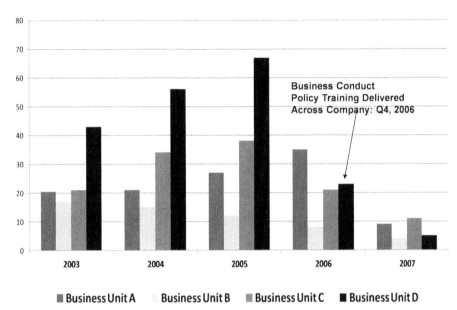

■ Business Unit A   ▨ Business Unit B   ▨ Business Unit C   ■ Business Unit D

The following example takes a different view of insider risk and focuses on the relationship of defective internal controls and security deficiencies to losses in several business units. This type of presentation might be used to provide further (root cause) explanation to trends in internal investigations. The numeric anchor for each of these business units to a ratio of employees to security defects gives the audience a clear focal point for action.

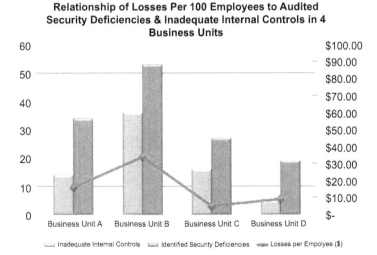

Relationship of Losses Per 100 Employees to Audited Security Deficiencies & Inadequate Internal Controls in 4 Business Units

TRACKING DISCIPLINARY ACTION

Even given a core business conduct policy framework, the differential application of sanctions within an organization can have serious implications for the investigative components of a corporate security department. Differing cultural environments often approach policy interpretation and enforcement in strikingly different ways with cases of employee misconduct being high on the list. Companies involved in mergers and acquisitions may bring significantly different approaches to a set of investigative findings and it is common to find very different results for the same infraction when compared between exempt and nonexempt employees.

Security can potentially be caught in the middle of poorly executed business conduct policy. It is important to track these trends in disciplinary actions noting when such inconsistencies may contribute to future potential for litigation and to guide investigations management.

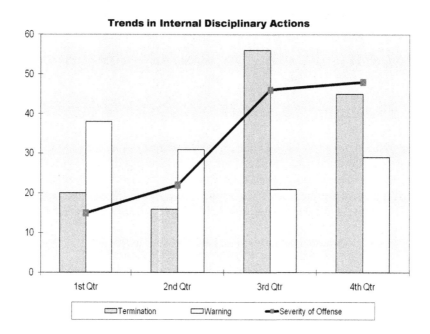

INSIDER RISK IN OUTSOURCED BUSINESS PROCESS

Let us take another view of outsourcing or vendor-related risk. Clearly, the definition of an "insider" has changed dramatically over the past several years as businesses have sought to reduce cost through outsourcing. Look at this combination of audit findings and the core business processes that have been assigned to others outside the four walls of this company. The internal control issues alone should be enough to make this company incendiary, but when we factor in what these "trusted" relationships are providing, how should we characterize insider risk? The finding on "shallow technical due diligence" brings new meaning to shallow audit review. Depending on how reliant your company is on these offsets and standoff relationships, if you are going to dig and measure the real picture of insider risk, you may need to ask for a big increase to your travel budget.

XYZ Corp. — Insider Risk Landscape

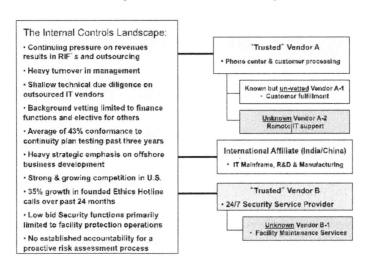

The Internal Controls Landscape:
- Continuing pressure on revenues results in RIF's and outsourcing
- Heavy turnover in management
- Shallow technical due diligence on outsourced IT vendors
- Background vetting limited to finance functions and elective for others
- Average of 43% conformance to continuity plan testing past three years
- Heavy strategic emphasis on offshore business development
- Strong & growing competition in U.S.
- 35% growth in founded Ethics Hotline calls over past 24 months
- Low bid Security functions primarily limited to facility protection operations
- No established accountability for a proactive risk assessment process

"Trusted" Vendor A
- Phone center & customer processing

Known but un-vetted Vendor A-1
- Customer fulfillment

Unknown Vendor A-2
Remote IT support

International Affiliate (India/China)
- IT Mainframe, R&D & Manufacturing

"Trusted" Vendor B
- 24/7 Security Service Provider

Unknown Vendor B-1
- Facility Maintenance Services

TRACKING LOSSES FROM FRAUD, WASTE AND ABUSE

Here is another view of insider risk. These trends all tell a story about lagging indicators related to ineffective supervision and weak internal controls. Business expense fraud tells volumes about management's failure to set expectations and monitor behavior, poor policy compliance, and questionable integrity within specific business units. This metric, in particular, is as good a barometer of insider risk potential as you can find. Weak controls around time keeping and internet compliance are measurable indicators of costly insider risk as well. Embezzlement and theft speak for themselves as risk indicators. One of the key indicators of management's connection to integrity and policy compliance will be the degree to which they probe on the subject's business unit supervisor and why that accountability failed to detect and deal with these issues before they concluded with this result.

Each one of these types in internal misbehaviors deserves occasional deep dives and incident postmortems to reliably identify the root causes and common denominators. Note that each of these tend to involve potentially time-consuming forensic and investigative activities, an insulting companion to the losses attendant to the incidents.

Losses from Corporate Fraud, Waste & Abuse

CONFIDENTIAL HOTLINE REPORTING

Whistle blower protection has established a variety of means of confidential internal reporting schemes, some into CSOs or ethics officers and others to outside service providers. The data from this source can provide critical indicators of internal risk with reputational consequences. When such programs are effectively advertised (and periodically re-advertised to maintain commitment on reporting), metrics like those seen below are highly useful in a dashboard directed to investigations reporting or reputational risk management.

Business Conduct Hot Line Reporting

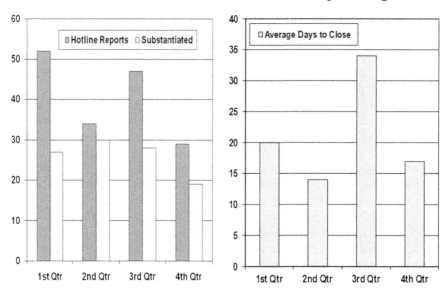

A SIMPLE DASHBOARD ON REPUTATIONAL RISK

Here is a fairly simple dashboard to engage top management on trends of concern related to insider and reputational risk. In this example, we are updating senior management on several areas having implications for reputational risk exposure. These five key indicators can easily represent an hour briefing with the CEO or the senior management team. Our objective here is to maintain engagement around some key risk measures of noncompliance around business conduct, findings from our root cause analyses, how we compare to peers around confidential hot line reporting, and our progress in expanded vetting for those with access. The bottom statistic relates to movement of a key performance measure on management accountability. There could be some interesting linkages between the measures in this discussion.

Organizational Integrity Dashboard: Our People / Our Reputation

	This Year	Last Year
NUMBER OF VIOLATIONS OF BUSINESS CONDUCT POLICY PER 1000 EMPLOYEES	4.4	8.2
% OF INTERNAL INCIDENTS WHERE FAILURES IN MANAGER OVERSIGHT IS CITED AS A CAUSAL FACTOR	39%	54%
% OF EMPLOYEE HOTLINE CALLS FOR FRAUD AND POLICY VIOLATIONS VS. PEER SECTOR AVERAGE	15% vs. 31%	31% vs. 34%
% EMPLOYEES & VENDORS HAVING LOGICAL & PHYSICAL ACCESS WITH NO BACKGROUND VETTING	9.5%	11%
% OF SR. MANAGERS WHO HAVE IMPLEMENTED PROCEDURES TO ENSURE COMPLIANCE WITH INFO SECURITY POLICY AND CONTROLS	94%	71%

If I were the CEO getting this briefing, I would likely ask the following questions:

- Where are the most prevalent sources of these violators, and what is local management doing to address this issue of lousy first-line management?
- What do you want me to do with this information? And, by the way, what are you doing to address these issues?
- What do you see as the milestones of moving an issue from red to green? How have you communicated your findings and expectations to those who need to hear it?

Pick your topics, and learn from the action and reaction. Expect probing around who (names please) the bad guys are in these examples.

Use caution in this area of metrics reporting

Metrics around internal investigations can be a risky business for all concerned. Keep these points in mind as you approach this area of risk management:

1. When your data targets a specific business unit and it may circulate within higher management, consider who in the unit's chain of command should be the initial recipient. Sharing for discussion and proposed issue resolution enables win/win.
2. Carefully consider what you intend to report and who will see it. Distribution should be carefully controlled.
3. If you have any doubts whatsoever about the reliability of your data, do not report them. The consequences of data unreliability are far reaching in the best of circumstances. It can be disastrous for a security program. Make certain you are reporting on root cause of internal problems, not just symptoms.
4. Depending on sensitivity, share your data with counsel to determine need for privilege.

UNINTENDED CONSEQUENCES—ANOTHER VIEW OF INCIDENT IMPACT ON PRODUCTIVITY

A significant number of data breaches are not caused by the malevolent acts of insiders or outsiders; they occur from unintentional acts of employees or persons with access to classified and proprietary information, often by electronic transmittal. Depending on the sensitivity of the material sent and the extent of distribution, the investigation, paper chase, and remediation can be both difficult and expensive.

In the chart below, we see four quarters of forensic and basic investigative activity devoted to 63 data spill incidents. One-hundred-thirty employees in this company were involved in resolutions, and that does not include the numbers that this company had to request at the receiving locations take time out of busy schedules to chase down and secure the data. The bottom line for one year's worth of unintended consequences in just this category: $1.2 million.

We could pile on and add both reputational and regulatory risk to the damage assessment, but I suspect you get the message.

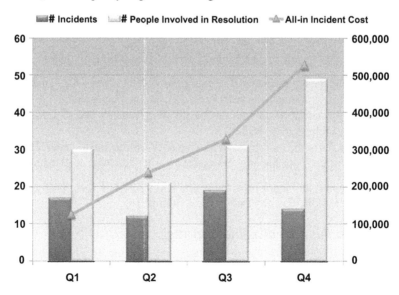

SUMMARIZING INSIDER RISK MEASUREMENT

Depending on the scope of your security mission, tracking internal incidents and the various views of internal crime and misconduct enables a critical assessment of the adequacy of internal controls. The knowledgeable insider presents the greatest human threat to a company's reputation and shareholder confidence. Outsourcing has redefined the meaning of "insider" and relying on a hands-off security posture with third-party vendors and "trusted partners" who have logical and physical access to our most sensitive information and operations demands a critical probing from skilled security professionals.

Picking a few key metrics to track and report up on a regular basis can provide a critically important and potentially unique lens on this sensitive side of operational risk. It is also an opportunity to collaborate with your corporate governance partners in building a process for connecting the dots on the state of internal controls.

TRANSITIONS—MOVING THE LENS FROM RISK TO PERFORMANCE INDICATORS

Our security programs have a variety of products that have been developed to serve specific clientele or management objectives. Portrayed here are a linked set of essential indicators that should be an integral part of the security manager's master plan and program measurement system.

An indicator is a sign, an index, a means to measure or visually point with some discipline around accuracy. We often see metrics associated with meters or dials, and we frequently use visual cues like the stop, caution, and go signals of a traffic light. KPIs are an integral part of business planning and strategy as are KRIs that guide enterprise risk management.

I have a bias on KPIs. I think in our business they have to be tied to KRIs and tell the story about how well those risks are being managed by all the accountable parties. This notion of accountability is important. We are only a part of the protection equation, and although we may own the tool kit and a big piece of the rule book, enterprise protection lives or dies in attentive business processes. I think it is fair to say that a good KRI signals a clear indication of which direction a designated risk is headed. Have our control measures enabled risk avoidance? What results are we using to obtain that conclusion? Is there a defensible line from the elimination of the exploitable security defect to a specifically directed security activity? Is this not the focus of our planning and that positive result the key measure of this program's performance?

Security's Metric Products

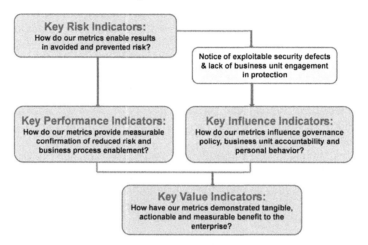

What about influence? When we have accurately identified the risk exposure from proactive or reactive exercises, deployed the right countermeasures, and effectively communicated responsibilities and awareness to employees and managers, we are using our unique pulpit to influence others who are part of the solution. Thus, our ability to influence results is a key performance indicator.

What about value? Proof of value can be elusive for us. It may be said that truly effective security is invisible, especially when it is effectively integrated into the daily business. Business executives understand the connection and the business rationale for an enterprise protection program. But they typically do not really understand what we do and why or how we do it. It is a critical part of the security manager's job to craft a message and educate top management on where and how we bring value to business strategy and the bottom line. This message has to include a variety of metrics that demonstrate in business terms our value story.

Where do we find value? Is value found in avoided risk? Do we add value to a business process when we enable it to do things that would otherwise be too risky? For example:

- Digging to learn where the exploitable vulnerabilities lie;
- Making it difficult to hire and retain bad people;
- Providing for safe and secure places to work;
- Educating busy, inattentive, and ignorant customers;
- Making life difficult for risky vendors and suppliers;
- Anticipating and planning for critical things tipping over;
- Providing flawless response when bad things hit the fan.

When we do a really solid job of building tangible measures of a program's performance in mitigating risk or enabling a positive business result, our metrics become a centerpiece of security's value proposition.

Measuring Security Program Performance

INTRODUCTION

You will better appreciate the fact that measurement begins at home when you have that one-on-one with the Chief Executive Officer (CEO) or Chief Financial Officer (CFO) who asks, "How do you measure your programs and their contribution to the bottom line?" I don't know how you can define and sell a security program without having the means and, ultimately, the evidence that measure how well it's working. But apparently a security manager who says, "Nobody's asking and I don't have the data" has somehow escaped the obvious oversight by management or is simply waiting for the shoe to drop on career advancement.

Or consider this more organizationally astute assessment by Andrew Jaquith: "[When] no good, consistent security metrics are available, companies find themselves unable to accurately gauge the suitability or effectiveness of different security options. Consequently, the amount a company can spend on 'improving' security has no natural bounds beyond the company's ability to pay."[1]

Let me be blunt. *I believe the security manager who fails to collect, validate, and communicate risk and performance measures is contributing to risk.*

Every security program that possesses an obligation or opportunity for delivering excellence in the corporate security mission requires planned, measured, and communicated performance objectives.

Many companies have employed a set of effectiveness measures like speed, quality and cost to drive value, service performance, and customer satisfaction objectives. If metrics have a logical home, it has to be around the "what" and "how" of measuring program performance. Unfortunately, "how" often ends up being "how many" or "how much." This results in a lot of people spending a lot of hours feeding Excel spreadsheets and then counting stuff like numbers of things processed, dollars and hours spent in specific activities, and how often they achieved a targeted completion rate—for example, number of forensic examinations of suspect desktops completed within the 95% target of five business days. Don't get me wrong—we need effectiveness measures like these to drive day-to-day resource management. The measures I'm looking for and the ones your clients need go to what these forensic examinations reveal about risky behavior and defects in policy compliance or supervisory oversight.

---

[1] Andrew Jaquith, *Security Metrics, Replacing Fear, Uncertainty, and Doubt.* Addison Wesley, 2007, p. 11.

In our business, risk metrics should be the drivers of performance metrics. Effective tracking of a trend in workplace violence should be driving deep dives into root causes and incident demographics. The learning that emerges from these analyses should drive development of strategies and tactics to reduce these incidents by specifically targeted numbers. Thus, a performance metric is grounded on a clearly allied risk metric. Together, they present the potential story of security's focus on preventable risk and the program's value proposition.

Every security program has its own unique standards of measurement. Security's stewardship of these programs is clear. What is often not clearly established is the custodial responsibility of individual business unit managers and employees for their critical part in enterprise protection. Security managers must analyze the relevant data, draw defensible conclusions, and communicate with this clientele on enterprise risk and security program performance. It is through this focus on shared results that metrics establish an actionable accountability model.

In the next section, we'll explore a variety of approaches to the measurement of security programs. There are several themes I try to frame because I believe security teams have several possible objectives to meet the needs of their bosses, customers, governance colleagues, and their own program management:

- What are those key performance indicators that should be driving your team and program's objectives?
- What should that dashboard or scorecard you've been thinking about look like? What contents are appropriate for which constituents?
- Do you seek to influence an outcome or sell an idea or proposal?
- Are the metrics providing alerts on a specific problem in a business unit or across a broader landscape?
- Do you see an opportunity to leverage a collaboration or improved alignment with a hard sell customer?
- Are you probing for operational excellence and building the performance metrics that are at the heart of managing execution?
- Has somebody up there in top management asked for some specific measures or metrics?
- Do you need to have that one-on-one with a subordinate to assess progress on those initiatives and goals you set for the year?

Effective leadership requires outstanding communication. Metrics support your script. Where is program performance in your communication strategy?

KEY PERFORMANCE INDICATORS

Key performance indicators (KPIs) can be so ingrained in a company's business strategy that it can be essential to reconsider how they fit in our corner of the business. We may employ KPIs in any of several security program areas. A few examples are offered in the graphic below.

Bottom Line: If you are not measuring, you are not managing. Performance measurement in all its facets is a core competency of all program managers.

KPI OBJECTIVES

Organizations use KPIs to evaluate their success in reaching long-term organizational goals. We may use them to set specific, measurable objectives for program performance. They may track our success in engaging the business in improved security practices or the progress of vendors in meeting contractual performance specifications. They may set standards for incident response and resolution or any number of desired outcomes tied to the allocation of security resources.

STRATEGY

In this example, the security manager has chosen four areas of program performance by which to assess his department's operations for the year: customer service, guard operations, incident response, and investigation outcomes. Under each, the security manager has identified multiple measures to track to indicate success in that sector of the business plan.

Customer Service. Set an 80% customer satisfaction target that may be measured by post-incident feedback, specific survey exercises, or as part of routine one-on-one customer meetings. Additionally, where business units request unsolicited risk assessments and implement a targeted percentage of security's recommendations, we have clear evidence of solid customer service and alignment with the business.

Guard Operations. Guard force operations typically take up a substantial part of the security department's budget. This security manager contracts with an outside vendor, facing issues of liability, coemployment, and vendor performance in an industry with frequently high-turnover employment pools. It makes sense to set measurable contractual expectations such as those found in service level agreements (SLAs). Our manager has selected four measurable SLA criteria dealing with supervision, turnover, and daily competency, each of which contributes to a qualitative picture of vendor performance.

Hierarchy of Key Performance Indicators

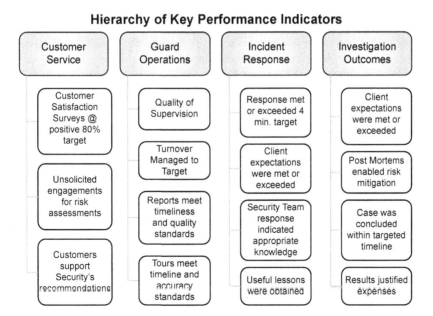

Incident Response. Targeting high-impact performance indicators in this area is a virtual imperative for a security program. Our security manager has set a response time standard that clearly reflects attention to safe and secure workplaces, and has identified measures of security team knowledge and customer responsiveness and the highly valued, actionable lessons-learned from incident post-mortems.

Investigation Outcomes. Throughout this landscape of performance indicators we see our security manager's attention to customer service, here with feedback on client expectations—a potentially sensitive area depending on the implications of investigative findings and results. There is also a continuing focus on management competency, as seen here in the measurement of case duration and cost assessment, as well as the opportunity to contribute to improved risk management through the investigative post-mortem process.

We must embed the imperative of connecting measurable results—critical success factors—with security program objectives. Key risk indicators and KPIs need to be the common tools you reach for as you craft the content of your various security programs. They serve to help you navigate the dynamics of risk, better connect and align with the business and its leaders, and effectively manage the often limited resources available to protect the enterprise.

COMMUNICATING PROGRAM PERFORMANCE WITH DASHBOARDS

"A dashboard is a visual display of the most important information needed to achieve one or more objectives; consolidated and arranged on a single screen so the information can be monitored at a glance."[2]

If you had to pick a reason for all this discussion about metrics, it would likely boil down to the need for informing and reporting[3]—visually and with desired results. In an earlier discussion, I pointed out the obvious problem of the security manager who has never been asked for program performance data and the assumption that they are pursuing other career opportunities. For those who have established reporting routines, you likely have some established framework and templates to guide your reporting. Regardless, these few that follow (and the others scattered about this book) are presented to provide some ideas for periodic, *customized* reporting up and across management and within your internal clientele. The idea is to build a more comprehensive pool of information than is available in a single-issue chart.

Several examples follow. The first is a basic security department dashboard that conveys status of a combination of five KPIs and key risk indicators (KRIs) for a quarterly report. There is a lot of information in this simple display. The color coding is an accepted means of conveying status and is complimented by just a short headline. Think about how these few key indicators could represent an hour briefing with the CEO or the senior management team. What do you want them to do with this information? What steps are you and the business taking to move the dials in the right direction and how will that progress be measured?

---

[2] Stephen Few, Information Dashboard Design, the Effective Communication of Data. O'Reilly Media, 2006, p, 34.

[3] I think these are different. The former is to enlighten and the latter is to merely document and record.

Security Department Dashboard

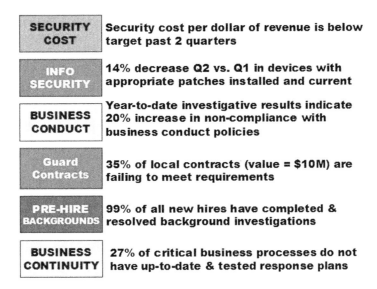

SECURITY COST	**Security cost per dollar of revenue is below target past 2 quarters**
INFO SECURITY	**14% decrease Q2 vs. Q1 in devices with appropriate patches installed and current**
BUSINESS CONDUCT	**Year-to-date investigative results indicate 20% increase in non-compliance with business conduct policies**
Guard Contracts	**35% of local contracts (value = $10M) are failing to meet requirements**
PRE-HIRE BACKGROUNDS	**99% of all new hires have completed & resolved background investigations**
BUSINESS CONTINUITY	**27% of critical business processes do not have up-to-date & tested response plans**

The second example takes a similar track but raises the informational bar a bit. The idea of following two key indicators for the top 100 critical business processes keeps our enterprise risk management agenda connected to business strategy, and the four KRIs in the center provide an opportunity to focus on both internal and external incident categories on an annual or quarterly basis. At the right, we see a separate opportunity to hit either progress or the lack thereof from root cause analysis and close out the discussion with three KPIs on core management initiatives.

Security Department Dashboard

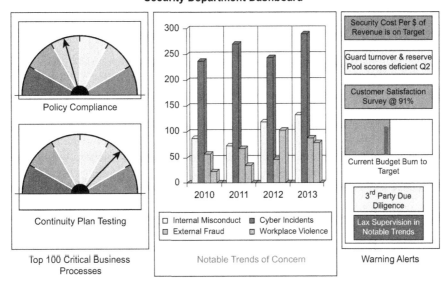

In this third example, we see a more detailed focus for protective operations that may represent a quarterly deliverable from the department head to the Chief Security Officer (CSO). There is a story on the progress made to mitigate workplace violence at Plant #4, the bottom left provides several summary updates, the recent quarter KPIs are provided with likely questions to follow on stalled progress, and six key areas of guard force activity for the past year are summarized.

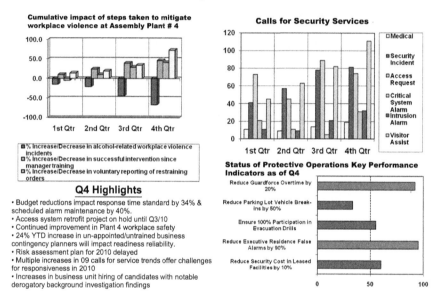

A more sensitive selection is seen in the following consolidation of charts on insider risk. The trending displays some key data to differentiate between what some may classify as "real" insiders or employees and outside vendors who have been given logical and physical access. There may be some dark humor in showing the dramatic spike in incidents involving "trusted" vendors—in this case largely attributable to cases investigated in outsourced suppliers engaged in inventory thefts and others in vendor fraud.

The root cause analysis focuses on both a two-year trending of several KRIs as well as the informative findings from deep dives into causal analysis on internal cases. There are interesting challenges in these data: a doubling of known but unaddressed vulnerabilities coupled with significant increases in supervisory failures to detect and to escalate both contribute to unacceptable levels of accountability.

These trends will require some definitive steps to reduce these areas of avoidable risk. If I were the CSO here, I'd be prepared (among other things) for pointed questions as to why we didn't see and address the fact that key security measures were inactivated.

The selection of an analysis of employee disciplinary sanctions for internal misconduct is interesting. When laid against the incidents in this time frame, the quarter-over-quarter trend suggests that some dialogue has been underway between security and human resources (HR) on the need to escalate more severe sanctions for internal misconduct. These are interesting data to be included in a dashboard on this topic inasmuch as they tend to close the loop on a common question from a senior manager: "What was the result of these cases in terms of the employees involved?" It also indicates a more engaging relationship between security and the employee relations representatives within HR.

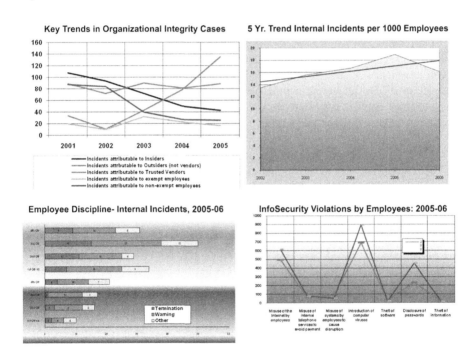

The final topic in this dashboard presentation brings in misconduct data from information technology (IT) security investigations. This is an important aspect of internal risk that can easily fly below the radar of senior management awareness. Monitoring and reporting on misconduct in this area is essential. Where IT security is separate from corporate security, joint metrics tracking and reporting are encouraged.

SUMMARY

There are scores of Excel-based or more sophisticated management dashboard software packages available, and your company likely has a variety available or mandated. Frankly, many of those that can be found in a simple online search appear to me to be incredibly busy, gimmicky and overdone. I also have several references listed that contain excellent ideas.

The value of a dashboard is to consolidate and aggregate relevant reporting data in a visual view of quantitative and qualitative information for a targeted clientele. If I had one point to reinforce on this topic it would be to focus on presenting *timely and validated risk and/or performance data*. Simply providing counts of activity or incidents fails to provide the *quality and actionability* of information—the takeaways and lessons learned—you owe the recipient.

PHYSICAL SECURITY IS MEASURABLE

Information security has extensively documented a broad and deep body of metrics. Given its reliance on an effective physical security, one has to wonder at the relative absence in at least a credible companion to this inventory.[4] Physical security is so basic to enterprise risk management that its relationship to a totally integrated enterprise protection strategy should be clear to anyone with the most basic understanding of security concepts.

This brief overview is followed by several discussions centered upon physical and operational security measures and metrics.

> Physical security typically represents the single largest security expense in a corporate security budget. The need for a body of KRIs to drive its focus and a companion set of performance indicators to demonstrate the effectiveness of program content should be clear to anyone with enterprise protection in their job descriptions.

Risk: Key risk indicators for physical security typically will focus on the consequences of vulnerabilities and defects in countermeasures. Physical security components within site security plans should contain performance measures. Proactive risk assessments and reactive, incident-based lessons-learned and root cause analyses all should ensure the development of metrics tied to findings and recommendations.

Cost: The people, vendors, and technology related to physical security operations are likely the single largest set of cost centers in a corporate security budget.

---

[4]A notable exception is found in the regulatory regimes of DoD, DoE, NRC, HIPAA, and a variety of sectors within the DHS Critical Infrastructure standards. We would do well to build a genericized compilation of relevant technical and operational performance measures and metrics that could be selectively adopted by individual companies and others.

Budgetary line items related to these programs must be based on measurable results beyond burn rates and activity counts.

Contract guard services: In a comprehensive benchmarking review of these vendors, we were able to fairly easily identify almost 100 measurable elements of work associated with contractually based security services. SLAs are too often unnecessarily constrained by procurement templates and coemployment phobia to apply real (not administrative) performance measures to these services.

Time: Time is a key physical security performance measure. On the one hand, we want to impose time on the adversary and from our perspective we want to ensure we will respond as quickly as possible to all matters requiring timely reaction. Barrier delay time, time to traverse a clear zone, time to reach an asset and escape undetected, and a host of similar measures all contribute to or constrain an adversary. When our security resources deter and delay enough or respond better than required, time becomes a qualitative measure of mission accomplishment.

Access management is measurable: Capabilities to limit unauthorized access and enable that which has been preapproved are clearly measurable elements of both physical and logical security administration. There is an incredibly rich array of industry standard measures that should be employed in this area.

Activities and component capabilities linked to command, control, and communications are measurable: The transaction cycle of event management from initiation, notification, reception, situational analysis, evaluation, dispatch, response, and post-event follow-up contain associated measures of reliability and quality.

Technology-based detection and assessment effectiveness is measurable: This should be focused on measuring reliability. I would hope that any deployment of this huge inventory of security technology has been guided by tested measures of detection reliability, assessment performance, time to failure and repair, and my favorite: false and nuisance alarm rates.

Personnel recruitment, training, and competence: Performance measurement of proprietary or contract personnel is a compulsory responsibility of management, and criteria are well established in HR terms or should be in contractual or SLA terms as well. The effectiveness of recruitment programs is measurable as is the relationship of training to performance.

Measuring operational effectiveness and quality of response: Given the critical first responder mission of these resources, this is the core element of security operations management. Hazard and risk mitigation, response in crises, contributions to business process execution, safe and secure workplaces, planned versus achieved results, customer satisfaction, and measurable results around hundreds of tasks and activities that comprise security plans and procedures all contribute to a required evaluation of physical security effectiveness.

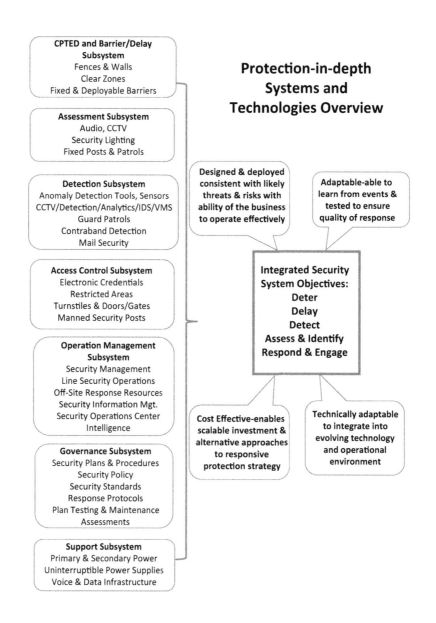

ALERTING MANAGEMENT TO HIGH PROBABILITY RISK

High-probability risk is *typically* a new CSO's early focus on making senior management aware of the key issues that keep him or her awake at night in this portfolio of security services. The five we have listed underscore some fundamental vulnerabilities that CSOs know are on their watch, and they are serious about eliminating plausible denial. The CSO is putting management on notice that several clocks are ticking in these high-risk areas. The objectives are (1) to engage discussion on steps that need to be taken to reduce these risks of significant concern, (2) obtain buy-in on policy reinforcement or sanctions for nonconforming business units, and (3) test the limits and affirm that security is on the right track with these concerns. This is advertising risk and marketing solutions with the people who are the source of that risk.

Top 5 Physical Security Concerns

RISK MANAGEMENT STRATEGY

It's obvious that this security organization has been highly proactive at assessing risk. It is equally obvious that this CSO's predecessor was asleep at the switch.

An ongoing risk assessment process is the cornerstone of an effective security program. What we see here are the consequences of inaction in this regard. Moreover, it is clear that security has not previously been aligned with business strategy, likely waiting for the phone to ring. The results are potentially very serious given their breadth and depth.

This is about advertising risk and marketing solutions with the people who are the sources of those risks.

There has been no prior notice of notable threat and vulnerability, and security has never before pushed back to ensure awareness. Given this risk-unaware environment, the procurement process has failed to conduct risk-based due diligence in both leasing and outsourcing. This is exacerbated by business units not stepping up to share the responsibility by assessing risks they own and intelligently managing access. The CSO has made line units aware of concerns and recommendations. They have not effectively responded. The CSO has made a decision to escalate to the CEO and audit committee.

This is a risky step for this new CSO, who may alienate many key constituents, and may be seen as "Chicken Little." The CSO is confident about giving adequate notice and has not received appropriate acknowledgment of risk from business units and the need for an improved state of security. This CSO may be seen as incapable of effectively influencing these business unit managers.

It is also risky in that this CSO is taking his first steps at testing the willingness of top management to buy-in to security's risk assessment processes and demanding change. But these vulnerabilities are too serious to remain unattended, and management's lack of accountability must be challenged. The CSO has no alternative but to escalate.

The data for this briefing must be embedded in the design and objectives of the multiple risk assessment processes at play here. These assessments should be focused on identifying vulnerabilities and detailing the anticipated performance metrics of the countermeasures selected to eliminate them. Management's concerns will center on the details of the responsible party's response to security's findings and recommendations.

Remember that change is the objective in this exercise! This is about fulfilling the CSO's obligation to inform, to be a positive change agent, and to establish a proactive security program that is connected to business strategy. It has to start with having reliable, actionable information and "telling it like it is."

MEASURING AND MANAGING YOUR REGIONAL SECURITY TEAM

A great many global corporations rely upon a regionally distributed security management team to provide a core set of services to the business operations in a specified geographic area. In a very real sense, these individuals *are* corporate security, especially as the distance from the headquarters flagpole increases, often to the opposite side of the globe. The service portfolio varies but typically includes the physical security program, risk assessment, awareness, and at least initial incident investigation. Other programs directed to business continuity, IT security, and more in-depth or sophisticated investigation activities may be assigned to this individual, shared internally or contractually on a site-specific basis, or provided directly by Corporate based on severity or criticality. Incumbents are often local hires to provide greater assurance of local knowledge and cultural alignment.

The further your security team is from the flagpole, the greater the impact on their alignment with plans and policy.

The relationship between the manager's immediate regional constituency and corporate security's senior leadership often presents challenges, and it is important to provide a set of performance measures with all parties aboard on expectations.

CHALLENGES

- *Cultural alignment*: Depending on the cultural/geographic base of corporate security operations, the regional manager may find him or herself mismatched to the established scope or nuance of security and investigative operations. U.S.-based investigative procedures, for example, may present both legal and cultural limitations and vice versa. Expectations need to be managed and procedures documented.
- *Cost Management*: Guard force costs are typically the biggest security expense in regional operations, and aggressive management of these costs is a job requirement.
- *Circle the Wagons*: Particularly where an incident can shine a light on local management's potential flaws or lack of adherence to policy, it is not uncommon for the regional manager to have pressure to "handle these issues at home."
- *Comfort Zone*: Ideally, we select these managers with a high degree of trust and confidence in their ability to stay energized and focused on their role as a full-service representative of the full range of security program content. Maintaining this scope can be a challenge.
- *Risk Assessor*: Risk is local with broad and diverse implications in a global business environment. Look across the Eurozone as an example. Establishing and maintaining trusted linkages with the right sources can be a challenge.
- *Relationship Management*: From a business alignment perspective, this is the essence of the local security mission. In practice, it is as much ambassador as security practitioner. The scope of relationships is as much outbound as inward-focused. Maintaining this balance can be a challenge.
- *Overreliance on Standard Performance Criteria*: Employee performance review can get bogged down in bureaucratic links to generic, HR-based competency assessment. This can significantly limit the critical link to the criteria that define success in the assigned role.

In response to these challenges, this CSO has established a small set of quarterly review measures[5] in collaboration with regional business leaders. This policy alignment enables security management at the corporate level to (1) communicate expectations around the regional manager's role as a representative of the approved corporate governance infrastructure and (2) provide clarity to the local manager's mission.

---

[5] using a 1 = low to 5 = high scale.

A summary review of the evaluative criteria used here relies heavily on relationship management, risk communication, and awareness. Since this report is a consolidation from local management, users, and corporate security management, there is a potential set of issues with this manager's attention to vendor management and incident reporting, both of which are critical tasks that drive both the quality of risk knowledge and cost management.

Work with regional business representatives and your HR organization to identify and develop your own set of unique business and risk drivers to populate your regional team's measures.

MEASURING AND MANAGING YOUR GUARD FORCE PERFORMANCE AND COST

One of the largest line items in most corporate security budgets is expense for what I call "security operations" and what others may refer to as "guard force" costs. I'm often amazed at the answers I get when I ask, "What metrics do you have for these activities?" Typical answers include hours of training, turnover rates, compliance with state certification, rates of conformance to preassignment standards, and guard tour checks. A deeper dive may reveal hours on patrol or hours of various post assignments.

I already know I'm paying for X hours of coverage. As a security manager, shouldn't I expect to be told what these hours have yielded for me in terms of risks found and mitigated and how customers were served?

Far too often, the only "metrics" people see are activity counts like hours of patrol or tours—nothing about what results are achieved with this costly time. Similarly, the number of training hours delivered is a "how much" statistic, when the important conclusion is about competence of performance, or "with what result?"

Why do so many companies use their service level agreements to measure the simple stuff and avoid the real areas of quality management?

In a recent benchmarking survey, respondents rated "average hourly cost for contract guard services" third in a 12-item metrics poll. The results were predictably similar, with billing rates within a very narrow field. Since most service contracts for these services tend to use a suite of typical requirements, hourly rates will tend to vary only on a geographic basis. The metric of interest in this contract space is the now-popular SLA. An example of one organization's routine may be seen on the following page.

SLAs often focus on cycle times because they are easy to measure. While critical in response times, fundamental guard force performance is more about service competence and proactive hazard mitigation. In addition to your typical SLA measures of training, turnover, and invoice accuracy, consider the following:

- Adequacy of supervision (use a one to five ranking scale) derived from inspection, report review, and customer feedback
- SLA performance—As noted in the example, there is an option to indicate penalties and additives to fee where such provisions are incorporated in the contract. Without them, there is little incentive for the benefits of performance measurements like this.
- Percent of random post/site inspections finding all required security tasks being performed to specified standard
- Percent of priority (define) calls for service with response to established standard of performance
- Percent of dispatched incidents for which a response time goal was specified that met or exceeded that goal
- Number of hazards, security defects, etc., identified and resolved per 24 hour period (focus on prevention and risk mitigation activities)
- If you are a regulated entity with security standards, the proactive identification and elimination of sanctionable defects is a KPI worthy of consideration.

Communication center activities too often fall out of the measurement focus (see the next section) and they perform a variety of critical functions. Accuracy around call-taking and caller prompting, dispatch and logging accuracy and responsiveness, and communication center staff knowledge of both routine and nonroutine procedures are all measurable and reportable.

I'll repeat my concerns about nuisance alarms: logging and labeling every alarm event received as valid or invalid is essential. Across U.S. businesses, billions of alarm events are logged and responded to with no simple indication of cause. The result is multimillions of dollars of wasted response time that should be better directed to real risk identification and management. If you depend on police response and have lots of invalid alarms, plan on discussions with the CFO who wants to bill your department for municipal false alarm fines.

Performance Measure		Region 1		Region 2		Region 3		Cumulative Fee Impacts	
Training & Cert, Compliance		10	10	10	9	10	8		
Alarm Response Times		0	0	10	10	10	10		
Emergency Response Times		10	10	10	10	10	0		
Dispatch Center Operations		0	10	10	10	10	10		
Lobby & Gate Operations		10	10	10	0	0	7		
Policy/Procedure Compliance		10	10	10	10	10	10		
Corrective Action Plans		8	5	8	8	8	8		
Special Event Support		4	2.5	8	8	8	8		
Patrol Plan Deviations		5.5	4	8	6	8	6		
Monthly Drills		0	0	7	8	0	0		
Invoice Accuracy & Timeliness		6	4	6	5	6	6		
Turnover Rate		3	3	2.5	3	3	2		
Score This Quarter	Score Last Quarter	66.5	68.5	99.5	87	83	75		

Security operations—and officer performance measures in particular—are incredibly important indicators that must be on the CSO's dashboard; I don't care if we are talking about a proprietary organization or one totally staffed by vendors—these are our customer-facing first responders. Their performance can define the competence of the total security organization. That "guard" may be the only contact the average employee or visitor will have with your company. You can have the best security technology money can buy, but if you put it in the hands of untrained, unprepared responders, then the investment is squandered. You need to be thinking about what defines results for this part of your security program.

Here is another, more granular way to communicate your vendor's SLA performance.

Service Level Agreement Ratings*:
Vendor: ABC Protective Services - Past 4 Weeks (Range: +5/-5)

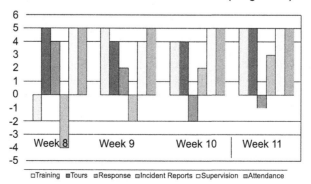

□Training ■Tours ▨Response ▨Incident Reports □Supervision ▨Attendance

Consider the following 10 measures/metrics you should consider for independent measurement of guard force vendor performance. Somebody reading this will say, "You can't do that, it's the vendor's job and they are contractually obligated to maintain performance metrics." Fine. But does that mean that you are going to pay a few million dollars a year to a contractor and simply accept their assessment of their performance? Remember that this expense is likely the largest line item in the security budget, and determining the level of quality for those services is owned by the CSO.

% of randomly reviewed incident reports found to be acceptable

% periodic management reports providing qualitative, actionable information

% sampled customer interactions rated positive per site per quarter

% of deficient versus acceptable responses to calls for service per site per quarter

Adequacy of supervision derived from independent report review and customer feedback

% random officer checks indicate knowledge of post orders

95% of the required two (2) off-hour and one (1) after-hour inspection have been adequately performed at 100% of staffed locations

% of independent site assessments by corporate security finding no notable defects

Exercises and drills conducted by management indicate an acceptable level of knowledge related to procedures and elements of response consistent with potential risk exposure

% assigned who indicate lack of knowledge of security plans, policy, or procedures from random test procedures

MEASURING VENDOR-BASED ALARM RESPONSE

Many companies rely completely on alarm company vendors for their installation, maintenance, and monitoring of both routine (opening, closing status) and risk event alarm systems. The costs for these critical system management activities are often lost in the occupancy costs across multiple sites in a regional network of business operations. Taken as a whole, these alarm vendor costs can reach millions of dollars, but company after company I've reviewed often fail to assess the performance associated with these costs and that of the those local managers who "own" site operations and integrity.

Earlier, I noted my risk-based concerns around alarm system reliability and response, so this example goes to the qualitative assessment of performance by alarm companies and by the company that fails to effectively provide actionable accountability around alarm management and notification procedures.

Here we have a situation where a variety of alarms are being annunciated, and designated contact persons are notified according to policy, with no response. This inability to reach the contact requires a response from local public safety. As seen here, these alarms were not valid threats, so the likelihood is a consistent pattern of fines or notice of no future response from police. Both the alarm vendor's failure to either maintain its system reliability or manage its relationship and the company's failure to meet its own local critical system management obligations are performance indicators requiring serious consideration.

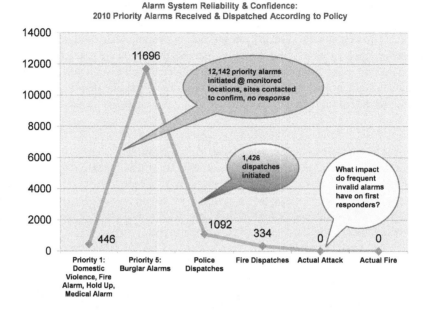

TRACKING PROTECTIVE SERVICES KEY PERFORMANCE INDICATORS

Protective services operations are the first line of defense in enterprise protection. It is essential to establish a variety of KPIs to evaluate and qualitatively measure these critical security services. We saw the SLA example with each of these incorporated, but they focused on the site's performance that may reflect more on your local corporate security management than exclusively on the vendor. This chart drills down on four areas this CSO believes are this vendor's KPIs for these sites and, importantly, focuses on results to the 95% target.

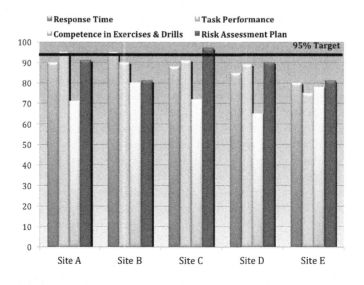

RISK MANAGEMENT STRATEGY

You can draw on over 100 performance measures for protective services operations but you need to select the key few that will tell your story or convey the message you seek to deliver. In this example, we are homing in on four that we deem critical measures in our vendor SLA. These few are more qualitatively focused rather than the simplistic administrative measures related to training, invoicing, and other SLA measures more useful for contract administration than the competence of a key element of the security program. Remember that the SLA process relies heavily on the vendor self-assessing, so having several independently measured performance metrics is essential to management oversight.

Owing to their criticality, we have established a 95% reliability target for the quarterly performance fee calculation. You can elect to apply any target, but some analysis of reasonableness is appropriate. For example, we should expect 99.9% reliability from our alarm system, but the same standard for across-the-board response time fails to take weather, traffic, and other delay factors into proper account.

Response time: In this example, I'm totally comfortable with defending a 95% target for response time for employee safety and critical area (high priority/high value) alarms. The meaningful metric for me is a 5 minute response time threshold from dispatch to arrival at the site of the call for service.

Task performance: This is admittedly a big bucket of expectations for a not-to-exceed 5% defect rate, but you would establish a short list of task categories that would be incorporated into the calculation. An example would be tested ability of trained first responders to successfully attend to incidents in their areas of expertise.

Competence in exercises and drills: A key indicator of likely success in risk event response may be found in the competence of protective service operations in planned (and unplanned) security exercises and drills. An effectively planned exercise can identify a wide range of flawed plans and procedures and flawed training and supervisory needs, while doing so under controlled conditions. Since we often rely on vendor competencies when real risk events unfold, the results of a well-planned and documented exercise can deliver a rich inventory of qualitative versus quantitative performance measures.

Risk assessment plan: A quality-focused SLA will hold the local vendor accountable for either developing and managing a comprehensive risk assessment plan or knowledgeably executing one provided by security management. Knowledge of risk and the countermeasures essential to mitigation is a fundamental expectation of security resources charged with enterprise protection. This is a process that can be measured and resulting metrics maintained by management for SLA evaluation.

SUMMARY

The easy out for SLA management is to be satisfied with having the vendor self-report its compliance and merely provide periodic counts of expended time, dollars, and reported activities. This completely fails to provide the essential information on what this time and money have yielded for risk management results. There is a flow-down effect from establishing the kinds of standards and expectations discussed here. If our vendor expects to succeed, it must have the demonstrated ability to provide meaningful, actionable performance metrics that result in an improved state of protection. If we in security management expect to succeed, we need to engage in measurable vendor oversight rather than merely paying the bill after checking the box that the monthly count report has arrived on time.

SECURITY OPERATIONS CONTROL CENTER METRICS

There are critical performance indicators that should be carefully maintained for the organization's global, regional and/or local security operations control center (SOCC).

OPERATIONAL CRITICALITY

It is clear that there are few functions performed by a corporate security organization that are more critical than an SOCC. It may be said that it is here that customer service, first response, and risk management combine to provide the most visible and essential corporate security services. Three major buckets of activity are found in well-established operations:

- Maintain and deliver situational risk awareness; monitor and communicate critical incident status, facilitate event escalation and crisis plan implementation.
- Provide 24/7 support to critical business operations and processes, and sustain the provision of safe and secure workspaces to employees and visitors.
- Provide for integrated monitoring of critical systems, apply intelligence, aggregate, prioritize, target, communicate, and escalate risk-related data reporting and assessment of security posture and anomalies.

Globalization and shared service business models have prompted many security organizations to build their SOCC capabilities to accommodate an enterprise support to facilities management, global travel, IT call center and security event management, supply chain event monitoring, and other 24-h business operations.

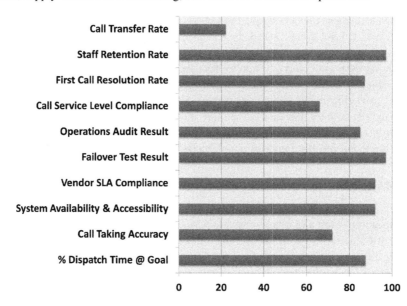

PERFORMANCE MEASUREMENT

This chart displays a variety of factors that may be measured, but there are many others that may be appropriate to individual business dependencies. In this example, multiple proprietary operator/dispatchers are posted on three shifts and receive heavy call volumes from North America and Europe. Call management—timeliness, accuracy and quality—is emphasized.

- Call service level compliance relates to the overall SOCC goal for customer responsiveness.
- % dispatch time @ goal-risk assessment and analysis has resulted in a 2-min goal for all critical calls and 3-min for noncritical. The performance objective is a running 90% average per reporting period. Using a more established call center performance measure, we would categorize this as average handle time.
- Call taking accuracy is measured by shift supervisors using direct observation, log review, and periodic incident post-mortem review. Communication skills and operator knowledge for customer responsiveness are key elements in this assessment.
- First-call resolution rates are transactions that are successfully completed within the initial call without a transfer to another individual.
- Transfer rates are calls that cannot be effectively handled by the initial call taker and must be transferred or escalated to another individual such as a supervisor or specifically designated desk. The performance issue here may be a training gap in the call-taker, inadequate customer direction for service, and the delay that accrues to the transfer.
- Operations audit is a scheduled or no-notice deep dive by a team into organizational performance. Its focus may be specific or more general.
- Staff retention (or turnover) rates are critical performance indicators in these operations. Where SOCCs are outsourced, turnover has imposed degraded operator competence and service-level performance.
- Failover testing is the essential resilience assessment and confirmation that is assigned to all critical business processes.
- System availability and accessibility is a measure of critical system and subsystem or process uptime reliability. While specific security head-end equipment is performing at 99.9%, other interdependent components or human factors processes may not perform as well, resulting in service-level degradation. This is a key performance contributor to call service-level compliance.
- Vendor SLA compliance relates to quarterly rating of vendors who provide core services to the organization that directly impact SOCC efficiency, quality, and service level. Examples are vendor-provided dispatcher/operators and equipment or infrastructure maintenance personnel.

These are just a few operational performance measures that may be monitored for internal management and reported as KPIs for SOCCs. If you think about it, high customer satisfaction in a SOCC may be the outcome of a life-saving event as well as the timeliness and quality of the response that is dispatched.

SECURE AREA RELIABILITY

Seven secure areas (spaces selected for more in-depth protection given the criticality or asset value housed therein) were selected for periodic penetration testing by security personnel. Ten probes using different attack scenarios are employed to test the intrusion detection, assessment, reporting, and response subsystems at each site. A probability of detection standard is established for each one individually. Secure areas A, D, and G will undergo subsequent analysis and retesting to restore confidence.

The second metric on false/nuisance alarms reflects a standard that secure areas will require not more than one false or nuisance alarm per zone per 24 hour period. Again, a basic measure of any alarm received is that it has a high degree of reliability, that it is a response to a threat. Measures and procedures also need to be applied to local business operations to ensure that operational discipline and device management are maintained.

Where vendors are used for periodic alarm and related electronic subsystem maintenance, establishing clear performance-based tasks and schedules is imperative. With secure areas, closeout, post-maintenance inspection is equally imperative.

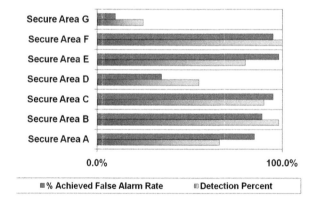

THE CRITICAL MEASURE OF TIME TO RESPOND

The objective is to inform your constituents that security is able to respond most quickly to emergency calls from within the company, thereby saving lives and limiting damage or loss. We seek to demonstrate how the value of a skilled security presence can help you convince management to maintain support for high standards of competence and training for in-house security staff.

RISK MANAGEMENT STRATEGY

We hear a lot about first responders. In the proactive security organization, our security operations teams are the ones that get the initial emergency call and move to assess it and respond from within. Is your organization up to the test of that call?

The 5 minute response time goal established for the security organization has obvious roots in the functions and demographics of the service population with risky work, an older population, and long public safety response times necessarily influencing officer staffing and deployment plans. Mandated headcount reductions in security coverage can arbitrarily increase these response times with increased risk for employees and invitees.

If you are not measuring time to respond to critical calls, you really don't understand your mission.

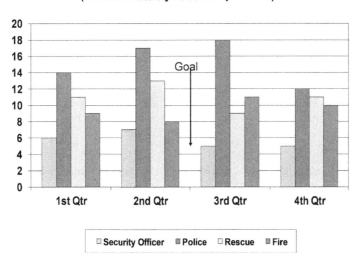

Response Times for Emergency Services (n = 235 incidents previous 12 months)
(40% of all life/safety incidents required EMS)

If you follow a disciplined incident reporting process, your logs will provide all the essential timelines of incident response by onsite and offsite resources, and training programs will ensure the competencies of security response personnel. Response time data should be the output of a planned program of incident management and call prioritization. Timeliness of response from call receipt to dispatch and constructive arrival are key measures of your responder deployment effectiveness, and should contain targeted objectives for monthly reporting.

Response times are critical, but what happens in a fire or other incident that requires a rapid evacuation of workspaces and before definitive response? We must rely on trained and prepared residents to initiate life safety procedures; thus, the notion of "first responder" is necessarily expanded.

It has consistently been demonstrated that we must have confidence in our ability to responsibly evacuate our business spaces within a planned timeline. In spite of the clear lessons of all-too-frequent and noteworthy events, all security managers are aware of the pushback that comes from business unit management when we propose to test emergency building evacuation plans on at least an annual basis.

In this example, we have a test objective of 20 minutes that obviously has to be adjusted for each set of sites. The result at site three serves to focus on the critical role of appointed and qualified floor wardens, and is noted to give slack to this individual but also to highlight the focus on the next exercise. These drills must be high on the risk management agenda, and I would suggest that the responsible manager at site eight needs an attitude adjustment with a strong management focus on performance review and bonus eligibility.

These two graphs tell a very important story about employee safety. Security management here is diligent in measuring KRIs, has focused on the competencies of security teams, and has set standards around response times and expectations for business unit responsibility in emergency preparedness. In this example, corporate security has said "what if" and added measurable value to employee and invitee safety and security.

We live in risky times, and our facilities require an integrated approach to physical security, life safety, and business continuity. The effectiveness of well planned, state-of-the-art technology is lost in low-bid guard force contracts. Businesses increasingly are unable to rely on public safety organizations to respond quickly to calls for service. Management needs to understand that response times and the competence of security personnel may mean the difference between life and death, between protracted downtime and quick recovery, and between costly liability and safety from litigation.

SUMMARY

In a specifically focused or larger management update briefing, a slide on either or both of these metrics demonstrates the benefits of an effectively trained and deployed security operations team and clearly shows the critical gap between onsite and offsite response.

MEASURING FOR OPERATIONAL EXCELLENCE IN SECURITY SERVICES

Operational excellence is among a family of business process improvement disciplines including Six Sigma, Total Quality Management, Kaizen, and other data-driven approaches to maximize efficiency, eliminate defects, and deliver measurable value to the customer that has been adopted by many global corporations. In this example, steadily increasing theft (>$1 million in 8 months) and confirmation from audit of inadequate internal controls at this company's central distribution center has led the CSO to craft a collaborative strategy with internal audit and center management employing several principles from the organization's operational excellence rulebook. The results you see above speak for themselves.

Operational excellence is about zero-defect processes that deliver a flawless customer experience. What are you measuring in these key areas of performance management?

In this particular company, the core process used is Six Sigma, which employs a framework with these basic elements: (1) define the problem and the goals to be achieved; (2) measure the current process, in this case the homing in on audit's documented internal controls; (3) analyze the data to identify defects and opportunities for defect elimination; (4) improve the process; (5) control the improved process; and (6) measure deviations from the improved processes. Defect identification involved a process called failure modes and effects analysis (FMEA), a tool used to identify potential process failures and score their consequences. But to give more definitive relevance to this process, the security team took deep dives into prior investigation findings and then performed a variety of covert risk assessments at the center to further probe vulnerability and internal control process defects. Then the team used those findings to postulate several loss scenarios.

Scoring involves several estimates on a 1 = low to 10 = highest scale; severity is estimated based on potential cost/other consequences, probability is estimated based on how evident the vulnerability might be to one with motive and opportunity; and detectability is the likelihood that the adversary's attempt would be detected given the effectiveness of the safeguards employed to protect the asset. Finally, the consequence is cost-estimated. This process is useful in demonstrating "what if" and selecting priorities among several scenarios.

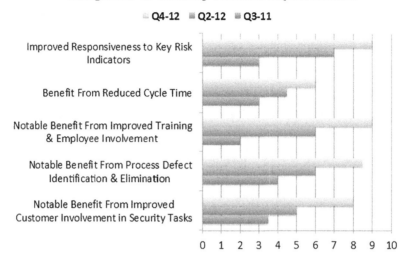

Reduced Distribution Center Loss Directly Assignable to Security Process Improvements

What was the result? Several benefits were sought in this analysis given the significance of growing losses and the conclusion that this was clearly an example of avoidable risk.

1. *Improved responsiveness to key risk indicators*: As is the case with most recurring loss scenarios, there were a variety of indicators that should have raised red flags for center management *and* for corporate security:
   a. Increased use of unvetted temps
   b. Inadequate inventory controls at receiving dock
   c. Center refusal to employ video in key areas of surveillance opportunity
   d. Lack of secure cages for in-process storage of high-value inventory
   e. Elimination of a security post within shipping and receiving areas
2. *Benefit from reduced cycle time*: Immediate reconciliation of incoming inventory and assignment of onsite investigator for immediate response to reported loss.
3. *Notable benefit from improved training and employee involvement*: Shift supervisors were engaged as a key element in the improved control processes. Performance reviews highlight loss prevention and security awareness, and team meetings are routinely held to review the effectiveness of security procedures and probe loss incidents.
4. *Notable benefit from process defect identification and elimination*: All contractors and temps are vetted prior to assignment, video coverage was installed in key areas of surveillance opportunity, and secure storage cages were constructed in several areas of the floor.

5. *Notable benefit from improved customer involvement in security tasks*: Center management is thoroughly engaged in the protection mission. Center personnel have accepted ownership of loss prevention accountability and have bought in to the advantages of teaming with security's expertise. It is also likely that security has learned to more intelligently push its involvement in risk mitigation.

MEASURE RISK EXPOSURE WITH SECURITY INSPECTIONS

It may not have happened here yet, but your metrics can provide the red flags and radar that will demand attention and response.

Capturing a variety of metrics data in a dashboard can work well for a periodic overview briefing to a selected audience or on a specific set of trends where the collection enables linking of findings. Another way to use the risk dashboard is to build a clear picture of exposure from risk assessments or, like the following, from some fairly simple inspections conducted by security officers after normal business hours. These are real results, and a statement that in 8 of 10 inspections, unsecured laptops likely containing sensitive customer information were found after hours has demonstrable impact. From this estimating base, calculating the potential financial impact is far more sound that merely throwing a "what if" on the wall.

We have several complementary objectives with this exercise:

1. Intelligently inform management on the potential for risk and/or loss in multiple areas of concern related to business integrity and continuity,
2. Engage management for follow-up, and
3. Obtain support for elimination of vulnerability while increasing participation in essential areas of risk ownership and accountability.

We recognize that testing provides essential indicators of vulnerability to customer-facing business processes, and effective communication of results eliminates plausible denial within management.

RISK MANAGEMENT STRATEGY

Have you ever heard, "But it hasn't happened here" from someone you are trying to inform and convince to invest in improved protection? Well, here are some metrics calculated to provide verifiable estimates of probability of loss given known vulnerabilities. This is not an ambush; we advertised we would be doing these tests and would inform on results. What you are presenting here isn't hype or scare tactics. Every probe category is based on well-established security expectations and common-sense safeguard policy. These data represent real results delivered against several test objectives you have advertised in your annual plan.

Think of the strategy in four levels or steps. First, protection programs and tactics are built around the achievement of clear, measurable results in terms of reduced exposure to risk—specify them! Second, by policy or accepted process, assessment programs *should be an essential component* of corporate governance, with results presented as required to senior management and internal audit processes, potentially to include the audit committee. Third, risk and protection performance assessments are structured around measurable criteria of effectiveness (success or failure) for the element(s) evaluated, and will be specifically measured on an advertised basis. Fourth, when you know the results of your metrics, thoroughly analyze them and report the results in a way that is responsive to management's format for action and accountability for results.

Probability of Loss Based on vulnerability tests conducted during the period 3/15/11-4/30/11

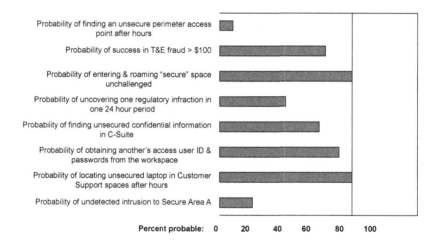

WHERE ARE THE DATA?

The data are in the quality of risk assessments you routinely perform on the adequacy of key protection measures and to uncover gaps in the quality of internal controls around critical assets and business processes. If you have appropriately structured your ongoing recorded measures and planned your risk assessment processes to provide comparative metrics, you will have:

- results of tests that yield a percentage of protection system or process failures and successes,
- training records showing preparedness of key players,
- documented frequency and results of prior tests,
- records of downtimes of critical systems or business processes, and
- specific benchmarks of protection system performance and the ability to gather test results against them

WHAT DO YOU WANT TO ACHIEVE WITH THIS INFORMATION?

We are really after an attitude of understanding and tolerance in this discussion. The best response I'd seek is "I support your objectives in assessing these risks and the discipline you have provided in arriving at these results. I accept our responsibility to assure remedial action on each of these corporate risks and ask our general auditor to track resolution of each of these findings."

MEASURING AND MANAGING COST

Cost is a constant focus of management, and we often fail to maintain the appropriate level of scrutiny until that inevitable phase of business operations that mandates some reduction in our budgets. Then we run around looking for a few of the less bloody "opportunities" like travel and delaying those long-needed capital expenses. Time is money. Look no further than how your team is spending its time.

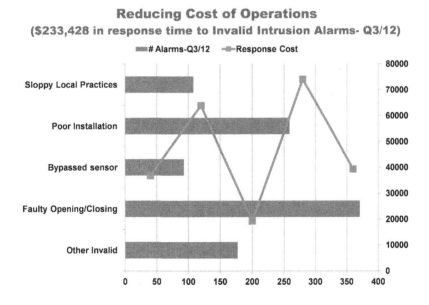

Reducing Cost of Operations
($233,428 in response time to Invalid Intrusion Alarms- Q3/12)

In this example, our CSO anticipated this frequent foible from management by thinking more proactively about the SLA with the guard force vendor. The CSO recognized the potential value of a more directed and analytical focus on the results of calls for service in addition to prioritizing specific kinds of activities, for example, response time to classified area alarms. Generally, what percent of calls for service are unnecessary, a waste of time? More specifically, for those we must dispatch and respond within an established standard, what percent are simply not valid?

Since this is a heavily populated 24/7 production complex with an extensive electronic security backbone to address regulatory requirements, R&D, and life safety objectives, there is significant time devoted to alarm response, and this seemed to be a fruitful target of opportunity. The first hurdle was in the reporting process. Alarm calls were simply dispatched and logged for time of arrival and clearance, but no report was made if the alarm wasn't the result of an actual security event like an intrusion. There was no process for indicating the *lack of validity* of the call, so nuisance alarms were lost in space. How many could this be?

A simple process of recording business unit location, alarm zone, and officer time was initiated for all alarms during the third quarter of 2012. These four categories of alarm initiation were selected based on common causes, and a fifth was added to account for causes that were undetermined but known to be invalid. A total of 1,008 alarms were logged into the analysis for the quarter. Tracking was done by security control center operator staff at the end of each day to routinize the process. To keep the result from paralysis of analysis, a consolidated $26.00 per hour rate was used, which provides for a small (10%) overhead for supervisory review.

The fact that, in one quarter, something just shy of a quarter million dollars in time was spent on chasing alarms that never should have happened provides what seems to me to be a solid opportunity for a discussion by this CSO with his management. Here are some thoughts on these findings:

1. *These alarms and related costs were avoidable.* Procedures are mature and training is current on business unit operation and practices.
2. There are outliers on frequency of alarms that deserve more focused attention, but the general conclusion is that the problem is more common and goes with the cost of protection operations.
3. Facilities here "own" the local system components, and when space is reconfigured or occupancy changed, security elements may not be updated for the new arrangements.
4. Some regulatory requirements mandate the posting of a guard until an approved representative arrives to clear the alarm cause. (These costs were not included in this initial analysis).
5. Where there is an established frequency of alarm zone annunciation over an extended period (for example, when poorly installed or maintained), there is a consequent loss of first responder confidence in the validity and criticality of the call. This can play to an adversary.
6. If this were a municipality, we would be faced with increasingly stiff fines and eventual notice of nonresponse by local police.

If you were the CSO here, what more would you have to say on this and what action would you recommend?

SHOW ME THE MONEY: TASK AND TIME ANALYSIS

You will know the axe is out when the company engages one of those firms that are paid to seek out every dollar of "unproductive expenses." That is when you learn about detailed time studies or task analyses. As painful as they can be, I strongly advise that you do one of these on your own for your higher expense functions. You will be able to show that you have scrubbed your processes for inefficiencies and defects, and be far better poised to defend the activities that are delivering results. If you do take this on, there is a lot of information available on line to help structure your approach. To simplify, you first need to rigorously identify the daily activities of the targeted work group. This is the work breakdown structure. You then have each member of the group log their time in not more than a 30-min increments to each task performed. Thus, in an 8-h shift, each individual would have at least 16 entries on that tour's log. I recommend at least a 30-day sample, and avoid a period where increased or decreased workload is scheduled.

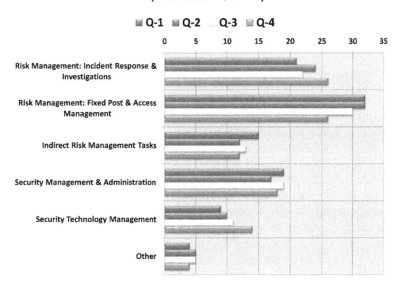

Percent of Security Operations Hours Dedicated to Six Major Activities
(Total Cost = $2.95M)

Like it or not, this is the most reliable means of identifying where security activities (and their associated costs) are expended. Mission priorities are assigned to specific families of time so that less productive or low-value tasks may be targeted for improvement, reduced, or eliminated. In the following example, the risk management mission of this guard force division is deemed prime, and the time devoted to indirect and administrative tasks will be subjected to increased scrutiny.

You will get a lot of push back from those who have to keep track, so take time to engage them in the process. I will tell you that when and if the call comes to pull back on expenses, this documentation pays significant dividends in being able to provide evidence of essential, value-centered work. Without this level of detail, you might just as well get out the dartboard and take your shots.

EXPENSE MANAGEMENT: THE INEVITABLE KPI

I think that if you have only one metric you routinely keep current, it'd better have something to do with your budget. Unless you are in the U.S. Congress, managing expenses is a basic expectation of your job. New risks and business initiatives challenge reliable estimates of cost. In the best of times, we have what we can document as legitimate resources. In response to crisis or more challenging economic times, it requires turning at a moment's notice. These "turns" are ideally addressed in a planful way; we've prepared contingency plans and we have prepared for 10, 20, or 30% hits to the budget. But then along comes the new CEO, the acquisition, the CFO, or your new leader with delusions of austerity.

If your first hunt for metrics comes in response to a demand from on high to cut your budget, you're likely too late to the game.

SLASH AND BURN

We have continuing evidence that the "slash and burn" senior executive is alive and well and security is often found in this person's cross-hairs. While we frequently own the consequences of this targeting owing to our failure to demonstrate value or visible contribution, these "downsizers" are typically more concerned about short-term financial results than the substance of security and reputational risk. Metrics will sort themselves out in the latter business environments. I'm more interested in having a portfolio of data that provides key indicators of consequential impact if specific security programs are reduced or eliminated. Frankly, scurrying around in panic-stricken defensive mode is, too often, too little too late. This is where a well-established, well-connected security metrics program can provide a compelling risk management and value story.

Are there a few metrics that provide the most effective defense? Certainly, but they are crafted from the unique business and threat environment within which you serve. Activity counts often get thrown out of court at the first hearing. Like my opening short story, I urge you to discuss with your CFO those few metrics you really should have for business reporting. They know what metrics resonate and can help vet the ones you may have. If there were one small set that I'd have in the bank, it would be like the examples in this discussion on performance management. How do our expenses compare to our peers and competitors? For example, we often see security program cost as a percent of revenue and the ratio of security headcount to employee headcount as credible comparisons—but use these carefully. Make sure you are comparing against similar programs with validated points of comparison.

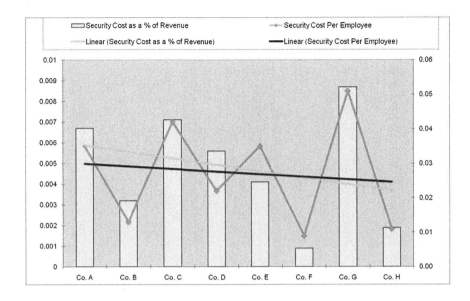

Be prepared to address the possibility that your costs are comparably higher or notably lower. You need to make sure that the service portfolios of the benchmark population are appropriately balanced for comparable services and other workload drivers. I'd also commend the following discussion on task and time analysis to your consideration. Unless you have thorough documentation and related data regarding the amount of time (converts to $$) being devoted to various activities aligned with some defensible assignment of criticality, simply trying to defend a gross line item in your budget is an exercise in futility. If somebody up there wants a target reduction in your budget, they are going to get it. Use your data to provide them with some measure of the potential consequences of those reductions. You will find possible examples in activities related to regulatory compliance, life safety, targeted risk mitigation tasks, business process enablement, insurance coverage, business continuity, timely incident response, asset recovery, and other activities. Several topical areas in the following discussions are supportive of this hunt.

Similarly, you often see security departments tracking investigation case volumes and costs such as in the example below. A problem with this particular treatment in my view is the absence of some measure of case complexity to anchor the relevance of the 24-month reduction in case cost. Standing alone, it looks like security management has done a good job of intake and closure on increased case volumes, but we don't know if clearance thresholds have been modified, if there are more cases of lower complexity and therefore able to be more quickly concluded, or if cases were exceptionally closed based on management decision. There may be a good story here with security adding value by doing more with less. A series of companion slides might display different types of cases or categories of complexity to put the overview into a more focused perspective.

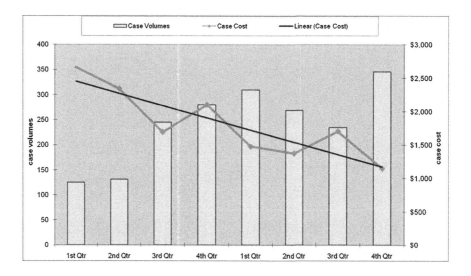

As previously noted, the graphs below display two frequently used metrics that track the ratios of security cost per company employee, headcount per security employee, and the guard force/physical security cost per square foot; the latter are often anchored to facility cost and the former tied to the service population. A source for geographic facility security cost is from the Building Owners & Management Association (BOMA). Since this is member-driven, your corporate real estate or facilities department may be able to access specific data for you.

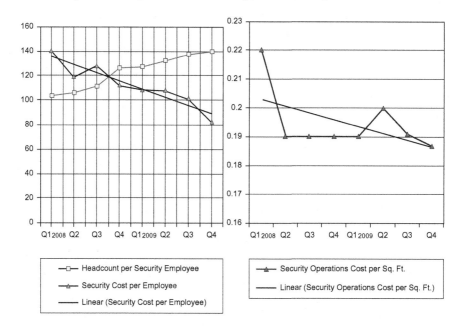

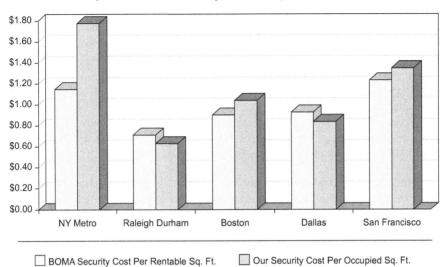

Comparison of FY-08 Security Cost Per Square Foot vs. BOMA* Data

☐ BOMA Security Cost Per Rentable Sq. Ft.   ☐ Our Security Cost Per Occupied Sq. Ft.

* Building Owners Management Association annual cost data—includes all personnel, security equipment and other related costs associated with facility protection

SHOWING THE ROI OF CONTRACT SECURITY FORCES

Consider this comment from a thoughtful colleague and security manager within a critical infrastructure organization: "I can't think of a more relevant issue for physical security than a series of metrics regarding contract security costs. The one item we've never been able to tie down during benchmarking was the ROI related to contract security. Obviously there are many moving parts to the issue, but when my director asks about value versus cost regarding contract security, we get back to proving the negative (minimal losses to theft, no intrusions, etc.)."

Return on investment (ROI) is fundamentally a measure of whether some activity is worth doing. Clearly, we can employ more sophisticated approaches, such as annualized loss expectancy (ALE), that estimate frequency and impact, and then apply various safeguard improvement options. But in my view, the ROI for contract security operations has to be tied to an operational risk management strategy. A lot of ink has been spent delivering the message that it's less expensive to deliver protective security operations with contract services rather than in-house proprietary. But how many companies have really dug down and evaluated what headcount (hours) they really need to provide the level of protection and service required? And what, with specific measures, are those requirements? I've worked these measures in a variety of domestic and international risk and business environments, and the business case is never a simple template in my experience. It may be cheaper to post a 24/7 uniform to control access in the third world and install a turnstile in Europe or North America.

This colleague serves in an organization where security compromise is intolerable, but is nevertheless in competition for increasingly scarce resources. In this case, I think the return is not a financial metric but a policy decision that concludes that the consequences of not having a competent security presence are intolerable. While the likelihood of an event may be perceived as low, we increase the potential by not making prudent investments in protection.

Herein is our dilemma: Is the perception of risk low because we are so effective or because there is little real threat out there? If the latter, then why do we have all this expense for security? Law enforcement has a deep reservoir of data on crime, calls for service, victimization, and clearance rates. Where do we look to support the effectiveness measures of our security operations teams?

1. **Defect detection and elimination.** What is the potential financial impact of various events that are within the response profile of your security force? The organizations we serve are complex and house thousands of processes and activities, many of which are prone to malfunction, breakdown, accident, human error, or malfeasance. A trained 24/7 security force can proactively identify and mitigate many of these defects. Does that demonstrate a potential return?

2. **Penetration testing.** Not a lot of apparent threats rearing their ugly heads? Find ways to test the effectiveness of your security measures. If you had 10 attempted penetrations for each of a variety of sensitive areas that demonstrate an 80% or 90% failure rate—that is, the would-be adversary did not succeed in getting to the asset the overwhelming majority of the time—does this not advertise the effectiveness of your security measures, including your security force surveillance and response capabilities? We know that we have assets that are potentially attractive to motivated individuals. That motivation can be deterred by clearly effective safeguards, including a professional security presence.

3. **Response time.** How long does it take for EMT or police to arrive at your facility? (Note that the time may be increasing due to local government budget shortfalls.) If your people are there in 5 minutes and can sustain a life or apply definitive care until EMTs arrive 5 or 10 minutes later, is there a benefit? How about responding to that water detection alarm in the computer room or being outside HR during a potentially hostile termination?

4. **Cost effectiveness benchmarking.** We are charged with protecting people, property, and corporate assets. How do you compare with other colleagues? Determine how many security officers you have per square foot of coverage, and how many officers per employee. If you show one officer per 5,000 square feet, and many other comparable organizations post more officers in the same area, you are demonstrating clear cost efficiency; a solid result in these hard times.

5. **Service-level agreements.** SLAs are fairly common in outsourced service contracts and deserve consideration for their ability to establish clear performance standards. Common elements for contract security are supervision, first call resolution, response times to emergency events, incumbent qualifications and levels of training, tour and staffing of specific posts. These may include both penalties for nonconformance and potential rewards for exceeding standards.

These are a few measures to consider when you are determining whether your contract or proprietary security force is delivering value for the cost. Clearly, much of the focus is on "what if." But that question is at the heart of management's obligation to manage risk on behalf of the shareholders or the public's safety.

CYCLE TIME: AN EXPECTED MEASURE OF PERFORMANCE

Security owns multiple processes that impact the business in a variety of ways. Just as we see above, time, in a variety of parameters, is a key measure for our programs. Clearly, response time to an incident or call for service is an accepted measure for our first responders, but setting cycle time target objectives for both internal teams and contracted service providers is a legitimate expectation of the business. Here are a few of the more obvious examples commencing with the impact of background investigations on the new employee onboarding process.

- Background Investigations (and reinvestigations): New hire processes clearly impact business units and Human Resource teams typically have established timeline targets to the hiring manager. The BI is at the end of the process and can make or break putting the candidate into the requisite seat. A 10 day target for the BI result seems to be typical and below is an example of one organization's monthly display of BI cycle time.
- Third-party due-diligence examinations: Where security is examining a prospective vendor/supplier or conducting a more focused investigation related to an acquisition or sensitive business relationship, customers will have expectations for a targeted delivery date of a final report. The unique perspective we bring to this prospective risk assessment process, especially given the sensitivity of the business processes being outsourced, demands responsiveness prior to a vendor selection.

New Hire Turn Around Time: 2011

Provides cycle time from offer extend to Background Screen completion

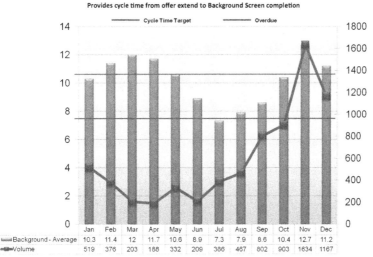

	Jan	Feb	Mar	Apr	May	Jun	Jul	Aug	Sep	Oct	Nov	Dec
Background - Average	10.3	11.4	12	11.7	10.6	8.9	7.3	7.9	8.6	10.4	12.7	11.2
Volume	519	376	203	188	332	209	386	467	802	903	1634	1167

- Logical and physical access credential processing: This is typically measured in hours and has obvious implications for the individual's productivity as well as essential security objectives.
- Various types of internal investigations and forensic examinations: An internal investigation can be very disrupting to a business, not to mention the subject. We are the finders of facts and HR, legal (possibly outside counsel for big $), the business unit manager and, potentially, compliance all await our findings in whatever form is specified. Setting expectations on time-to-complete is a measurable standard. It is also critical to set time objectives for IT forensic examinations and restoration of capability resulting from an incident.
- Periodic exercises and drills that impact business process productivity: We are all familiar with annual evacuation drills, business continuity tests of various types, and levels of engagement and other security-related exercises that may be required. Set the timelines and measure conformance. These are essential tasks, but it pays dividends to be able to say you can reliably estimate time commitments.
- Scheduled risk assessments involving business unit staff: These assessments are an essential element of effective security administration, but typically require the receiving business unit to dedicate time to what they often see as disruptive and a waste of time. Part of the accommodation is to specify and measure the time required and expended from start to finish.

Here is another example of cycle time metric reporting on several areas of risk management. A focused graph like this would be a good input to a quarterly dashboard report to management. There are multiple performance indicators seen here that reflect on both the security organization and the reliance on business unit buy-in to what may be policy-based performance goals.

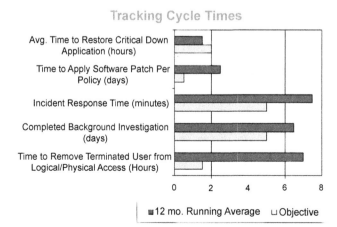

INFORMATION SECURITY

Information protection is so clearly a priority for the corporate security agenda, regardless of whether it is assigned to the chief information officer/chief information security officer (CIO/CISO) or is found in the CSO's service model. A comprehensive enterprise information risk management program involves virtually every element of corporate security's program. Collaborative planning and policy coupled with integrated safeguards and incident response are the minimally essential ingredients in this corporate governance relationship.

I "owned" this mission in my CSO portfolio for many years. However, because the threat landscape has so expanded and the literature on security metrics is so rich with material crafted by professionals far more qualified, I'm simply going to include the following metrics[6] that have been conceptually stolen from a highly respected information security expert, Andrew Jaquith, whose excellent book on metrics is footnoted below. The concepts and examples he explains so well in this text has broad application across the corporate security spectrum.

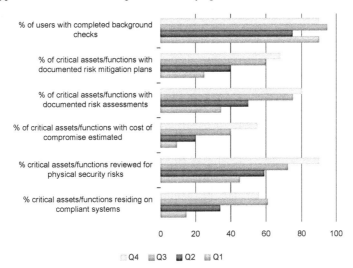

Andrew' Jaquith's book will give you everything you want to know about this topic, but if you Google *information security*, you will get more than you can digest.

METRICS ARE BIDIRECTIONAL: FAILURE AS A PERFORMANCE INDICATOR

There is an adage: Expect success but plan for failure. Threat is dynamic. Performance to plan is risky business. Here are four measures you need to have in your inventory.

---

[6] Andrew Jaquith, *Security Metrics, Replacing Fear, Uncertainty, and Doubt*. Pearson Education, Inc., 2007, p. 100.

We need to estimate the cost of compromise. If you haven't determined the consequences of loss or compromise, you cannot reliably calculate how much you should spend to ensure protection and availability.

What percent of loss events are attributable to a failed security measure? If you can demonstrate that a security measure prevented or responded so effectively that a loss was avoided or minimized, so too must we be able to calculate the implications of those that fail.

If your program lies within a critical infrastructure or your business processes are subject to regulation, the potential for review of security compliance yielding sanctionable findings is always present. There may be a similar situation where direct or indirect government contracts exist, or your company has contractually imposed security requirements from a client company. Fines or loss of business attributable to violations are not performance metrics your program needs.

Business continuity processes establish a recovery threshold to build plans and measures to ensure that outages will not exceed the point of unacceptable business impact. When plans fail or the recovery resources are found ineffective, those owning the process and delivering the scheduled resources are presented with a clear metric with loss implications.

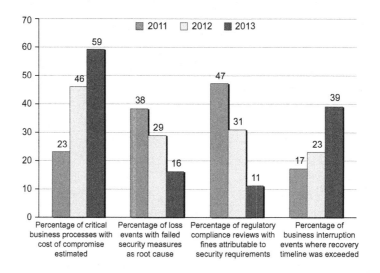

MEASURING PROGRESS OF ANNUAL PLANS AND OBJECTIVES

I trust that everyone reading this has to have some sort of business plan each year that sets some stretch goals in addition to adding up the columns of cost for the standard line items you have included for the past many years. Typically, we are given a budget target, but if you have been using your metrics effectively, you will have had an opportunity to demonstrate results and advertise specific value for security's programs. It may appear that this security manager has fully appreciated the fact that metrics are bidirectional: they can go counter to the best-laid plans, and now this individual has to go before the boss and explain what is going on with these six initiatives. There are some obvious issues at the heart of this story.

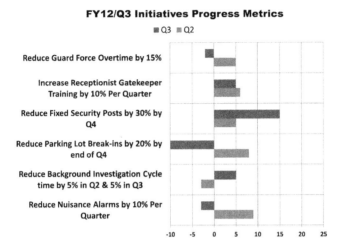

FY12/Q3 Initiatives Progress Metrics

- *Nuisance alarm reduction*: Invalid intrusion alarms are wasting time and erode the confidence of responders in alarm-related calls. Moreover, many of these alarms are within classified spaces and require posting a guard until the resident arrives to confirm secure status. This is most often resident error, but identifying and eliminating invalid alarms can be a challenge.
  The plan: A 20% reduction over these two quarters. They actually increased by 9% in Q2 and so the 3% reduction in Q3 still leaves the goal short by 14%.
  The explanation: 40% of these alarms came from 3% of the spaces containing intrusion alarms. Resident attitude adjustment needs to be cranked up several notches.

- *Overtime and fixed post reductions*: On top of this demand on security operations' time, security has succeeded in getting business units to assume some entry control duties—using the receptionist for entry control meant that the overtime budget was out of control in Q1.
  The plan: Our manager has committed to a reduction in the guard force vendor's overtime by 15% while reducing and/or redeploying 30% of the fixed posts on campus. He has reduced these posts to 20%, but delays in receptionist assignments slowed that program. Q2 saw another spike in overtime due to campus construction and shareholder events, and Q3 has yielded only a 3% repair to that 5% increase. These events were known and should have been factored into the plan.

- *Gatekeeper training*: This reduction in entry-based security posts will partially be met by business unit assignment of a receptionist. This company has adopted a "gatekeeper" model that emphasizes a focused security set of tasks in a concierge role.
  The plan: To address these new assignments coincident with the reduced security posting, a 20% increase for Q2/3 gatekeeper training has been planned. Unfortunately, lead security officers provide this training, and all of these shortfalls in initiatives have impacted them most severely. The good news is that business unit delays in reception assignments relieved this plan to an excusable degree.

- *Reduce background investigation cycle time*: Hiring has spiked and the number of candidates being submitted for vetting has caused delays to the 10-day cycle time SLA.
  The plan: Several temps were hired in Q2 to increase output, but this effort failed to impact the backlog until the beginning of Q3. This effort is now on target, and recent completion cycle times are meeting the SLA.

- *Reduce parking lot vehicle break-ins*: This campus is within a large urban area with large open employee and visitor parking lots and easy access to several major highways. Vehicle break-ins and thefts spiked in Q1 and were major concerns requiring this commitment.
  The plan: A 20% reduction was initially met with a continued increase, but tactics were revised, lighting improved, and an agreement was reached with the local police to do casual patrols. Q3 saw real progress that has continued into Q4.

SUMMARY

This is not a "be careful what you ask for" story. This is how our plans so often unfold. The point of metrics is to understand the "why" and "how" of the data being conveyed. There were a lot of moving parts in these initiatives that impacted our manager's best efforts.

IS COMPLIANCE A KEY RISK INDICATOR OR A KEY PERFORMANCE INDICATOR?

Think about it. How are you measuring compliance to established security standards? How serious is the notion of compliance in your company? Is your reputation in the marketplace linked to conformance to an established set of laws, rules, or standards? Are there protection mandates in the contracts you have with your customers and key suppliers? What are the implications of inadequate security with regard to your insurance? We are a key player in the governance of these internal controls.

OBJECTIVE

Our goal is to track, analyze, and report on risk-related conditions and events that are subject to mandated or self-imposed compliance; and, additionally, to identify root causes so as to eliminate defects in safeguards and establish accountability for corrective actions.

RISK MANAGEMENT STRATEGY

Every organization experiences serious events or conditions that must be escalated to a designated individual or authority for notification and remedial follow-up. These are the incidents that make it to the Board's risk management or audit committee. They may require regulatory or customer notification. They are likely to have noteworthy financial impact. You don't want them on your watch, especially if the failed control belongs in security's portfolio.

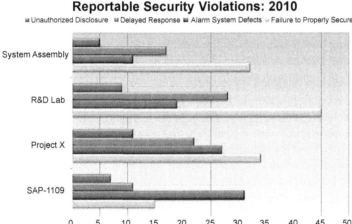

Reportable Security Violations: 2010

To add insult to injury, most are avoidable. The rules and responsibilities are—or should be—known. The nearby graphic is typical of security's normal approach to metrics: We maintain counts of "what" and "how much." The essential next step is what security management does with these data. If you accept the fact that what you see here indicates avoidable risks, the next step is to dig deep and uncover the root causes.

Compliance standards all possess embedded measures for monitoring conformance. For example, if certain types of information must be protected to a specific standard, inspections will reveal the status of safeguards, and automated tools and protective systems can monitor for and alert to attempts to compromise protection. Processes to ensure or verify personnel reliability may be measured, as can response to potential threats to protected assets. In sum, there is a diverse inventory of sources for actionable metrics.

In the best of circumstances, an internally directed compliance review or risk assessment identifies the internal control defect or security vulnerability, nails the cause, and addresses the exposure before an event occurs. Your value metric is the number of vulnerabilities you have proactively discovered and fixed. In the worst-case scenario, the defective control that you knew about somehow never got fixed. Somewhere between best and worst is the case in which a previously unidentified defect directly contributes to a notable event. Both of these metrics also need to be tracked—at least, while you are around to track them.

Look at the four indicators being tracked by the department in this graphic.

- **Unauthorized disclosure** relates to proprietary information that has been transmitted by any means in violation of standards of protection.
- **Delayed response:** We can all envision certain types of incidents, alarms, or calls for service that establish standards for first responders. Time from dispatch to arrival is logged for verification of adequate response time.
- **Alarm system defects:** Alarms installed to monitor sensitive areas or assets must meet specific standards of reliability. Standards for tracking faulty, false, or nuisance-induced annunciations are checks on system reliability and responder confidence.
- **Failure to properly secure** relates to the missteps of persons accountable for following established protection standards, whether the cause is malicious intent, negligence, or a flawed understanding of their responsibility.

If you work in a business environment where regulatory compliance is a critical measure for the viability of the company, or simply need to better understand your obligations under various legislative standards, I strongly encourage your examination of the Security Executive Council's Regulations and Compliance Management (RoCM) tool. Although it is a work in progress, it represents a significant body of researchable information on security-related legislation and regulations.

In further extension of the few examples offered above, here are some additional key compliance indicators:

- Pass/fail rate from government-conducted security inspections (keyed to program life cycle)
- Response time to special access area alarms in excess of mandated threshold
- Percent of personnel submitted for clearance found to have material derogatory backgrounds
- Percent of programs with tested conformance of safeguards and internal controls
- Number of reportable security defects found in outsourced suppliers per audit or inspection
- Percentage of compromise incidents where compromise is ruled out versus in
- Percentage of control deficiencies identified as a percent of total controls in the safeguard process
- Elimination of sanctionable penalties associated with frequency and severity of compliance deviations
- Number of unauthorized persons found in controlled space per period
- Cost of investigation and resolution of data breaches by business unit per period
- Security cost as a percent of total regulated program revenue

- Number of unaccounted laptops with encryption disabled
- Number of defective or unsecure physical access controls found by tours per 24 hour period
- Number of false or nuisance alarms per protected area per 24 hour period
- Average time to clear identified control deficiencies
- Number of information protection violations per 100 employees
- Percent of controlled access areas with fully tested business continuity plans
- Percent of unused access credentials for onboard personnel per reporting period
- Percentage of tested population having accurate awareness of security procedures
- Number of security violations by personnel with approved access as a percent of total approved population
- Incident post-mortems involving compromise of specific types of internal controls having regulatory implications
- Fines or enforcement actions avoided by timely identification and corrective action
- Security-related award fees achieved compared to total fee potential
- Number of notices of corrective actions required by regulators

Think about what is reportable in your company and what protocols are in place to ensure reporting compliance. The rules are clear if you are in a regulated business environment, but may not be in a less formal setting.

SECURITY CONTRACT COMPLIANCE AUDITING

Contracts with product and service suppliers are an integral part of many corporate security service delivery programs. Ensuring the effectiveness of performance terms and related compliance monitoring is a critical management objective that requires knowledgeable and engaged resources along with the right data for performance measurement.

BACKGROUND

Many companies spend millions of dollars annually for thousands of hours of service from contract guard vendors, and often solely rely on the vendor's own periodic reporting for compliance assessment. SLAs typically apply a relatively small sample of performance requirements across different aspects of the contractual agreement. In this example, this company is concerned with coemployment risk and takes a relatively hands-off oversight posture. The vendor is required to ensure that all personnel who may be assigned under this contract are submitted for background investigation and drug testing, both administered by contractors of their choosing. Hiring, training, and retention standards are specified, and the contract indicates that the company's security contract administrator may audit compliance. This audit function is assigned to the purchasing department, and the company is heavily outsourced and lean on management.

RISK MANAGEMENT STRATEGY

A new director of security has correctly prioritized a thorough review of operations, and this contract represents 62% of the corporate security budget. The vendor is required to submit a variety of data pursuant to an SLA, and places a request of purchasing for audit reports with this result: There are none. Purchasing is "too busy with RFPs" to engage in audits. The security operations manager who "owns" these services also serves as a lead investigator for site incidents and has relied on facility managers and the vendor's supervisory team to jointly manage guard operations.

The security director has seen a variety of signs in incident reports, shift reviews, and simple observation of post assignments indicating that this vendor may require more active oversight. A subsequent review of this one report confirms these concerns. It shows that in the past two quarters at the company's two largest sites, this vendor has reported 103 individuals slated for assignment or actually assigned have been dismissed or reassigned, likely to other clients with lower retention standards. This represents a 32% rejection rate for the quarter. Of more immediate concern is the finding that 70% of this group either failed to meet preassignment standards or had to be dismissed prior to the end of their 90 probationary period. A deeper dive indicates that turnover has spiked over the past three quarters, and the supervisory team has been reassigned to a new contract in another part of the region. Follow-up discussions with selected facility staff further reveal that service quality has deteriorated and response times have noticeably increased in areas specified as requiring a not-to-exceed 5 minute response.

An initial thought that the contractual standards might be excessive indicates that they are totally appropriate. Clearly, something is amiss in this vendor's recruitment efforts or in the available pool of candidates. It is also clear that the company has totally failed to exercise its responsibilities in basic contract management, and this one metric report is only the tip of the iceberg.

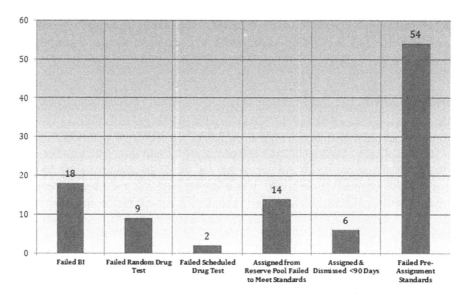

QUESTIONS

If you were presented with this set of facts and concerns, what steps would you take to immediately improve the quality of personnel and service from your guard force contractor? What other data would you demand from the vendor? What steps should be taken internally to ensure the appropriate level of contract compliance? If your actions with this vendor created coemployment concerns from purchasing and legal, how would you answer them? What would be an appropriate response from the vendor's management?

MEASURING FOR INTEGRITY: BACKGROUND INVESTIGATIONS

A comprehensive background investigation (BI) program is critical to the health and integrity of any enterprise, in good times and especially in bad. A worsening of the economy can have a striking impact on the honesty of the employee candidate pool, and it can also affect the quality of internal and external background vetting.

A KPI for this process is that persons who fail to meet established standards for employment are not hired. The quality of procedures associated with vetting prior to the BI and the actions taken by hiring authorities in the face of a materially derogatory BI also provide noteworthy measures.

RISK MANAGEMENT STRATEGY

If we look at business contracting from our unique perspective of enterprise risk, we note several potential implications:

- When the business is doing poorly and hiring has stopped or slowed, hiring managers may seek to be exempted from hiring freezes by citing a critical need for an essential position. They may exert pressure to lower investigation standards to streamline the process on replacements and new hires, and they may overlook flaws they would find undesirable in more competitive times.
- Outsource providers may push back on contractual requirements for background investigations altogether or attempt to impose their own less stringent standards of selection.
- Even in the best of times, headhunter agencies encourage creative writing and embellished work experience to maximize their candidates' qualifications. Today's job pool is alive with unemployed professionals being represented by these agencies.
- During recessionary periods, there is strong evidence that the honesty quotient in the employment pool declines and the unemployed may embellish their personal histories and qualifications.

We need to feel confident that our background vetting programs are effectively verifying candidate assertions of prior salary and experience, education, supplementary compensation (bonus, perks, incentives, etc.), and benefits. We need to be tracking the ratio of cases with no derogatory findings against ones with various types of potential disqualifiers, also focusing on the variance between different business units.

2011 Background Investigations: % of Derogatory Findings in 5 Business Units

This chart clearly shows some switches that need to be reset with these business units and the HR staffing team. The hiring managers are not effectively probing interviewees on the veracity of their personal histories, and the HR recruiters are simply leaving any semblance of vetting to security's background investigators. These candidates have fabricated their prior experience to suit the job descriptions and held up the hiring manager by inflating their prior salary history. This picture also should alert the reader who employs outside background investigation vendors to ensure they are getting the truth, lest every step in the process would fail.

These trends will tell stories about the level of due diligence being done by HR recruiters, headhunters, and hiring managers, and you may need to use these data to reset some switches. You may find data for measuring these trends in your investigative post-mortems and employee termination-for-cause statistics.

In the following chart, we offer another look at background investigation data that offer a significant target for discussion with HR about their oversight of external recruiters. These vendors may fail to reinforce the need for complete honesty in the application and personal history documentation process. Keep in mind that the services of these headhunting firms are tied to the applicant's success in meeting all the requirements of the prospective job. Exaggeration and bending the facts about prior employment, education, previous compensation—and that missing hole in the work history that went to time off for the felony conviction—sometimes get lost in creative writing. Your discussion with HR should also probe recruitment pool issues that may be contributing to these across-the-board increases in derogatory findings.

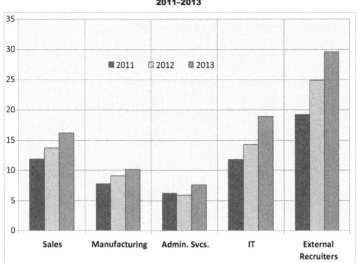

It's pictures like this that feed my commitment to the background vetting program belonging within corporate security's accountability with HR/staffing as the customer. When we see HR owning the whole process, there is too much of a vested interest in filling empty seats. If background investigation services are outsourced by HR, security should own the policy framework, vet prospective vendors, and provide audit oversight of the vendor. Monthly or quarterly metrics to reflect their performance to contractual standard should be part of the security dashboard.

SUMMARY

Stay on top of what your background investigation data are telling you about the candidate pool in your company and your key vendors, especially those providing services for critical business processes with reputational impact. I often push back on companies I talk to that are not rigorous in background vetting. I'll ask them to talk to a colleague who has a solid program and check on the number of applicants they have rejected. "Their rejects are probably working for you," I'll add. Make sure your management takes this basic risk mitigation process seriously. Be the company that is sending your rejects to your competitors.

MEASURING EXECUTIVE PROTECTION PROGRAMS

In many discussions with my colleagues over the years, one of the most elusive areas of measurement that we probe is in programs related to executive protection (EP). If we focus on performance indicators, we typically exhaust the key ones after listing level of protectee satisfaction with services, percent of travel itineraries modified based on our risk assessments, and my favorite, absence of faulty alarm systems or failed responses to executive residences. And yet, this is an often a costly and labor-intensive part of the corporate security service suite.

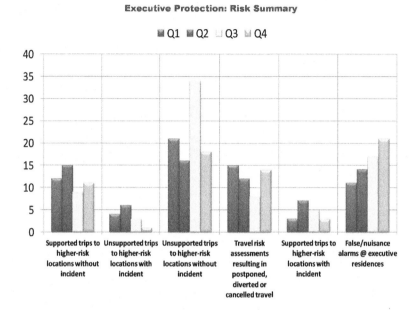

It seems to me that risk, or preferably the avoidance of risk, is a logical way to measure program performance in this area. In this chart, we see a half-dozen activities that this CSO is using to track EP-related risk indicators. The discomfort associated with faulty residential alarm systems is obvious to anyone in our business, so tracking system reliability to a 95% target and response time within a set standard or less should be considered. Executive travel typically boils down to those itineraries we agree are more risky and require a security presence, and those to risky destinations where our services were not employed, and the frequency of incidents in either of these categories. Percentages of trips where EP team intervention were required (whether accompanied or not) is a practical measure as well.

Due to Internal Revenue tax implications, EP services are required to be accounted for, so these metrics are often found in team documentation.

BUSINESS UNIT CRITICALITY, RESILIENCE, AND CONTINUITY PLANNING

How well employees perform when responsiveness is essential is directly proportionate to adequacy of our planning, training, and testing. Performance indicators are all over these objectives. While crisis planning and incident management are typically found in the corporate security suite of responsibilities, many of these organizations also have business continuity/contingency planning in their portfolios. This assignment makes a lot of sense.

- Security is one of the few 24/7 functions in the business
- The concept of protection of business-critical operations should extend to response and recovery
- The continuity planning requirement of assigning criticality to business processes enables a more comprehensive and prioritized asset protection strategy
- Incorporating awareness of risk to continuity within 24/7 security operations personnel provides a knowledgeable and preventive resource
- Increasing business interruption threats are IT-based and require IT security resources for threat identification, definitive response, forensic examination, and recovery assistance
- Crisis management operations invariably involve a variety of security resources

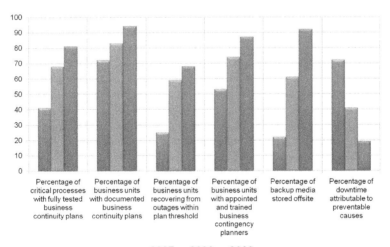

Impact of Board & CEO Scrutiny on Business Resilience

■ 2007 ■ 2008 ■ 2009

In this example, we see a selection of six key elements of business continuity administration being tracked and reported to the Board and CEO at their request. This company has experienced several outages from both natural and man-made events, and the Board has demanded action to increase assurance of more responsive preparation and adequacy of response. Although there are multiples that could be presented, these six represent common evaluative elements subject to effective measurement of compliance:

- Business units with documented continuity plans
- Critical processes with fully tested continuity plans

- Business units with appointed and trained continuity planners
- Business units recovering from outage within plan threshold
- Downtime attributable to preventable causes
- Backup media stored offsite

Think about the interrelationship of these program elements: plans tested and in place overseen by qualified people, increasing rates of recovery, and reduced rates of preventable downtime combined with backup media safely stored offsite for assured restoration of critical business processes.

What's the bottom line in this previous chart? When you want to get resistant business units engaged for results, get top management engaged on the implications of affirmed threats to safe, secure, and resilient business operations. Threat management ultimately relies on some sort of accountability model. A key component of the overall protection strategy has to be based upon the principle that the owner of each process is accountable for integrity and security and the employees who operate the process are the first line of defense. Use your metrics to shine a light on that accountability model.

In the next chart, we see the importance of employee awareness in this engagement strategy. In this company, corporate security directs the contingency planning program and subjects the top 50 A-1 processes to various types and frequencies of assessments to ensure that their uninterrupted availability is tested and assured. We can see that each of the 50 processes had awareness tasks phased over the four quarters of the past year. To maximize awareness of those risk issues that have the highest potential to occur, security's contingency planning team worked with each customer to tailor the awareness program format and content based on historical incident experience and issues identified in prior risk assessments. Throughout the year, a number of quick and easy to more detailed knowledge and readiness tests were applied to affirm currency and quality of awareness.

Contingency plans are always arrayed around the most critical business processes and involve both specific steps to be taken to mitigate impact and timelines associated with compensatory measures. The key measure is found in the percentage of critical functions that followed established protocols and procedures when a threat event presented itself, and the story is about incremental improvement in conformance to established plans within each affected business unit. The trend line shows a fairly dramatic increase (47–85%) in responsiveness over the period, a result that dramatically affirms improvement in the effectiveness of the awareness programs.

SUMMARY

Corporate security must be an enabler of its constituents being alert to risk and knowing what to do when things go bump in the night (or day). We have limited resources and must depend on our customers to be the eyes, ears, and, as demonstrated here, the initial responders to threats to critical business operations. We empower them to do the right things when we provide measurably effective awareness of responsibility.

We have a unique story line that comes from gathering, analyzing, and understanding threat and risk data. This lens on risk has to translate into a "what if" dialogue to intelligently engage our customers on the potential incidents we know could occur. This is an absolute for the reliability and availability of most critical business processes in the company.

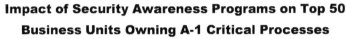

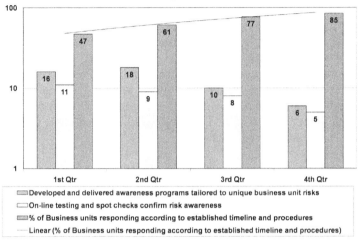

Impact of Security Awareness Programs on Top 50 Business Units Owning A-1 Critical Processes

Developed and delivered awareness programs tailored to unique business unit risks
On-line testing and spot checks confirm risk awareness
% of Business units responding according to established timeline and procedures
Linear (% of Business units responding according to established timeline and procedures)

MEASURING SECURITY AWARENESS PROGRAMS

Security's ability to educate and empower its customers in its risk management responsibilities is a fundamental element of any business protection strategy. Our objective is to develop a security awareness program focused on key areas of employee safety, corporate integrity, and business process security and resiliency.

If you are a sole practitioner security manager (an army of one) or a CSO with a sizable service portfolio and staff to match, at the end of the day, measurably effective security really boils down to a measurably aware and engaged employee population. They live with the assets and own the accountability for protection of those assets. So, we better have a plan for keeping them smart on risk and their responsibilities for secure asset management. We need to communicate and "sell" to build and maintain an aware, engaged base of customers.

What does this have to do with metrics? It's about measuring the elements of preparedness and awareness, and communicating them to reinforce the positive and correct deficiencies where found. Our performance is measured by the degree to which those we target for awareness demonstrate working knowledge of expectations and skills with the tools we have provided.

RISK MANAGEMENT STRATEGY

If your company thinks the security organization is the owner of security-related business risk, get your résumé up to date. We are paid to understand the range and depth of risks confronting the business in its various environments, to build strategies to mitigate them, *and to educate our constituents on their responsibilities*. Business process owners' awareness is a fundamental element in a security risk mitigation strategy.

Just as your company has to market its products or services, corporate security must market and "sell" the employee's role in personal and asset protection.

If you expect key individuals and groups to conform to policy and procedures, you must use focused communication to ensure that they're aware of those requirements. So, what is security's brand at your company and to whom do you sell it? Think about it. You have products to sell to senior management, the Board, employees, partners, vendors, and visitors. What is your tagline, your brand that guides and frames the message for your constituents? How are you "selling" accountability for business protection? Look at this chart and ask yourself what the results might be if they were measures of your awareness program?

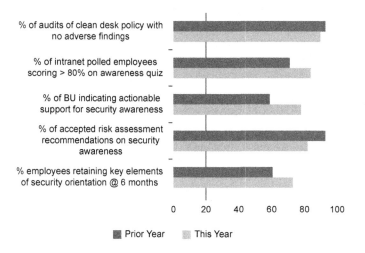

Awareness: A Few Key Indicators

Security awareness is measurable. Actionable measures and metrics for risk awareness may be derived from a variety of sources:

- Risk assessment findings provide qualitative data that need to be fed back to appropriate business units to make them more aware of their accountability.
- Risk events and profiles identify unmanaged exposures that need to be communicated. You can determine the absence or degree of measureable improvement in risk exposure or conformance to policy by conducting follow-up testing of your awareness initiative to see how well the messages got across.
- Formal feedback surveys and interviews can identify the level of security awareness within targeted populations. A useful technique is to use the corporate intranet to quiz users and engage in random polling on risk or procedural responsibilities.
- Incident post-mortems, lessons learned, and victim interviews provide a rich source of information on gaps in security awareness.
- Security department customer satisfaction surveys can ask how well respondents understand security's messaging and how effective the communication medium is.

- Policy audits, such as clean desk policy checks, can be performed by evening shift security officers during rounds.

Corporate security and brand protection is every employee's job. The quality of your connection—your actionable messages—with them is a key element of security management.

THE ABSENCE OF AWARENESS IS A KEY CONTRIBUTOR TO RISK

Two key measures of the effectiveness of a security program are (1) how well security communicates the responsibilities it expects employees to meet and (2) the affirmation that those expectations are being met.

We are paid to anticipate risk. That expectation drives our multiple efforts to identify vulnerability through a variety of means including risk assessments, countermeasure tests, and incident post-mortems. When we use probes like these to better understand what happened and why, we may find that those in the best position to prevent or act responsibly were not aware or were negligent of their role in enterprise protection. We need to test and affirm employee awareness of security responsibilities, and periodic surveys of targeted populations are an effective way to accomplish this.

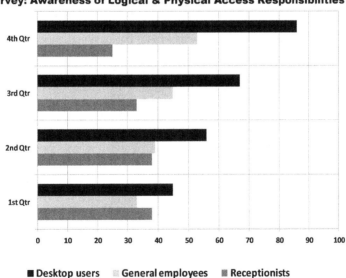

Survey: Awareness of Logical & Physical Access Responsibilities

■ Desktop users   General employees   ■ Receptionists

In this example, our security organization has focused on a simple test of aware-ness of access control responsibilities by targeted receptionists and desktop users, and a sample of the general employee population. Receptionists are gatekeepers and should be empowered to maintain access integrity while welcoming visitors. In a more process-oriented way, the myriad of desktop users must follow established authorization procedures to gain access to preapproved business applications. The corporate intranet offers a variety of user-friendly means to quiz and reacquaint specific employee categories with security policy while identifying soft spots in awareness. Security officers on tours have frequent contact with receptionists and employees at access points and can plan and advertise events such as "access awareness days," which could consist of a simple quiz and handouts like badge reels or small reminder cards. Similarly, information security teams can engage desktop users at logon or other times to test awareness of security procedures.

Security awareness is a centerpiece of a measurably effective corporate security program. That principle requires us to craft and effectively communicate specific guidance to address potential areas of risk. I use "guidance" because many organizations abhor the term "policy." Use whatever description for your expectations you feel is appropriate to your culture, but do not fail to identify critical expectations and advertise them. Logical and physical access control integrity is a fundamental security principle that touches virtually every employee, and it is too easy to allow an unknown tailgater to go unchallenged or to write off a simple computer security procedure because it's inconvenient.

Surveys deliver the data: The data you need to understand levels of awareness are in planned or random surveys of targeted employees or other stakeholders (like vendors in possession of proprietary information or processes), risk assessments, and post-incident analysis. Your various business environments may offer a variety of means to gather and reaffirm awareness data on security policy. Be creative; engage employees in the process. If this is done well, it will also help you build good public relations for the security organization.

Testing delivers the data: In this example, security has employed a logical access password cracking tool to test the strength of this key safeguard. The story here reinforces the importance of training to an engaged and aware population. We know that training and awareness programs have a shelf life, so for critical components in the delegation of security accountability, testing and performance feedback play a key role in the maintenance of employee commitment.

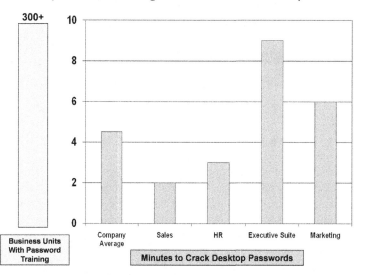

**Logical Access Password Strength
(Password Cracking Exercise Conducted in Q2)**

ABILITY TO INFLUENCE THE BUSINESS IS A KEY PERFORMANCE INDICATOR

The ability to influence people, policy, and results has to be a core competence of any manager. Depending on where you sit in the hierarchy, it is particularly critical for managers in corporate security. Your metrics are one of the most important tools in your ability to influence because they provide the evidence for your pitch.

Why should influence be the focus of your security metrics? Think about the results you are seeking with your metrics—how the measures and data you are communicating achieve some improved state of security or safety. Remember that one of the key requirements of an effective security metric is that it is *actionable*. It shouldn't just count things; it needs to inform and create a storyline that leaves the audience with the need to address the risky conditions or root causes you have set forth.

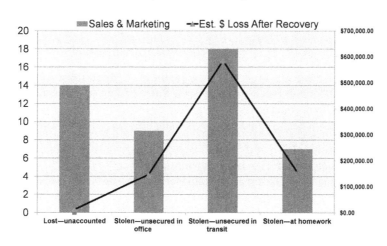

Lost & Stolen Laptops From Sales & Marketing Division (2010–2012/Q2)

In this example, a new security director has determined that relationships between corporate security and several business units are either nonexistent or seriously deficient. In exploring the root causes, one obvious consequence is some fairly significant nonreporting of incidents noted in the sales and marketing division. A referral from the purchasing department indicated a consistently high run rate for laptop purchases within this division over the past 10 quarters, so an inquiry was initiated. Nine laptops were reported as stolen from sales office spaces across the company since the beginning of 2010, and 10 were reported as stolen from employee vehicles or on travel in the same period.

When tallying purchased laptops against those stolen, there were significant variances that required investigation. The investigation's results are seen in the chart. Clearly, there is more than nonreporting going on in this company. Is this a notable example of an influence moment? Is this a snapshot you could use to influence behavior?

- Fourteen were somehow lost after assignment to the division but apparently replaced
- Eighteen, not 10 as reported, were lost in transit
- Seven were stolen from employee residences
- Using available benchmark data against known onboard data content, investigation and replacement cost, this division alone accounts for a $900,000 loss to the company.

So, if you were this security director, I think you would have a clear picture of a major set of notable risks that likely go beyond this specific case. Is this an opportunity to influence on a broader scale or are you just an investigator closing out an investigation?

- What conclusions would you draw about this business unit if you were this security director?
- How would you relate these findings to the discussion you would plan on having with the division SVP?
- Who are the supervisors who own these yahoos who are asking for new laptops? What questions are being asked about the negligence that led to their loss?
- How would you propose to influence the supervisor's decision on addressing the implications of these findings?
- What sanctions should be applied to those who failed to report?

Let's assume the SVP doesn't see the problem ("I think most of these were encrypted…") and thinks this is just part of the cost of doing business. How are you going to escalate to his manager?

Perhaps there are deeper opportunities to influence policy and behavior here:

- What is the status of IT policy around laptop security and accountability?
- What checks and balances exist on purchasing requests?
- How could you use this example to influence the enterprise risk management agenda?

Influence is a key performance indicator for corporate security. Keep a few good metrics in your toolkit to tell a powerful story and provide a great opportunity to influence.

WARNING SIGNS OF SECURITY'S DECREASING INFLUENCE

If you accept that security's influence is a KPI and that influence is a core competency, what indicators might we employ to assess our organizational influence quotient?[7] I think the answer is found in your ability to answer "yes" to three questions:

1. *Does management believe the program is adding value?* Absent that, you are a liability in a competitive marketplace.

---

[7]You can view this from both a personal and organizational perspective. Your ability to sell your advice and conclusions has a clear connection to how others trust and see your credibility. So too, the security organization must be perceived by consumers as deserving of trust and confidence in the competence of its people and accuracy of its products.

2. *Does the program have the influence to help eliminate risky business practices?* If we clearly and competently advise on risk and things don't change, what's wrong with this picture?
3. *Do employees and management accept the concept of shared responsibility for asset protection?* If the business thinks you protect the company, you have failed to ensure that line business managers are the accountable custodians of assets and that your mission is to provide the tools and flawless first response.

There are multiple alarm bells that may indicate that the security program is falling short of success in these critical areas. What does this have to do with security metrics? Everything! Our measures and metrics are the stories, our script we share with management, to influence and assign accountability for maintenance of standards of protection.

Consider the following 15 indicators of decreasing influence and examine your own program to see if any of them apply. If you think they may, what steps could you take to affirm your concerns and how would you propose to reverse the trend?

1. *Imposed budget reductions made without consideration of increased risk.* I'm aware of a number of examples of this, especially in these challenging economic times. But while we may want to rack this up to tough decisions on priorities, we have to ask how well we have made the case for exposure to risk and the cost of protection.
2. *Realignment of security at a lower level, impacting unfettered access to the top.* This is a frequent, follow-on partner of risky budget cuts, but it may have even greater impact on the program. The more we are insulated from access to those who influence policy and behavior, the less able we are to make change happen. Every level imposes its own agendas, and yours may not make the list.
3. *Increased number of risky external relationships with no security review.* Outsourcing is a business paradigm and is likely to remain—if not increase— as we attempt to compete globally. Where the processes being outsourced are acknowledged as inherently risky, to what extent are your programs engaged early on to be an integral element in the due diligence process? How are the contractual conditions structured to incorporate elements of security oversight or affirmation of compliance? Are you a *real* part of the strategic business model?
4. *Increasing frequency of inadequate first response to security incidents.* You don't share this one, you *own* it! You are paid to understand the more likely events that are assignable to your portfolio! Your resources (plans, people, equipment, etc.) should be prepared to respond in a highly competent and timely manner to mitigate the threat.
5. *Failure to uncover common contributing causes to multiple, diverse security incidents.* This one may seem less clear than the four previous indicators, but it may be the most critical given the unique perspective on risk your data should provide you. If you have captured your lessons learned on various types of incidents, you should have a body of data on the *real* contributing causes of

events and what needs to be done to mitigate future risk. If you haven't, you don't understand your obligation to learn on behalf of your employer's risk management objectives and to influence policy and behavior on eliminating future events with similar common denominators.

6. *Continuing findings of exploitable vulnerabilities.* You have conducted a risk assessment or a post-incident lessons-learned exercise that revealed exploitable gaps in security measures. You have notified responsible managers and business units of these gaps and recommended ways to close them, but in spite of your advice, the vulnerabilities persist. Where and why has your ability to influence change broken down?

7. *Increased (or unresolved) audit findings of security program deficiencies.* Serious security deficiencies are on auditors' watch lists. When the identified vulnerabilities go unresolved, management will wonder why security has not been successful in either directly or collaboratively impacting the elimination of the known problems. Increased deficiencies are a clear red flag that the security program, at some level, does not take the threat seriously. This may escalate to the Board's audit committee and you don't need this sort of top management attention.

8. *Increased bypassing of basic security safeguards.* Propped doors, card readers consistently in access mode, hiring people with adverse background findings, discounting specific asset protection procedures—the list goes on. You have installed safeguards that are being disabled. Have you effectively sold the rationale for these security measures? Are you tracking the consequences? What do you need to do to gain the confidence of employees and managers?

9. *Decreasing ability to influence or have a say in sanctions on internal misconduct cases.* Your investigation has validated that an employee has been involved in wrongdoing. Now the employee's advocates totally discount (or worse, even fail to consider) your views on precedent and sanctions. While security does not decide the outcome in these cases, your ability to bring your findings to bear is a legitimate test of your influence.

10. *Increased frequency and/or severity of security infractions, accidents, crime, or other preventable risk events.* The risks on our watch are dynamic. We have a responsibility to develop and maintain metrics on the direction of key trends and recommended mitigation strategies. What are we to conclude when the trends continue to grow after we communicate information on increasing risk and attempt to engage appropriate parties in solutions? Are they listening and taking positive action based on our good advice? We need to look inward at how we frame our messages for influential impact.

11. *Security is not consulted before management makes changes to processes, products, or relationships with evident security risk impact.* Note the word "evident" in this sentence. Ignorance is one thing, but when it's clear that changes involve probability of risk, and management still decides not to include us, we are a marginalized player at best.

12. *Management fails to approve security's recommendation for development and communication of a new or revised security policy to mitigate a consistent pattern of risk.* What should we conclude when we have a convincing story on what steps should be taken to mitigate risk, and they decide to leave things as they are?

13. *Increased downtime of critical security safeguards that fail and go unattended.* Think about this one! You have a "critical" safeguard (like a duress alarm in the executive suite or consistent unauthorized access to a sensitive area) that is unreliable and nobody is fixing it! Are you watching the dials on your dashboard? There are two possibilities: Either you are unaware of these vulnerabilities or you have failed to take appropriate action. In both cases, count on your stock taking a big hit sooner rather than later.

14. *Security fails to effectively analyze its data on security incidents and thereby invites future risk that will seriously deplete leadership's confidence in us.* While this closely resembles #3 above and some others, it really goes to the failure to establish a comprehensive, disciplined, and ongoing process of incident and workload analysis. What are the trends and the common denominators? What steps are working and where are the gaps?

15. *Decreasing engagement of essential internal partners in matters of clear security concern.* This is not an isolated shortcoming; it is a summary result of all the failures mentioned in this series. You have not connected the dots between your security and risk message and the responsibilities of your organization's employees and business leaders. You either haven't spoken their language or they have tuned you out.

I think one of the key mission elements of a corporate security organization and its leadership is to use its unique perspective as a lever to drive behavior, risk management policy, and business strategy. Effective security executives are influential as a core competency.

So, this has been a brief look at 15 danger signals that may indicate failing influence on critical issues or can clearly damage the credibility of the security organization and its leadership. Metrics provide an early warning system. Metrics enable positive influence over your constituent's actions, attitudes, and conformance with policy. You have the data—now take an objective look at the competence of your data management capabilities. What metrics really make a difference in your contribution to value and your ability to influence results and standards of protection?

MEASURE INFLUENCE BY TRACKING ACCEPTANCE OF RECOMMENDATIONS

All nonrevenue-producing organizations like corporate security are in the influence business. Influence is a measure of effectiveness, and we need to apply various processes to evaluate security's effectiveness. There are a variety of ways security can do this, but the method described here may yield the most informative results.

Our objective is to track the recommendations security makes to other business units and to determine what percentage of them are accepted. The result sought is to better assess our ability to influence change and effectuate risk management improvements in our clients' security practices.

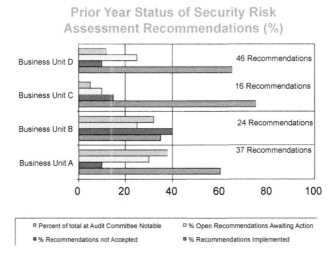

RISK MANAGEMENT STRATEGY

This chart displays the status of security risk assessment recommendations delivered to four different business units in one year. The percent of recommendations accepted or implemented, compared with the percent not accepted, should serve as a strong indicator of the degree of influence security holds over the recipient business executive. Recommendations awaiting action are merely in a queue for eventual analysis. The real ringer here is the percent of the total recommendations that are deemed audit committee notable (ACN), a status typically warranting very high levels of resolution priority.

Let's take a look at Business Unit A, which received 37 security improvement recommendations during the year. 15 of those were deemed ACN and 22 were satisfactorily resolved. Looking behind these numbers, we would find that none of the four recommendations *not accepted* were in the notable category. This is significant because it may mean that the influence of the audit committee is stronger than that of corporate security. But it is very important to note that this escalation option open to security indicates a high degree of confidence by audit and the Board of Directors in the integrity of the process employed by security in performing its risk assessments and analyses and framing a resolution strategy with the business units. Other points of interest might be the aging of unresolved recommendations, especially if they fall within the ACN category.

The remaining business unit examples follow the same pattern, with the exception of Unit B, which has rejected 60% of security's recommendations, claiming that only internal or external audit has the competence to evaluate its business controls. Security's recommendations in this unit are under external review for final findings. The data that form the conclusions and substance of the recommendations made by security are embedded in the risk assessment process employed by the security department.

This chart displays the work of a highly proactive security executive who has obtained the confidence of senior management. This example is about more than being influential. If we are to be a legitimate and full partner of the corporate governance process, our role clearly involves setting expectations on business unit stewardship of security policy. If your responsibilities only extend to physical security operations, your programs still fall within this process. Physical security is the front line of protection for all corporate assets and is clearly accepted as a key element in information security and business continuity as well.

SECURITY'S VALUE PROPOSITION: VALUE IS A KEY PERFORMANCE INDICATOR

Organizationally adept security executives are all concerned about ROI. But how should we translate this universal business metric to an accepted measure of security's value to the goals and bottom line of the enterprise? Proof of value can be elusive for us. It may be said that truly effective security is invisible especially where it is effectively integrated into the daily business. Business executives understand the connection and the business rationale for an enterprise protection program. But they typically don't really understand what we do and why or how we do it. It is a critical part of the CSO's job to craft a message and educate top management on where and how we bring value to business strategy and the bottom line. This message has to include a variety of metrics that demonstrate in business terms our value story.

Security's value can be elusive especially when we consider that truly effective security is blended into the business. We have to sell the story of our positive impact to the bottom line.

FINDING A CORPORATE SECURITY VALUE PROPOSITION

A business strategy has to speak to the desired value proposition for the enterprise. Developing a value proposition is based on a review and analysis of the benefits, costs, and value that an organization can deliver to its customers, prospective customers, and other constituent groups within and outside the organization. It is also a positioning of value, where Value = Benefits − Cost (cost includes risk).[8] Individual

---

[8] Cindy Barnes, Helen Blake, David Pinder, *Creating & Delivering Your Value Proposition: Managing Customer Experience for Profit.* Kogan Page Publishers, October 2009, p. 28.

program cost isn't simply the expenses assigned to a security budget line item. It includes the costs incurred by the business in the execution of its program. The challenge is in the measurement of benefits.

This concept of benefit delivered minus cost should be a key element of security management strategy. What are the benefits of individual security programs to specific internal customer groups and how are the costs rationalized by both sides? Given our mission, how should the concept of avoided risk be valued? Is there a measurable value in our ability to enable risky business practices to deliver their products and services?

Security's value proposition is driven by a combination of facts—real results—and perception. In many ways, we are back to that earlier discussion of how we demonstrate a risk avoided or prevented. But there are real deliverables offered across our spectrum of services that can (and should) be assembled to demonstrate where and how we deliver value to the bottom line. A few examples are seen here.

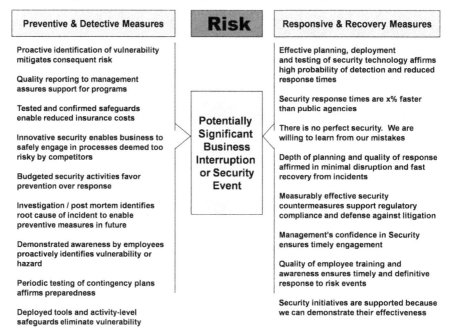

Preparedness & Competence = Anticipated Value

Preventive & Detective Measures	Risk	Responsive & Recovery Measures
Proactive identification of vulnerability mitigates consequent risk		Effective planning, deployment and testing of security technology affirms high probability of detection and reduced response times
Quality reporting to management assures support for programs		Security response times are x% faster than public agencies
Tested and confirmed safeguards enable reduced insurance costs	**Potentially Significant Business Interruption or Security Event**	There is no perfect security. We are willing to learn from our mistakes
Innovative security enables business to safely engage in processes deemed too risky by competitors		Depth of planning and quality of response affirmed in minimal disruption and fast recovery from incidents
Budgeted security activities favor prevention over response		Measurably effective security countermeasures support regulatory compliance and defense against litigation
Investigation / post mortem identifies root cause of incident to enable preventive measures in future		Management's confidence in Security ensures timely engagement
Demonstrated awareness by employees proactively identifies vulnerability or hazard		Quality of employee training and awareness ensures timely and definitive response to risk events
Periodic testing of contingency plans affirms preparedness		Security initiatives are supported because we can demonstrate their effectiveness
Deployed tools and activity-level safeguards eliminate vulnerability		

I'd like to think that much of what has preceded in this book contributes in its own way to demonstrating ideas on benefits assessment and ultimately, security's value. But at the bottom line, I like the notion that *security delivers value when it enables the business to do what would otherwise be too risky*. Enabling enterprise risk management is the link to our prime mission, but the value proposition has to incorporate a more fundamental connection to the unique business drivers of shareholder value and corporate culture.

If you have done an effective job of planning and designing your security programs and initiatives, you will have built-in KPIs for each one that measures the value the work has, is, or should be bringing to the business. Don't be afraid to seek out these answers with your customers. They may see benefits from a different perspective.

MEASURING SECURITY'S VALUE

While I can provide a number of views of risk and performance and some ideas about their measurement and messaging, untold hours of discussion with colleagues over the years always circles around the question—the frustration—regarding how to measure and communicate security's value. Can we develop some key value indicators? Where and how does corporate security deliver value to the company's people, operations, and bottom line?

I'm a firm believer that our value has to be connected to our success in measurably impacting the risks on our watch. What are the measures, and how are you communicating the critical messages? Sure, every program is delivering some statistics, typically lists of incidents or activities that they sell as "metrics." But real metrics inform and create a story line that implies the need for action. Lists are the nails you use to build these stories.

I recently worked for several months with an outstanding corporate security organization that serves a very successful global manufacturing company. The CSO launched a major initiative to identify a body of metrics across the security organization "to tell the value story to management, to demonstrate in measurable ways where and how we bring value to the bottom line of our company." Suffice it to say, this security management team exercise found value delivered in guard force operations, investigations, background vetting, risk assessments, supply chain protection, workplace violence response, and a variety of previously unprobed corners of security service delivery. Let's explore one example: their fire and life safety first responders. The picture of responsiveness and value in this example illustrates a host of best practices.

The data seen in the following charts underscore the relationship of KRIs and KPIs. This is a production environment employing thousands of workers, so there are known risks to life/safety. This organization is addressing probable risk through aggressive awareness and by providing certified EMTs on all shifts. Because the production environment has a known risk of fire, a highly trained fire prevention and response capability is engaged. Both areas of risk have clear and potentially significant implications for impact on business continuity and productivity. The value story here leaps off the page! But behind these data is the intended takeaway for management:

First, we know it takes offsite rescue/EMT services 5 to 6 minutes to arrive on scene, and we respond in fewer than 4 minutes.[9]

1. Survivability and recovery are dramatically improved
2. Injured are returned to work significantly faster

---

[9] Whether proprietary or contractual, having qualified first responder qualified individuals on all shifts is a guaranteed value proposition.

3. Impact to business process is minimized
4. Employee injury claims will be reduced
5. Employee morale is served by a perceived sense of safe workplaces
6. It pays for us to have our own dedicated and qualified onsite resources.

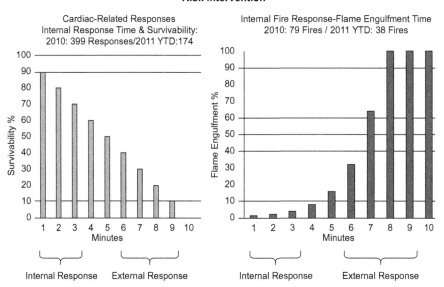

Risk Intervention

Second, we know it takes offsite fire services 5 to 6 minutes to arrive on scene, and we respond in less than 4 minutes.

1. Fire, chemical, or environmental incidents at industrial facilities present potentially serious life/safety, production, financial, and reputational risks to business; the impacts of these incidents are significantly reduced by faster, more definitive response.
2. Many industries possess onsite operations that require special equipment and training essential to effective emergency response. Offsite responders may not have these resources, producing adverse consequences when they are relied on to respond.
3. Onsite services keyed to these risks can engage in routine preventive and awareness operations that will significantly reduce incident occurrence and impact.
4. It is clear that such capabilities can deliver positive results in terms of insurance cost.

It is possible to document a variety of financial benefits associated with these risk avoidance and response capabilities. In this example, over 500 individuals with at-work injuries and life-threatening events were served in time to make a difference. The same value story may be told for these fire services.

Their industrial operations involve the potential for fire, presence of hazardous materials, and employee safety risk, so it wasn't much of a stretch to take an early look at their operations that focus on prevention and response to these areas of business and employee risk. The going-in assumption was that management would see security providing these services as wasteful inasmuch as there are qualified fire departments they are already supporting with our taxes—why pay twice?

So we categorized several areas of preventive service and incident response as seen here. The number of incidents noted (n) are real and the $ costs use verifiable costs of response by the company's first responders compared to the cost that would be levied by the public safety agency. The bottom-line comparison was impressive: Company cost = $4.5 million and the alternative would have been $16.45 million. But the real value story is about the quality of response:

- Individuals returned to work deliver productivity,
- Faster, better prepared and equipped response equals less production downtime impact,
- Assurance of faster, qualitative response contributes to employee safety and morale,
- Preventive operations result in measurably lower construction and insurance costs,
- Proactive inspection programs mitigate fire, safety, and business interruption risk,
- OSHA and other regulatory sanctions are avoided through aggressive inspection,
- Company and individual health insurance costs are reduced, and, most importantly,
- Several employee lives were saved by these corporate security first responders in the course of this year.

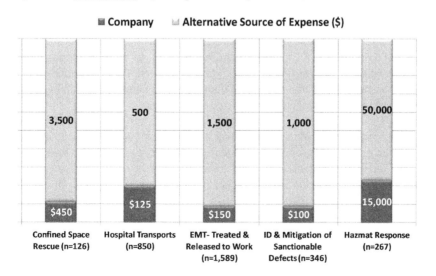

Corporate Security: Fire & Life Safety Service
Comparison of <u>Per Incident</u> Proprietary Service Expense Vs. Qualified Alternative Source

■ Company   ◻ Alternative Source of Expense ($)

3,500	500	1,500	1,000	50,000
$450	$125	$150	$100	15,000
Confined Space Rescue (n=126)	Hospital Transports (n=850)	EMT- Treated & Released to Work (n=1,589)	ID & Mitigation of Sanctionable Defects (n=346)	Hazmat Response (n=267)

Now, the average reader won't have a service like this in their organization. But think about what services you do deliver that can tell your unique value story.

Protective operations: Are your officers trained to respond to health and safety events and have they done so successfully in the past? Are their tours organized to identify and eliminate hazards to safety or exploitable vulnerabilities that could result in measurable loss such as business interruption or asset compromise?

Risk assessments: Do you have a program that proactively examines the range of security-related risks to critical assets? What would the cost of compromise have been for those vulnerabilities your team found and eliminated? What fines or litigation were avoided by elimination of a failed security measure or risky practice?

Timely response: When security programs deliver faster, qualitative responses to risk events, you measurably reduce the cost of impact.

Awareness: When you deliver learning to the business you impact intelligent accountability and contribute to prevention of loss.

I led a proprietary security organization and always had to be prepared to address the legitimate question of the rationale of those costs versus contracting out. I frequently engaged in comparing costs for selected security services and found that our fully loaded costs were far more cost efficient and cost effective than those we found in established areas of purchased services.

The idea here is to think about how what we do prevents and avoids bad things from occurring and reduces the consequences when they do. We add value in many ways but often fail to document and tell our story. What is your story?

DO BUSINESS UNITS VALUE SECURITY RECOMMENDATIONS?

I've discussed influence as a performance indicator, but it is a value indicator as well. Our ability to influence internal customers starts and ends with their perception of the effectiveness and value of security programs. We have to test this perception on a periodic basis, because the results provide opportunities to consider the effectiveness of our programs and alternative approaches to both risk and relationship management.

An obvious way to track customer confidence is to look at whether business units are accepting security's recommendations in key areas. In the example from which the graph below is drawn, the security director has been tracking several program criteria that should be valid indicators of both security's perceived credibility and the state of business unit engagement in their accountability.

There's a little good news and a lot of bad in these results. The good news is that there is a program to track results in several core areas. The bad news is that there seems to be a dramatic disconnect between security and the rest of the business.

First, here is a consistent set of adverse trends across the range of programs. Next, these findings may indicate more fundamental exposures to corporate risk that are not being effectively mitigated by established security measures, and that points to weakness in the security director's leadership. Finally, I have to conclude that senior company management has failed to communicate that it expects business units to play a role in brand protection and corporate integrity. This is clearly impacting the security director's ability to lead and influence results.

Consider these findings:

1. **Business units ignore or decline recommendations for improved security** *occasionally, but trending up.* This is about as basic a measure as you can find. You have delivered multiple recommendations to address security gaps, but your findings have had a minimal impact on the state of protection. Did the business fail to connect the findings to real business risk? Security needs to take a hard look at the quality of its findings and presentation, and should consider a new approach to visibly escalating noncompliance.

2. **Business fails to address repeated security violations** *increasingly frequently.* If this company had any sense of the relationship of security risk to corporate risk, this would be on the audit committee agenda. This result clearly shows the security director's failure to lead and influence with the facts, exacerbated by an unsupportive tone at the top.

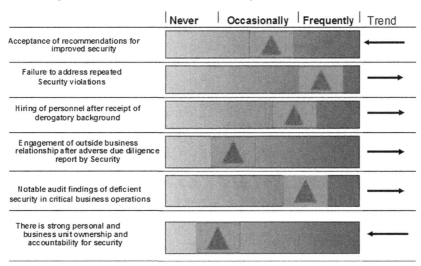

Confidence in Security Functions
Quarterly Results from Business Unit Acceptance of Recommendations

	Never	Occasionally	Frequently	Trend
Acceptance of recommendations for improved security				←
Failure to address repeated Security violations				→
Hiring of personnel after receipt of derogatory background				→
Engagement of outside business relationship after adverse due diligence report by Security				→
Notable audit findings of deficient security in critical business operations				→
There is strong personal and business unit ownership and accountability for security				←

3. **Business hires personnel with adverse background findings** *occasionally, but trending up.* Business units don't know how to relate a bad background to a potential risk in their midst. Security hasn't adequately communicated the consequences of hiring people who have not been truthful in the process. The director needs to engage with his counterpart in HR to validate this program. Here is another area in which security should be helping senior management to connect the dots.

Are we adding value when we communicate the existence of bad security?

4. **Business units engage in risky outside business relationships after security has issued an adverse due diligence report** *infrequently, but trending up.* Security is showing the business that there are risks in a proposed relationship, but business chooses to partner anyway. The business doesn't get it, so security needs to work with audit to maintain a risk watch on these outsourced operations.

5. **There are notable audit findings with regard to security deficiencies in critical business operations** *frequently, and trending up.* This is a clear and independent assessment that reinforces a failure in the status of corporate governance and security management leadership.

6. **Business units show little ownership or accountability for security in their operations** *frequently, trending up.* This is an obvious consequence of significant shortcomings in the objective of shared responsibility for asset protection.

Summary: Is this quarterly assessment a reflection of totally inadequate security management or an indictment of this company's senior leadership's failure to provide the security director with a clear charter and mandate to impact corporate policy and behavior? Perhaps it's a combination of both. Remember that this is an ongoing assessment process that has been sending trend data regularly to the security director.

- Why and how does this presentation demonstrate a value proposition for security?
- What would you do to turn this company around on these KPIs?

USE METRICS TO DEMONSTRATE SECURITY'S ALIGNMENT WITH BUSINESS OBJECTIVES

Your objective is to identify multiple products, services, and positive results that the security organization brings to help meet the enterprise's business goals. In addition, you should enable increased understanding and appreciation by senior management and other key stakeholders of security's value and contribution to the bottom line.

RISK MANAGEMENT STRATEGY

How effectively are your security programs aligned with the objectives of your constituent businesses? The Conference Board recently published a survey of several hundred business executives that revealed a perceived lack of value of the security functions within their organizations. Security leaders must use multiple data sources and metrics to identify security's positive impact on the business and its bottom line and present that information to management.

Here are some examples you may be able to identify in your own enterprise. Data sources for many of these examples are clear in the brief descriptions below.

- Penetration testing yields data on the effectiveness of safeguards and supports claims of reduced opportunity for attack. Protection effectiveness supports resilient business operations.

- Pre-contract examination of the risk potential of third-party vendor relationships identifies vulnerabilities to enable favorable contract terms and post-contract inspections, thereby reducing risk and consequence of loss.
- Examination of incident trends and incident post-mortems produces metrics that either affirm the effectiveness of internal controls or justify the redirection of resources, yielding improved risk management practices.
- When metrics are employed to measure and improve the effectiveness of safeguards, results may clearly support security's contribution to customer and shareholder protection. An obvious example is in the resilience of protection measures around confidential customer information. Similarly, revenue-producing business activities benefit due to more efficient means of protection.
- Focused metrics also generate evidence of cost reduction through reduced consequences of risk and reduction in insurance premiums where effective safeguards are demonstrated.
- Metrics associated with fast recovery from business interruption incidents consistently show the advantages of a resilient business continuity program. Similarly, a more security-aware employee population enables faster notification and improved engagement in protection.
- Virtually all of the security-related regulations imposed in response to financial and domestic security crises of recent memory require metrics to provide verifiable measures of compliance and thereby minimize the imposition of fines, sanctions, or other impacts to shareholder value. Focused metrics enable tracking of incident costs and post-implementation value comparisons of new security measures.
- Advertised and demonstrably effective security measures not only enable customer satisfaction but may also be a draw for new customers and sales. Being "the secure choice" is a plus to the bottom line.
- Deployment of proven security technology consistently demonstrates the potential for reducing security operations costs. The ROI for an access control system that eliminates X number of manned security posts is a frequent example.

If you have the opportunity to present to management on the value of security, be sure to carefully identify only the results or functions that *reliably* offer support to your program. The key is to determine which metrics will best demonstrate your clear connection to the objectives of the enterprise you serve. This is the way to demonstrate security's value.

A SIMPLE ANALYSIS YIELDS VALUABLE RESULTS

In the following graph, the value story is in a response to continuing losses due to theft in this company's inventory depot. A newly appointed security manager examined relevant loss data and then evaluated the potential security defects linked to inventory storage and movement. He experimented by redeploying guard hours (the red line) to a new inventory control point and then added well-advertised CCTV (the green line) to key intersections within the depot. Losses in the first 6 months totaled

$1,381,938, and in the last 6 were reduced by almost 50% to $730,560. These savings were achieved at a cost to date of $37,200. The follow-on story here will be to push this trend line down and further assess how continuing thefts are being accomplished through undercover operations and a detailed examination of inventory controls by internal audit. Does security deliver value in this case?

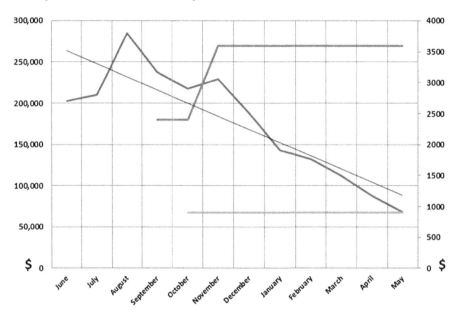

SECURITY'S BALANCED SCORECARD

No discussion of security's value is complete without consideration of a balanced scorecard.[10] I offer it here because its concepts are so embedded in business and performance management and the elements of operational excellence. If you do nothing more than consider the four questions related to these quadrants, it seems to me impossible to escape having to develop at least a few measures and metrics associated with them.

But a deeper dive into the questions pushes the envelope to a more meaningful objective, in my view. Of what we do and deliver, what is *really* perceptible to top management and shareholders? That gets back to my opening question of what is really visible about what we do. I know from a personal phone call that driving the CEO to have a compulsory minimum 12-character password with not more than eight numbers is perceptible. But I also know from others' experience that delivering safe products, a secure environment, and a perception of honesty and integrity are perceptible, and our programs can measurably contribute to those stakeholder perceptions and those of our customers as well.

---

[10] See R. Kaplan & D. Norton, "The Balanced Scorecard: Measures That Drive Performance," *Harvard Business Review*, January–February 1992, pp. 71–79.

I know that there are programs we can deliver that have been designed to specifically attack a known risk or vulnerability at a reduced cost of security operations and then quantify the positive impact those initiatives have provided to an improved state of security. Kaplan and Norton would probably agree that those continuous improvement efforts have provided measurable value.

Business Alignment & Security's Balanced Scorecard

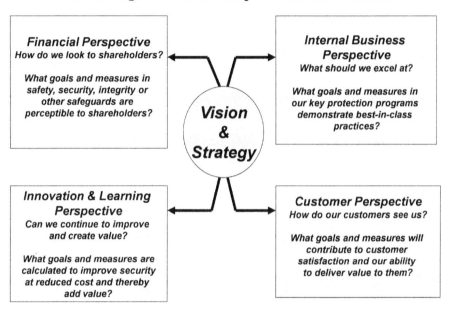

Consider taking this scorecard representation to your boss or a few senior executives and see where the answers to these three questions would take the conversation:

- What four perspectives do they believe are relevant to your company's business,
- How do they see security delivering value within these quadrants?
- What measures would they adopt to demonstrate value in each one?

The following discussion delves into benchmarking's contribution to performance management. You may find the four areas of measurement of value in some deeper dives into these processes.

BENCHMARKING SECURITY OPERATIONS

Metrics cannot escape the need to explore and demonstrate measures of security's cost efficiency, and therefore contribute to a value story. There are a variety of measures that accomplish this, but as we have seen in the annual Security 500 data, there is popularity in those that measure security cost per square foot and per employee, as well as security cost as a percentage of annual revenue. As you approach building your benchmark survey, even at the fairly simple level shown in the following chart, you need to consider the limitations and success factors described in the previous discussion.

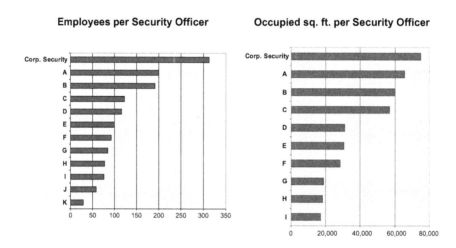

Benchmarking Security Operations:
Comparison of Our Protective Service Operations Vs. 11 Industry Peers

Employees per Security Officer

Occupied sq. ft. per Security Officer

To achieve a level playing field with verifiable data, you need to benchmark with trusted peers or seek out industry sources that annually maintain comparative data. The nearby charts depict two examples of peer benchmarking data. In these examples, a CSO has contacted several colleagues in his industry who frequently exchange security-related information on a regular, trusted basis. (This may be done directly or through your or your company's membership in a trade organization.) In both cases, he needed to carefully qualify a common baseline for comparison. Since physical security operations are common and typically larger expenditures, this CSO calculated the cost served by proprietary or contracted guard force operations and employee data housed within these occupied spaces. You can go crazy with qualifiers, so try to keep it on as common a baseline as possible.[11]

This CSO's data are represented in the top bar of each chart, with each comparator in descending order. Thus, his company's security department serves 310 employees

---

[11] Instead of peer benchmarking, you could work with your facilities or corporate real estate representatives to obtain security cost data from either the Real Estate Executive Board (REEB) or the Building Owners & Management Organization (BOMA), both of which maintain security cost-per-square-foot benchmarking data. REEB permits the data to be sliced many ways: asset type, geography, and industry are the main classifications.

per officer, and his closest peer's serves 200. Similarly, this CSO's security operations respond to 75,000 square feet of occupied space, and his nearest peer responds to 62,000 square feet. In both examples, using these two common criteria, the median spread between his department's level of efficiency and those of multiple peers is significant.

Square footage included only those occupied spaces where security services are provided and include payroll, taxes, and fringe benefits for directly employed security personnel, contracted guard force expenses, contract administration, security monitoring, all directly expensed security equipment/systems plus maintenance expenses associated with them, ordinary supplies necessary to operate a security program, vehicles and maintenance, and all other supplies/materials/miscellaneous expenses not captured above.

This chart paints a very nice picture for our CSO. But (again referring to the limitations noted in the general discussion above) if you consider the possible factors that may influence the numbers the bars represent, the picture can get less clear. For example, company E has 100 employees and about 32,000 square feet per officer versus the big numbers you see for our gloating CSO. What if his colleague at E company is in much riskier urban locations and shared spaces, has a lower appetite for risk, and has accepted the cost of posting officers at more points of control? Is our CSO more efficient or are these two companies just approaching their deployment strategies based on different sets of risk and business drivers?

There is no doubt that there are clear, cross- and in-sector business-relevant security metrics that should be probed, validated, and shared among CSOs. Comparative data contribute to learning. Vetting why one peer is able to deliver a service or manage an area of risk with significantly different (better?) results moves the dial for all. Where we find similarities, they tend to validate resource allocations.

Anyone working as a corporate security professional is confronted daily with an array of industry-specific risk and performance indicators that are far too extensive and diverse to address in this volume. I've worked with sector-specific groups, and it's clear that the most meaningful metric on their management's expectation list is something totally unique to that company. For example, in working with a great group of hospital security administrators, when I offered security cost as a percent of revenue, they quickly translated to security cost per patient day—their more tailored connector to the revenue stream. I remember working in a program for securing weapons-grade nuclear material, but if you were to ask top management about risk, they would say that their main concern was the inventory of gold required for one of their product lines.

SECURITY EXPENSE VERSUS COST OF LOSS

The following chart paints a different picture on security's cost to value estimate by comparing it to the cost of loss. The assumption here from the bean counter's view would likely be "if it's costing us more to secure us than we lose to security incidents, where is the value in that equation?"

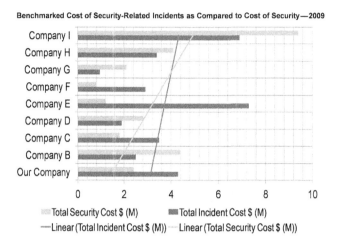

Benchmarked Cost of Security-Related Incidents as Compared to Cost of Security—2009

But this chart also begs a few questions:

- What is the relationship between the amount of security resource cost and the cost of loss? Would any incremental increase in resources provide a more aggressive reduction in loss?
- Our company has about a 2:1 ratio of losses to security expenditures. Company I has about a 6:1 ratio. Would it be reasonable to argue that we are doing a significantly better job in utilizing our resources than they are?
- Five of these peer companies are spending more in 2009 on security than they lost to events. Is this due to the impact of better security measures compared to those who had greater losses than expenditures?

Value is elusive. There may be a host of great success stories as well as some indicators of failed programs throughout this chart. It tells more of what we don't know than what we do know. The value story has to be anchored to specifics that clearly connect the dots between several pieces of the puzzle. Here are several questions to ask yourself—or to drive real discussion among your security team:

Value Linked to Managing Assigned Risk:

1. What do we really know about the consequences and root causes of the risk we propose to attack with our fixed security resources? Are we satisfied that a security solution is the correct set of actions to address the root cause?
2. Can we establish a clear relationship between what we propose to do to eliminate or reduce the risk and the eventual results?
3. Can we accurately estimate what it will cost to execute our solution and specifics related to the beneficial impact on loss exposure?
4. To what extent can we measurably demonstrate a cost benefit from process defect identification and elimination?

Value Linked to Managing Program Cost:

1. Can we establish a direct link between what we spend to address the activity and an equally direct link to a definable business benefit?
2. To what extent are the beneficiaries of the activity willing to directly support the cost of the service we provide?
3. To what extent have we thoroughly assessed the direct and indirect cost of activity-based tasks to provide assurance that all available efficiencies and cycle times are in place?
4. To what extent can we deliver on assurances that selected security activities have been vetted against available best practices and process improvement opportunities?

Value Linked to Business Enablement and Customer Service:

1. Can we cost-efficiently deliver a service for which we are uniquely qualified and positioned that will measurably enable the business to engage in an activity that would otherwise be too risky?
2. To what extent do our services enable the business to work more competitively and cost effectively in a litigious and regulatory business environment?
3. To what extent can we establish that our suite of responsive services directly and measurably reduces impact from business interruption and increases workplace safety and a personal sense of security?
4. To what extent can we factually demonstrate that our business is measurably more available, reliable, safe, and secure than that of our competitors?

Value is not anchored to resource commitments—it is linked to benefit received, which is a matter of how well you document and verify those benefits. That's why you need to have measures and metrics in your toolkit. They are the supply chain for security service value demonstration.

A FEW METRICS YOU SHOULD REALLY CONSIDER

It's always a dangerous proposition to suggest that there is a tiny selection that qualifies as "must or should haves." Also, in spite of the apparent commonality of elements in the security manager's job description, I have found that we often talk a different language, at least when it comes to metrics. Here are just a few limitations:

- Lack of a common set of measurement terms and definitions to focus discussions on various metric targets. Example: What is a "security incident"?
- Differing databases and methods for recording and compiling incident, activity, and workload data. Examples: FBI, CAPRisk, local, or industry-specific?
- Significantly different threat types and capabilities, business risk profiles, service populations, and related resource requirements.

- Fundamentally different appetites for risk and expectations from management with regard to security's performance indicators.
- Lack of common acceptance among security executives on which activities versus which incidents define security program effectiveness.

Throughout this book, I've tried to put forth a variety of metrics you can consider and test out for yourself; the following is a summary of few "buckets" that categorize and aggregate a body of representative measures and metrics. As a reminder, just make sure that the ones you select avoid the running tallies of month-to-month counts of events and hours of services delivered. These lists and counts are just the input side of your metrics.

KEY RISK INDICATORS

Risk is the reason you have a job. What is the measurable impact of security programs on risk? If you are counting how many each month, you are missing the point.

- Rate of change (+/−) for frequency and severity of security infractions, accidents, crime, or other *preventable* risk events. The key concept here is that investigation clearly confirms that the event was avoidable but stupidity prevailed.
- *Internal misconduct and security policy violations per 1000 employees.* This is about ethics, reputation, and management's communication of expectations. You have given your "trusted" insiders the knowledge and opportunity. How well are the controls working?
- *Reduced risk of attack through more measurably effective protective measures.* If you have attractive targets, this is about the tested effectiveness of security measures reducing the likelihood of adversary success. Is all that money delivering better security?
- *Workplace violence per 1000 employees.* This is about safe, secure workplaces and avoidance of litigation. Benchmark data for industry sectors are available from the U.S. Department of Labor/Bureau of Labor Statistics.
- *Number of security violations by personnel with approved access as a percent of total approved population.* You trusted them and they are found wanting. What are the root causes and what do they say about your internal controls and culture?

INFLUENCE INDICATORS

- Percent of third-party relationships modified, avoided, or terminated attributable to security-related due diligence examination. The business isn't just inside your four walls anymore. What have you delegated, and are the jewels just as safe there as they are under your direct supervision?
- Number of security policies signed off, endorsed, and advocated by senior management. Policies drive cost. This is a basic measure of confidence in security management.

- Percent of exercises and drills indicating effective security response and employee awareness. You have assigned the resources and set the expectations. Now, how well are they working?
- Percent reduction in security-related incidents with ineffective management oversight cited as a causal factor. You can't reach every employee or process but you can try to reach all the supervisors and managers with the information they need to be accountable.

KEY PERFORMANCE INDICATORS

- Percent of critical business processes with current risk assessments.
- Percent of risk assessment recommendations accepted and tested as effective.
- Percent of reduction of security-related incidents attributable to improved security measures.
- Percent of customer satisfaction survey scores above target.
- Number of safety, security, or regulatory compliance defects identified by security officers per 24 hour period. Or, percent of calls for high-severity risk events dispatched and response at or below targeted timeline.

VALUE INDICATORS AND FINANCIAL PERSPECTIVE

A sample of measures that support demonstration of a return on security program cost.

- Percent conformance of budgeted activities to performance measures in annual plan.
- Reduction in security cost as a percent of revenue or as a validated peer comparator.
- Reduction in direct cost of security incidents or critical process disruptions.
- Reduction in cost of compliance with security-related regulations or cost to insure.
- Operational and physical security as a percent of occupancy cost or total security cost per population served.

VALUE INDICATORS: CUSTOMER PERSPECTIVE AND BUSINESS PROCESS ENABLEMENT

- Customers captured or retained, award fee contribution or client satisfaction acknowledged as attributable to proactive or reactive security measures.
- Percent of interrupted business processes satisfactorily restored within targeted timelines.
- Measurable reduction in cycle time or cost of essential security controls. Reductions in employee interaction with time-consuming security measures.
- Increased market penetration attributable to security measures; facilitating secure business process in risky markets.

So, how is the value of a business process measured in your organization? What are the attributes of that activity that management accepts as value delivered, and how are the metrics defined?

If I were to hear you bemoaning the lack of your management's knowledge of security's value, to whom should I look for accountability? While they can clearly see the cost of your programs, they are likely clueless on what results those costs deliver! What indicators drive the management of your resources? Are you measuring the [real] results and communicating the metrics—or just waiting for someone lacking your depth and breadth of knowledge to do it for you?

SOME CLOSING THOUGHTS

I thought it would be interesting to close out with a definition of *security metrics*. I think this nicely frames the critical elements of what I hope the preceding examples have left for your consideration:

> *"For an entity (system, product, facility, asset, or other) for which security is a meaningful concept, there are identifiable attributes that collectively characterize the security of that entity. A security metric, or combination of metrics, is a quantitative (and qualitative)[12] measure of how much of that attribute the entity possesses."[13]*

The notion of "meaningful concept" and how you "characterize security" within your organization isn't a simple black-and-white consideration.

- Corporate culture is incredibly influential on how security is defined and approached.
- The diversity and complexity of the risk environment and how policy makers perceive the likelihood of threats push or limit security engagement in business process management.
- The ability of security management to inform, educate and craft security measures that "fit" versus seen as unconnected and costly, will significantly enable the quality of rank-and-file awareness and *measurable* engagement essential to enterprise protection.

As I've had the opportunity over the past four-plus decades to view security, I'm often shocked at the lack of it. I've concluded that where this level of ignorance is permitted to exist, I'll find a broken process surrounding all things related to security information management and focused communication. Folks may be generating a lot of words and numbers, but this data sits unattended, misunderstood. I'll not find "a measure of how much security an entity possesses" here. This is an organization simply waiting for something to happen or not knowing it already has.

In the organizations that really understand their risk exposure and attendant responsibilities, I've found a security manager who worries about data availability and reliability, learns from it, and seeks to reach the right people with actionable information. Metrics here are a valued security product, and measuring is a core management competency.

---

[12] I've taken the literary liberty of adding "qualitative."
[13] The System Security Engineering Capability Model, Carnegie Mellon University, 1995.

Index

Note: Page numbers followed by "b", "f" and "t" indicate boxes, figures and tables respectively.

A

AAR. *See* After-action reviews
"Acceptable" risk
  annual percent of interrupted business processes, 90
  critical assets percent, 89
  factors, 89
  incidents percent, 90
  security incidents percent, 90
  threshold identification, 88
Access control dashboard, 64f
Accountability assurance, 13. *See also* Data integrity assurance
Accountability management, 52
ACN. *See* Audit committee notable
Actionable security metrics, 9–10. *See also* Corporate security metrics
  business drivers and objectives, 10
  data to work, 11
  file cabinet, 10
  types and locations of data essential for, 10f
Advertising failure to act, 71
  corporate security organization, 71–72
  leveraging learning, 72–73
  RCA, 71–72
After-action reviews (AAR), 71
ALE. *See* Annualized loss expectancy
American Society for Industrial Security (ASIS), 18
Annualized loss expectancy (ALE), 151
ASIS. *See* American Society for Industrial Security
Audit committee notable (ACN), 178
Avoidable risk
  business risk profile, 76
  idea, 75
  metrics on, 54–55
    business risk environment, 55
    examples, 55
    good security programs and internal controls, 55
    test for gaps, 55
  risk management strategy, 76–77
  summarization, 80

B

Background checks, 25
Background investigations (BI), 153, 163
  measuring impact, 55
    employment suitability standards, 56
    material discrepancy, 56
    predictors of potential future behavior, 56
    worst-case scenario, 55
Benchmarking. *See also* Metrics management
  limitations, 34–36
  with peers, 27–28
  security
    best practices, 34
    challenge, 29
    current state, 30–32
    finding value in, 28–29
    KPIs, 32–33
    KRIs, 33–34
    models establishment, 30
    qualitative or quantitative, 32
    valuable responses, 36
Benchmarking security metrics programs, 36–38
  business drivers, 37
  current status, 39
    global companies, 39f
    metrics poll-utility/importance, 41f
    principal objectives, 40
    working group security leaders, 41
  driving need, 37
  observation, 38
  roadblocks to metrics development, 37–38
  single *vs.* multisector benchmarking, 42–43
BI. *See* Background investigations
Board-level risk assessment, 50
Building Owners & Management Association (BOMA), 150, 190–191
Business integrity, 95–98
Business risk profile, 76
Business unit leader, 23
Business unit scorecard creation
  annual business unit security scorecard, 91f
  data, 92
  objective, 90
  risk management strategy, 90–91

C

Charting security-related losses, 60
Chief executive officer (CEO), 58, 117
Chief financial officer (CFO), 63, 117
Chief information officer/chief information security officer (CIO/CISO), 155
Chief security officer (CSO), 1–2, 45, 122
CIO/CISO. *See* Chief information officer/chief information security officer

Cleaning crews, 65

Committee of Sponsoring Organizations (COSO), 82

Competency management, 51

Compliance efforts, 83

Compliance risk measurement, 73. *See also* Security awareness measurement

   reportable security violations, 73f–74f

   risk management strategy, 73–75

Conference Board, 186

Confidential hotline reporting, 112

Confidentiality limitations, 34

Corporate security, 58, 94b

   value proposition finding, 179–181

Corporate security metrics, 1–2, 18

   contract security guards, 18

   expanse, 18

   state of art, 19

      business partners, 19–20

      real obstacles deserve real solutions, 20–27

Corporate Security Officer (CSO), 19, 22

COSO. *See* Committee of Sponsoring Organizations

Cost management, 129, 145

   alarm initiation, 146

   contract security forces ROI, 151–153

   expense management, 148

   slash and burn, 148–151

   task and time analysis, 147–148

Coupling solid risk assessment, 88

CSO. *See* Chief security officer; Corporate Security Officer

Cultural alignment, 129

Customer service, 119

Cycle time, 153–155

D

Dashboards, 120

   CSO, 122

   in misconduct data from IT, 123

   root cause analysis, 122–123

   security department, 121f–122f

   value of, 124

Data integrity assurance, 14

Data security assurance, 15

Defect detection and elimination, 152

Defective access control, 62

Definitional limitations, 34

E

Effective access management, elements measurement of, 60–62, 63f

Employment suitability standards, 56

Enterprise risk councils (ERCs), 47–48

Enterprise risk management (ERM), 95

Enterprise-wide board risk management, 46

   accountability management, 52

   competency management, 51

   conceptual risk picture, 46–47

      purpose of research output, 47

      SEC, 47

      security mitigation strategies, 47

   ERCs, 47–48

   infractions, 51

   leading indicators, 50–51

   security's role in risk management, 48

   supply chain protection, 51

   system reliability management, 52

   "what if" analysis, 50–52

EP. *See* Executive protection

ERCs. *See* Enterprise risk councils

ERM. *See* Enterprise risk management

Executive protection (EP), 165–166

Exploitable security defects identification in business process, 52, 53f

   caution on likelihood, 54

   data, 54

   risk management strategy, 53–54

   vulnerabilities, 53

Extreme Presentation Method, 16, 17f

F

Failure modes and effects analysis (FMEA), 141

Full-time equivalents (FTEs), 35

G

Gatekeeper model, 158

Global supply chain study, 48

Guard force

   communication center activities, 131

   performance and cost, 130

   security operations, 132

   SLA, 131, 132f–133f

   vendor performance, 133

Guard operations, 119

H

Human resources (HR), 25, 47, 123

I

IAHSS. *See* International Association of Hospital Safety and Security

Incident analysis, 101

   data, 101–102

   risk management strategy, 101

Incident response, 120
Indicator, 115
Influence, 177
    ability to influence business, 173–179
    indicators, 194–195
    measurement by tracking acceptance of recom-
        mendations, 177–178
    warning signs of security's decreasing, 174–177
Information security, 124, 155. *See also* Physical
        security
Information technology (IT), 92–93, 123
    contractor risk, 92–93
Insider risk, 41, 105f–106f, 109
    areas of concern, 100
    management, 100
    measurement, 115
    in outsourced business process, 110–111
    tracking losses from fraud, waste and abuse,
        111–112
Internal controls establishment, 13, 14f
    accountability assurance, 13
    data integrity assurance, 14
    data management and analysis, 14
    data security assurance, 15
    relevance to business process, 14
International Association of Hospital Safety and
        Security (IAHSS), 42
Investigation outcomes, 120
IT. *See* Information technology

K

Key performance indicator (KPI), 20, 32–33,
        118, 195
    hierarchy of, 119f–120f
    objectives, 119
    strategy, 119–120
Key risk indicator (KRI), 32–34, 80–82, 84f,
        120, 194
    "acceptable" risk
        annual percent of interrupted business
            processes, 90
        critical assets percent, 89
        factors, 89
        incidents percent, 90
        security incidents percent, 90
        threshold identification, 88
    at CSO level, 82–84
        COSO, 82
        design and roll-out, 83
    deeper dive on multiyear trends to highlight
        risk, 85–86
    at enterprise level, 80–81

risk assessment program effectiveness
        measurement, 87–88
    risk indicator dashboard, 86
    risk management strategy, 86–87

L

Line security manager, 22
Loss
    elements measurement of effective access
        management, 60–62, 63f
    identification and advertising causes, 59
    risk management strategy, 60
    strategy, 62–65

M

Malicious incidents, 107
Material discrepancy, 56
Metrics management, 1
    building program, 7
        actionable security metrics, 9–11
        business drivers and objectives identification, 8
        construction process, 7f–8f
        internal controls establishment, 13–15
        metrics intended to inform and influence, 9
        qualitative security measures and metrics
            program, 15
        risk-related metrics, 11–12
        security's multiple benefits to business,
            12–13, 13f
    corporate security metrics, 1–2, 18–27
    great data, great opportunity but bad
        presentation, 16
        Extreme Presentation Method, 16, 17f–18f
        PowerPoint slides, 16
        purpose, 16
    metrics program assessment, 2
        metrics self-assessment tool, 2, 3t–6t
        SWOT, 2
        uses, 6–7
    six-step process, 1
Multisector benchmarking, single *vs.*, 42–43

N

National Fire Protection Association (NFPA), 18
National Institute of Occupational Health & Safety
        (NIOSH), 70–71
NFPA. *See* National Fire Protection Association
NIOSH. *See* National Institute of Occupational
        Health & Safety
Nuisance alarm reduction, 157
Nuisance alarms, 77
    reduction, 79

O

Operational excellence measurement in security services, 141–143
Organizational integrity dashboard, 86–87, 86f
Organizational variability limitations, 35
OSHA. *See* U.S. Occupational Safety and Health Administration
Outsourcing, tracking risk in, 92
    broken windows in boardroom, 96–98
    business integrity and reputational risk, 95–98
    data, 93–94
    information technology contractor risk, 92–93
    KRIs in business continuity, 94

P

Penetration testing, 152
Physical security, 124, 127f. *See also* Information security
    access management, 125
    hazard and risk mitigation, 125
    integrated operational security system elements, 126f
    operational security measures and metrics, 124
Process-specific risk assessment, 50
protective services operations KPI, 134
    risk management strategy, 135
    SLA management, 135–136

R

RCA. *See* Root cause analysis
Real Estate Executive Board (REEB), 190–191
Recovery time objective (RTO), 33
REEB. *See* Real Estate Executive Board
Regional security team
    challenges, 129–130
    management and measurement, 128
Regulations and Compliance Management (RoCM), 74, 160
Reliability, 6b
Reliable benchmarking data, 28
Reputational risk, 95–98
    measurement, 104
    simple dashboard on, 113–114
"Requisite", 89
Return on investment (ROI), 37, 151
Risk appetite, 83
Risk assessment
    plan, 135
    program effectiveness measurement, 87–88
Risk exposure measurement, 143b
    attitude of, 145
    data, 144
    risk management strategy, 143–144

Risk indicator dashboard, 86
Risk management strategy, 53–54, 57
    CEO, 58
    corporate security, 58
    CSO, 58
    risk assessments, 57–58
Risk personified–knowledgeable insider, 98–99, 99f
    confidential hotline reporting, 112
    cost of bad employee, 103
        considerations, 103–104
        objective, 103
        reputational risk measurement, 104
    incident analysis, 101
        data, 101–102
        risk management strategy, 101
    insider risk in outsourced business process, 110–111
    management, 100
    using metrics, 104–106, 105f–106f
    reputational risk, simple dashboard on, 113–114
    security, 100, 100b
        incidents impact measurement, 106
        strategy, 106–108
    summarization, 115
    tracking disciplinary action, 110
    tracking internal investigations, 108–110
    tracking losses from fraud, waste and abuse, 111–112
    unintended consequences, 114–115
    visibly effective security programs and internal controls, 100
Risk reporting, 83
Risk treatment, 83
Risk-related metrics, 11–12, 45
RoCM. *See* Regulations and Compliance Management
ROI. *See* Return on investment
Root cause analysis (RCA), 71, 122–123
RTO. *See* Recovery time objective

S

SEC. *See* Security Executive Council
Sector limitations, 35
Secure area reliability, 138
Security awareness, 172
    programs, 169–171
Security awareness measurement, 65. *See also* Compliance risk measurement
    risk, 65
    risk awareness assures preparedness, 67, 67f
        logical access password strength, 69f
        risk aware organization, 69
        security practitioners, 67
        test of, 68

security organization, 66
surveys deliver data, 66
testing delivers data, 67
Security benchmarking
    best practices, 34
    challenge, 29
    current state, 30–32
    finding value in, 28–29
    KPIs, 32–33
    KRIs, 33–34
    models establishment, 30
    qualitative or quantitative, 32
Security contract compliance auditing, 161
    audit function, 161
    questions, 163
    risk management strategy, 162–163
Security Executive Council (SEC), 30, 45
    RoCM, 160
Security operations control center (SOCC), 136
    operational criticality, 136–137
    performance measurement, 137–138
Security practitioners, 67
Security program, 117b
    ability to influencing business, 173
        influence measurement, 177–178
        risk management strategy, 178–179
        warning signs of security's decreasing
            influence, 174–177
    absence of awareness, 171–173
    annual plans and objectives measurement,
        156–158
    business unit criticality, resilience, and continuity
        planning, 166–167
        contingency plans, 168
        corporate security, 168
        employee awareness, 168
        key elements, 167
    cost management, 145–153
    critical measure of time, 138
        risk management strategy, 139–141
        security operations team, 141
    cycle time, 153–155
    EP measurement, 165–166
    guard force performance and cost,
        130–133
    high-probability risk, 126–128
    influence indicators, 194–195
    information security, 155
    KPI, 118–120, 158, 195
        objective, 159
        risk management strategy, 159–161
    KRI, 158, 194
    measuring for integrity, 163

    candidate pool, 165
    risk management strategy, 163–165
    measuring for operational excellence in,
        141–143
    metrics, 155–156, 186
        analysis yields valuable results, 187–188
        benchmarking security operations, 189–191
        risk management strategy, 186–187
        security balanced scorecard, 188–189
        security expense *vs.* cost of loss, 191–193
    performance with dashboards, 120–124
    physical security, 124–126, 127f
    protective services operations KPI, 134
        risk management strategy, 135
        SLA management, 135–136
    regional security team management and
        measurement, 128–130
    risk exposure measurement, 143–145
    risk management strategy, 127–128
    risk metrics, 118
    secure area reliability, 138
    security awareness programs, 169–171
    security contract compliance auditing,
        161–163
    security manager job description, 193
    security value proposition, 179–186
    SOCC, 136–138
    value indicators, 195–196
    vendor-based alarm response measurement,
        133–134
Security project involvement, 24
Security value proposition, 179
    business units value security recommendations,
        184–186
    corporate security value proposition finding,
        179–181
    security value measurement, 181–184
Senior security manager. *See* Corporate Security
        Officers (CSOs)
Service level agreement (SLA), 119, 152
Single benchmarking, multisector *vs.*, 42–43
Site risk assessments, 24
Site security operations, 24
Size limitations, 34
SLA. *See* Service level agreement
SOCC. *See* Security operations control center
Social media review programs, 71
Strengths, weaknesses, opportunities and threats
        (SWOT), 2
Supply chain protection, 51
SWOT. *See* Strengths, weaknesses, opportunities
        and threats
System reliability management, 52

T

Termination, 107
Third-party due-diligence examinations, 153
Tracking disciplinary action, 110
Tracking internal investigations, 108–110
Tracking preventable risk, 56
    cost assignment to preventable security incidents, 58–59, 59f
    risk management strategy, 57
        CEO, 58
        corporate security, 58
        CSO, 58
        risk assessments, 57–58
Transitions, 115–116

U

U.S. Occupational Safety and Health Administration (OSHA), 18
Unified risk management, 48

V

Value indicators, 195–196
Vendor-based alarm response measurement, 133–134

W

"What if" analysis, 50–52
Workplace accidents, 108
Workplace violence, 69, 70f, 107–108
    hostile workplace factors, 70
    investigative postmortems, 70–71
    potential for, 69–70
    risk awareness and avoidance, 71
    social media review programs, 71

Printed in the United States
By Bookmasters